A Nurse for All Seasons

A Nurse for All Seasons

Elizabeth Robinson Scovil
1849-1934

New Brunswick's Pioneer
of Professional Nursing

Virginia Bliss Bjerkelund

Author of
Meadowlands: A Chronicle of the Scovil Family

Chapel Street Editions

Appreciation of Place

Chapel Street Editions exists within the unceded and unsurrendered territories of the Wolastoqiyik, Mi'kmaq, and Peskotomuhkati people. The work we do is born from the stories carried by this land and its inhabitants. The animals, plants, soil, water, and air make this place home for the Indigenous people who belong to this land, for the descendants of those who took this land and made it a belonging, and for those who have since come from away. Chapel Street Editions holds a deep appreciation for our place within this land and the stories it tells. We honour the land's Indigenous caretakers and are grateful for their wisdom and guidance.

Published by
Chapel Street Editions
150 Chapel St. Woodstock, NB Canada E7M 1H4
chapelstreeteditions@gmail.com
www.chapelstreeteditions.com

ISBN 978-1-988299-52-5

Library and Archives Canada Cataloguing in Publication

Title: A nurse for all seasons : Elizabeth Robinson Scovil 1849-1934 : New Brunswick's pioneer of professional nursing / Virginia Bliss Bjerkelund.
Names: Bjerkelund, Virginia Bliss, 1929- author.
Identifiers: Canadiana 20230566502 | ISBN 9781988299525 (softcover)
Subjects: LCSH: Scovil, Elisabeth Robinson, 1849-1934. | LCSH: Scovil, Elisabeth Robinson, 1849-1934—Family. | LCSH: Nurses—New Brunswick—Biography. | LCSH: Nursing—New Brunswick—History. | LCGFT: Biographies.
Classification: LCC RT37.S36 B54 2023 | DDC 610.73092—dc23

The photographs beginning on page iv have been restored, repaired, and enhanced using the Neural Filters in Adobe Photoshop.

Book design by Brendan Helmuth

Chapel Street Editions, Ltd. gratefully acknowledges the financial support of Arts Culture New Brunswick.

Dedication

With admiration for Elizabeth Robinson Scovil,
my Great Aunt Bessie, whose formidable presence
is one of my earliest memories.

Table of Contents

Foreword

Virginia Bliss Bjerkelund first presented her Great Aunt Bessie — Elizabeth Robinson Scovil — in *Meadowlands: A Chronicle of the Scovil Family*, a non-fiction novel set primarily on a 900 acre hay and horse farm at Scovil Point across the St. John River(Wolastoq) from Gagetown, New Brunswick. Aunt Bessie is a featured character in *Meadowlands*. She was the anchor of this branch of the Scovil family from the late 1800s through early 1930s. But this is only part of the story. Elizabeth Scovil made a decision in 1878 at the age of 29 that warrants a biography.

Her decision to enroll in the newly established two-year nurses' training program at Massachusetts General Hospital led her to become a primary figure in the professionalization of nursing and nursing education in Canada and the United States. *A Nurse for all Seasons* is a biography that tells the story of these vocational and professional accomplishments. It is also a fascinating immersion in the rapidly changing social dynamics of late Victorian and early modern times.

Unlike many biographies that present the details of their subject's life in a chronological narrative, *A Nurse for All Seasons* rolls out a sequence of chapters that individually focus on Elizabeth Scovil's overlapping careers. She was a pioneer of professional nursing and nursing education. She developed an associated career as the author of highly successful books on the healthcare, development, and family life of children.

She was a prolific journalist who was a founding associate editor of *The Ladies' Home Journal* and *The American Journal of Nursing*. She was an associate editor and frequent contributor to *Canadian Nurse*.

She was a practicing nurse, the nursing Superintendent of a major hospital and nurses' training school, the co-founder of the

Victorian Order of Nurses, and a friend of Florence Nightingale. She was much sought after for keynote addresses at conferences of Canadian and American nursing organizations. Nurse Scovil became a leader in articulating a philosophy of nursing that encompassed the details of practice and the ethics of the profession.

As the author of unprecedented and best selling books for women about pregnancy, childbirth, and the care of infants and children. She put a new level of information, knowledge, and awareness into the lives of thousands of women that increased their skills and confidence. As an associate editor and regular columnist of *The Ladies' Home Journal,* she addressed and responded personally to questions from mothers about the illnesses, healthcare, and development of children.

As a writer and journalist for the publications of the nursing profession in North American, she advanced the modernization of practice and the role of nurses in upgrading medical ethics. As a speaker at conferences of nurses, she urged her compatriots to develop the discipline of practice and the ethic of care that makes nursing, and therefore women, a powerful force in the creation of a more enlightened and socially progressive society. As the co-founder of the Victorian Order of Nurses, she helped make nursing care readily available in the rural areas of Canada. As a founder of the National Council of Women of Canada, she was at the forefront of what has become the international feminist movement.

Virginia Bjerkelund has organized and composed this biography in a way that provides the reader with a deep and broad immersion in the intellectual and socially significant context of her great aunt's contribution to the modernization of nursing and to the emergence of women from the Victorian era into a more egalitarian world. She develops her story by including extensive quotation's from Elizabeth Scovil's books, journalism, lectures, and letters. The result is a fully rounded exposure to the intellectual processes and ethical philosophy that gave her a socially progressive voice to which the nursing profession and thousands of women in general responded.

One incident, in particular, highlights her influence. When she travelled to British Columbia to deliver the keynote address to a national meeting of the Victorian Order of Nurses, women came to the stations where it was known her train would be stopping en route across Canada to thank her for writing the books that had been so helpful to them as mothers and keepers of family households. Aunt Bessie never had a family of her own but her advice and counsel was highly valued. When Mary Scovil, the author's mother, challenged her aunt's expertise in writing about such matters, nurse Scovil replied; "The watchers see most of the game."

In *A Nurse for All Seasons*, the author has provided us with a front row seat for watching the intellectual life, the vocational trajectories, and the significant social influence of Elizabeth Robinson Scovil play out across the critical transitions of the era in which she lived.

Keith Helmuth, Publisher
Chapel Street Editions

Mary Eliza Robinson Scovil, mother of Elizabeth Robinson Scovil (E.R.S.)
circa mid-1860s. (Scovil family archive)

Samuel James Scovil, father of E.R.S.
circa mid–1860s. (Scovil family archive)

E.R.S. in Saint John, age 19, 1868. (PANB)

E.R.S. as a young nurse in Boston, circa 1878.

Frontispiece to the book *Morning Strength*,
1896, Herny Althmus, Philadelphia. (Scovil family archive)

Meadowlands – House and barns. Scovil Point, NB. (Scovil family archive)

Meadowlands house from the St. John River (Wolastoq). (Scovil family archive)

E.R.S., Morris Scovil, author's Grandfather, and four-year old, grandniece, Virginia (author). Amherst, NS, 1933. (Scovil family archive)

E.R.S. with grandniece, Rosemary Scovil, and grandnephew, Roger Scovil Jr.
Greenville, SC, 1934. (Scovil family archive)

Morris Scovil, Bishop's Stortford, England, 1934.
(Scovil family archive)

Elizabeth Robinson Scovil, age 85. Bishop's Stortford, England, 1934.
(Scovil family archive)

Chapter One

Introduction

Great Aunt Bessie has always lived with me—a powerful presence from my earliest memories. Now she is frowning, forcefully reprimanding me for not having put this book together years ago. She follows me about, whispering in my ear to set aside time each day, as she did, to write her many books. With the discipline that comes from a nurse's training, from a lifetime of instructing others, and from a talent for public lectures, she pushes me to complete the story of the ethic by which she lived. She carries an indelible message engrained in her character that prompts her, as the eldest surviving sibling, to shoulder family and societal burdens that must be endured, lessened, and if at all possible, removed.

I do not have her steadfast focus, but rather a rambling determination to joyfully research a considerable collection of information and discover the many layers of Great Aunt Bessie—the Elizabeth Robinson Scovil of public fame. She was a pioneer in the profession of trained nursing, a millionaire on paper before the stock market crash of 1929 when she was eighty, a feminist who helped found the National Council of Women of Canada, an innovative author and journalist, and a deeply religious woman with a practical bent who, for example, found a quick solution to paying for a new barn door needed on her brother's farm at Meadowlands by producing a new book of spiritual reflection and insight for her publisher.

By peeling back the layers of her life, detailing the many roles she played, and recounting her accomplishments I have produced a portrait of my Great Aunt Bessie that I hope will secure her place in our cultural heritage and social history. I have been aided by the crystal clear memory of my mother and her stories about her interaction with Aunt Bessie—critical, sad, funny, and profound—that she passed on to me all through my life. There are also more than two dozen letters written over a period of thirty years in Bessie's Victorian hand, family photographs, her own photograph album, her Birthday Book, her published books, newspaper clippings, the manuscripts of lectures and articles in my possession, and in university and provincial archives, plus my own tiny child's memory that have given me the material needed to compose this biography.

My earliest and most deeply etched memory is her stern face, hair pulled back in a bun, her upper neck and head glued to her lower neck and shoulders by a black velvet band topping a complicated white lace collar over a discrete black dress. She is looking out of a square, birds eye maple frame, guarding my mother's dressing table. I hoped, partly for my mother, that one day, when I looked, Aunt Bessie would be smiling, but I was always disappointed. Through my mother's stories of her childhood came her ambivalent feelings of dislike, admiration, and dependence on her father's older sister. I assimilated my mother's need for a smile from Aunt Bessie, but she remained, in that photograph, steadfastly unsmiling.

After more than ninety years I am still hoping the memory of her face will smile approval at my effort to collect what I can of her essence and her life's work, to discover why she made the choices she did, to learn how she overcame considerable obstacles to achieve remarkable results and why I am still so fascinated by her. I check her photograph, near my desk, from time to time hoping for further insight.

* * * *

Elizabeth Robinson Scovil was born on April 30, 1849, either in Saint John, New Brunswick, according to the Scovil family bible, or at Meadowlands, the family farm across the river from Gagetown, if we wish to believe her gravestone in Bishop's Stortford, England. I am inclined to believe the former as the record of his children's births is written in her father's hand.

Bessie probably told her nephew, Morris, at whose house she was staying when she died, that she wanted Meadowlands on her stone as her place of birth as she was so fond of that farm and eventual ownership of it meant so much to her. In fact, she was the one who changed its name from "The Farm at Scovil Point" to "Meadowlands" when she first visited in 1880 after her parents were willed the property by her father's uncle, Samuel Scovil. The lushness of the large hay fields that bordered the St. John River prompted her to call it Meadowlands. In addition to this intervale land, the farm included extensive woodland and totalled nine-hundred acres. It was located directly across the river from the village of Gagetown. The site is still referred to as "Scovil Point" on some maps.

I know very little about Bessie's first nineteen years, except that she was educated privately in Saint John, until the age of sixteen. Her parents produced eight more children, only three of whom survived childhood illnesses. Sophie Allaire came a year after Bessie, but she died before she was four, allowing Bessie to enjoy a sister playmate for only a short time. She remained the only surviving child for ten years until Jack arrived. Two more tenacious boys followed and flourished, my grandfather, Morris, and Barclay.

Wherever she was born, Elizabeth was not the first child of her parents. Samuel James Scovil (1816-1883) and Mary Eliza Robinson (1824-1894) were married on July 23, 1845 at Christ Church Anglican Cathedral in Fredericton. Their first child was Mary Eliza who lived only two years. Elizabeth was their second child. She grew up in comfortable circumstances in the largest city of New Brunswick, Saint John, where her father was a banker as well as being a licensed attorney.

What is well documented in newspapers of the day and elsewhere is the catastrophe that struck Bessie's family when she was nineteen. Samuel James Scovil, her fifty-two year old father, went bankrupt. His branch of St. Stephen Bank, an investment and lending bank, bought gold on the New York market and, unfortunately, sold it for less than was paid for it—several times. With the bankruptcy, his name was dragged through the mud in the press and in drawing rooms. He was in gaol briefly on the Kingston Peninsula where he took refuge near his clergyman brother. The family had to leave Saint John to live with his wife's relations, the Robinsons at Pine Grove in Douglas, across the river from Fredericton, land now occupied by York Manor Nursing Home. This arrangement did not last for just a few months; the family lived there for most of eleven years until Bessie's father was willed The Farm at Scovil Point.

Based on my mother's comments about her aunt's attachment to her clergyman uncle, William Elias Scovil, and his family on the Kingston Peninsula — easily reached by riverboat from Fredericton — she probably spent extended time there, perhaps keeping an eye on her younger cousins. As a young lady in her twenties from a well-connected family, she would have taken an active part in the Anglican Church centred around Christ Church Cathedral in Fredericton and in the city's social life generally. In a letter dated November 1937, Bessie's youngest brother, Barclay, writes the following to my eight-year old cousin, Roger Scovil (Junior) in Greenville, South Carolina:

> When a young woman, she [Bessie] taught school in Fredericton, N.B. With my mother and myself she moved to Cambridge, Mass. We stayed there about a year and all returned to Fredericton. My sister returned to Boston, Mass. and entered the Massachusetts General Hospital for nurses, one of four such schools in the United States. During her early training she scrubbed floors and did other such pleasant work.

This bid for independence, unusual for the times, occurred two years before Bessie's parents and three younger brothers settled on the inherited farm. By 1880 two satisfying events took place — graduation into a profession for Bessie and independence for her immediate family on The Farm at Scovil Point. The new graduate's first position was at St. Paul's School, Concord, New Hampshire—a private school for boys—where she was in charge of the infirmary.

On page three hundred seven of *A Survey of the Scovils or Scovills in England and America: Seven Hundred Years of History and Genealogy,* by Homer Worthington Brainard, published in 1915, a thumb nail sketch of Elizabeth Robinson Scovil informs us that, among other accomplishments, she was in charge of the infirmary at St. Paul's School for ten years and superintendent of the Newport Hospital, Newport, Rhode Island from 1888 to 1892. If the ten years at St. Paul's were uninterrupted this would have been impossible; she could not have held both jobs between 1888 and 1890.

I have come to the conclusion from this reference and from comments in her letters, that she had at least one break from St. Paul's, returning after a rest for her troublesome eyes at Meadowlands. She may also have gone back to St. Paul's after her more demanding four years (according to the above dates) at Newport Hospital. Private nursing was another option she sought; it allowed recuperating time between assignments.

Barclay, her youngest brother, contributed much to Brainard's survey, although his 1937 letter to little Roger differs somewhat from that thumbnail sketch. "She [Bessie] was for 10 years in charge of the Infirmary of St. Paul's School at Concord, N.H. She then became matron of the Newport, R.I. hospital, holding the position for six years." This is likely to be correct as he adds; "I went there quite often to see her from New York. I worked at an importing dry goods house on Broadway for seventeen years." Barclay was only seventy-one when he wrote this, three years after Bessie died, so there is no reason to suppose that his memory was failing.

*   *   *   *

This account of my Aunt Bessie's life, unlike most biographies, is not strictly chronological. Her various activities overlapped in such a way that the story can best be told by focusing each chapter on one of the major roles she played and her associated accomplishments.

From 1890 until 1906 she was an Associate Editor of *The Ladies Home Journal,* for which she wrote a monthly column of advice for mothers. In addition, she contributed featured articles. Bessie was a Contributing Editor of *The American Journal of Nursing* from its founding in 1900. For twenty years she composed a monthly column titled "Notes from the Medical Press," and occasionally contributed full articles as well. She was also a Contributing Editor of *Canadian Nurse* from its founding in 1905 until 1924.

From early in the 1890s into the 1930s, Bessie wrote and published twenty-three books on health, family life, and religious themes, including a book of poetry. Her books on the health, development, and care of children were best sellers. Her stature was such that in May of 1900 she gave a paper before the third annual convention of the Nurses' Associated Alumnae of the United States, which took place in New York. Her address was printed in full under "Official Reports of Societies" in Vol. 1 (1900) of *The American Journal of Nursing.*

As Canada began to have a core of nurses graduating from its own training schools, Miss Scovil became a department editor of *Canadian Nurse*, a new national journal for which she regularly prepared articles. In addition, the speeches she gave at conferences of nurses and of hospital superintendents in Canadian cities during World War I were also published in *Canadian Nurse.*

When Lady Aberdeen, wife of the Governor General of Canada, was thinking about establishing the Victorian Order of Nurses (VON) in the 1890s, she sought the advice and support of Elizabeth Robinson Scovil. Miss Scovil was such an effective advocate for the VON that she was asked to speak at public meetings across Canada to promote and assist in the formation of local chapters of this community based expansion of nursing services. Lady Aberdeen's social innovations included organizing and establishing the International Council of Women and the National Council of Women of Canada. Elizabeth Scovil was president of both organizations during their start up periods. She remained active in both organizations and was an official delegate from Canada to the International Council meeting in London in 1904 where she delivered an address to the entire gathering.

On this and two other trips to London, Elizabeth met with the woman who placed nursing on a professional footing, the icon, Florence Nightingale. These meetings were no polite cups of tea but deep exchanges of views on nursing and related subjects. The polite cups of tea were reserved for her audience with Queen Victoria.

In the summer of 1903, family ties pulled Bessie away from professional nursing in the United States back to Meadowlands in New Brunswick where her brother's wife, Harriet, was ill with diabetes. Harriet died in September, leaving five children ages five to fourteen, including my mother, Mary. Aunt Bessie's care of the children and the household was expected to be temporary until a satisfactory full-time housekeeper could be found. When that proved impossible and it was clear her brother, Morris was not likely to remarry, Aunt Bessie remained at Meadowlands to help him raise the children and manage the household. Though tucked away in the country, a half-day riverboat journey from Fredericton, she continued to write, to edit, to advocate for greater independence of women and to travel and lecture across North America and abroad.

Though the stock market crash on Black Thursday, October 24, 1929, greatly diminished the value of her investments, Bessie could still finance twice-yearly voyages across the Atlantic with her brother Morris for the rest of her life. They stayed with his eldest son, Morris A. (also known as Morrie) and his family at Bishop's Stortford in England for six months and with his youngest son, Roger and his family in Greenville, South Carolina for the other six. Sister and brother, Bessie and Morris sometimes detoured to Nova Scotia to visit his youngest daughter, Mary and her family, which included me.

In the fall of 1934, Elizabeth Robinson Scovil and her brother, Morris, were concluding their annual six-month stay with the family of her nephew, Morris A. when her health noticeably weakened. They were anticipating their annual return voyage to the U.S. and wintering in South Carolina, but it was not to be. Her strength rapidly failed and she died that fall at age eighty-five of heart failure, and is buried in the ancient town of Bishop's Stortford, about thirty miles northeast of London.

With this introduction to my Great Aunt Bessie, we are now ready for a detailed account, chapter by chapter, of the extraordinary life of a woman from New Brunswick who left a legacy of service across her times and into ours.

Chapter Two

Influences

Were there towering events, exciting inspirations, gloomy cautions, or frightening examples that influenced Elizabeth Robinson Scovil to make important decisions in her life? Were there public figures, authors, or family members who helped her to lean in one direction and away from another? How weighty were the accumulated messages from generations of family who were staunch Loyalists and Anglican clergy, even from those as far back as Henry III and Robert the Bruce, who received history book recognition, mostly for positive deeds? We will never know, precisely, though certainly some of these ancestors played a part in shaping the life of this unusual woman. Not all accomplishments of her forbears are to be praised. Although it may be uncharitable to look first at a scandal, I am doing so because of the devastating effect and the timing, November-December 1868, when Bessie was an impressionable young woman, just nineteen. But, before that, an introduction to the family will set the stage.

Bessie's father, Samuel James Scovil (1816-1883) was the younger and only brother (two sisters of four reached adulthood) of the Reverend William Elias Scovil (1810-1876). William Elias was the third Scovil rector at the Trinity Anglican Church at Kingston on the Kingston Peninsula, near Saint John, New Brunswick. He succeeded his father, the Reverend Elias Scovil who married his first cousin Eliza Scovill (1783-1869) and succeeded his father, the Reverend James Scovil as the rector of the same parish.

The Reverend James was appointed rector in 1787 and moved with his wife, Amy Nichol (1742-1832) and family from Waterbury, Connecticut in 1788 to a jurisdiction under the

9

British crown where the growing population felt the need of a resident clergyman. There was no rectory and no church, though the former was quickly built, and was used until recently. Trinity Church at Kingston was then built and consecrated on November 5, 1789. It is the oldest Anglican church in the province of New Brunswick, though it did not acquire its imposing spire until 1857. The rectors — James, Elias, and William Elias — spanned ninety years of continuous service to the community and surrounding population. William Elias and his wife, Frances Lee (1822-1913), produced five surviving male children: William, Thomas, Charles, Ernest and Samuel who all turned their backs on careers in the Church and so an unusual dynasty came to an end.

Samuel James, brought up in the Kingston Rectory, where his grandfather, his father and eventually his brother were all in holy orders, married Mary Eliza Robinson (1824-1894) in 1845. She was the granddaughter of Colonel Beverley Robinson, the Younger, a prominent United Empire Loyalist who brought the Loyal American Regiment, raised by his father of the same name in New York, to the safety of British soil — first to Nova Scotia and then soon to settle along the Saint John River near Fredericton. The Colonel himself chose an extensive tract of land, establishing a farm that he named "The Naswaaksis" across the river from what became Government House in Fredericton.

The Colonel's son married the daughter of Major Anthony Allaire, an officer in the Loyal American Regiment. They lived in the Allaire home, called Pine Grove, an extensive farm, where the York Manor Nursing Home is now located. Samuel James Scovil claimed the hand of their daughter, Mary Eliza, and they were the first couple to be married in the newly consecrated Christ Church Cathedral in Fredericton by Bishop Medley, its first rector. The groom was twenty-nine. The bride was twenty-one. They made their home in Saint John.

Samuel James and Mary Eliza's first born in 1846, Mary Eliza, lived two years, nine months, and twenty-six days. The second, Elizabeth Robinson in 1849, seemed determined to make her mark in the world and survived to become my great Aunt Bessie. Sophia Allaire was next in 1850 but died before she was quite four. Then, a much-wanted son, Samuel, was born in 1852, but survived only until he was three. Samuel John (Jack) was born in 1856, survived, eventually married and had three children who lived into adulthood. Next came Morris in 1860, who also survived childhood and became my grandfather. He and his wife, Harriet Lavinia DuVernet, had had five surviving children of which my mother, Mary, was the next to youngest. Another early death follows with Henry Barclay, born in 1864 but who died before his first birthday. Barclay Allaire, born in 1867, when his mother was forty-three, lived until he was eighty. Barclay, like Bessie, remained unmarried. He became very interested in genealogy and contributed to the 1915 book by Homer Worthington Brainard, *A Survey of the Scovils or Scovills in England and America: Seven Hundred Years of History and Genealogy.*

In the autumn of 1868, Samuel James and Mary Eliza Scovil were living in Saint John, enjoying an affluent and pleasant life with four surviving children to support and care for, Bessie, Samuel John (Jack), Morris and Barclay, ranging in age from nineteen years to twenty months. Samuel James owned commercial shipping, carried on an insurance business, and was a qualified attorney-at-law, or at least he activated his attorney's papers occasionally and may have practiced at one time. In addition, he was a lending and investment banker. A flier on file in the Saint John Free Public Library dated March 4th, but giving no year, shows him as

> Agent at St. John for the St. Stephen Bank, office — No. 5, Water Street, Market Square. Investments made in and sales effected of Bank Stock, Mortgages and Securities of every kind. Sums of £10 and upwards received on deposit, for which receipts will be given, bearing interest at the rate of 6 per cent, and payable either at call or fixed periods, as may be agreed upon.

He re-registered his attorney's papers in 1868, at the age of 52, when his financial world began to dangerously crumble and move toward the disaster of bankruptcy.

Samuel James' financial problems and those of his bank appear to have become serious partly because of a quality he would have learned at his father's knee — trust. He trusted his New York agents. However, to understand the impact of the circumstances it is useful to know what appeared on the *Saint John Morning Telegraph* editorial page on December 3, 1868 in an article headed, "Mr. Scovil's Gold Account Books Reveals some Curious Facts." The article goes on to state, "His purchases and sale of gold from Sept. 17 to Nov. 10 amounted in gross to $5,474,000 — a fact which substantiates our statement that Mr. Scovil dealt in millions in these operations."

When the investment bank of which he was an agent failed, it was proposed that Scovil be charged in Saint John under the Absconding Debtor's Act, but the fact he had already arranged to be held in Kingston gaol complicated matters. In the 4th of February 1869 hearing in Saint John, Judge Watters ruled he could not adjourn proceedings to Kingston in order to obtain evidence from Mr. Scovil because "he had no power to hold judicial proceedings in King's County that had been commenced in the County of Saint John" (*Saint John Morning Journal*, 5 February, 1869).

The 1983 University of British Columbia Press published the book, *Canada Home, Juliana Horatia Ewing's Fredericton Letters, 1867-1869* (edited by Margaret H. and Thomas E. Blom) offers an additional view of "The Scovil Affair." In a letter dated Sunday, 29 November 1868 to her mother in England, Juliana Ewing paints a picture of a thoroughly disreputable Samuel James, suggesting he was a rogue and an intentional swindler:

> There have been some rather disgraceful commercial failures which will make it a very hard winter to many innocent people and which makes us thankful we have no money invested here! One gentleman

who has ruined lots of poor single women and people in a "small way" by his bankruptcy was put in honorable captivity in his own house under care of the Sheriff—(but assisted by a friend) he locked the Sheriff up and bolted. He has since been taken. The Bishop [Medley] is very full of all this, and a good deal worried, as he has church money invested as well as money of his own, and confidence in all kinds of securities is greatly shaken.

Although more dramatic and somewhat divergent from the newspaper accounts, this gives an indication of how widespread were the effects of Samuel James' bankruptcy. Juliana Ewing mentions multiple "failures" including the Commercial Bank and the Westmorland Bank as well as the St. Stephen Bank, all New Brunswick institutions. No wonder "confidence...is greatly shaken." Unfortunately, Mrs. Ewing writes nothing further by way of creating a more balanced picture, which she might have done after Samuel James's letter of apology and explanation was published in the Saint John *Morning Telegraph* on Saturday, December 5, 1868 under "Affairs of Mr. S. J. Scovil":

> The following letter from Mr. Scovil to one of his creditors....appears to be a candid expression of the deepest contrition for the enormous losses which Mr. Scovil's business operations have brought down upon so many confiding depositors....
>
> Kingston Gaol
Saturday, 28th Nov. 1868

> Dear Sir,
> It has been said, "better deal with a knave than a fool." By my want of caution and business capacity, I have brought ruin upon myself, my nearest and dearest friends and all who have placed such unlimited confidence in me.

You inquire whether the St. Stephen Bank is not liable for your deposit? That Bank stands in precisely the same relation to me as any other creditor, except that I paid the Bank no interest—whereas to others I paid, to some 6 and to a few 7 per cent per annum. My losses have been enormous. It is a dreadful business, but my unfortunate creditors have no remedy, except against me personally.

The preference I gave to the Bank and others was intended to preclude them from any further share in my assets. I had already given to persons appointed by my depositors, full permission to examine my books and papers, as I wished to give my creditors all the information they desired. I was anxious also to make an assignment, the exact terms of which I visited my Solicitor that night to discuss. It was arranged, then, before I knew of any writs against me for, which I had not given bail, that I should leave St. John and come here to be confined in the gaol of my native town, Kingston. I left with this intention, came and voluntarily surrendered myself to the Deputy Sheriff here.

My coming here has placed me in the position of one absconding from his creditors. It has, however, placed all my property at their disposal, which I do not regret, if they prefer this mode of proceeding to a well considered assignment to their own nominees, in which the rights of all classes would have been carefully guarded and preference creditors excluded. From the bottom of my heart I lament the loss you in common with so many others have sustained.

It is a sad, very sad, heart rendering [presumably he means rending] affair; and even in the absence of any criminal intention, has overwhelmed me with

14

the deepest sorrow and despair. It was my aim, and I have spent days and nights of toil and anxiety, to pay every one his just dues. I have miserably failed, and if my failure had only affected myself, I should not, as now, be compelled to drag out a wretched existence of sorrow and shame.

Your humble servant,
S.J. Scovil

What misery Bessie's father must have suffered writing this letter, but his early lessons of right and wrong clearly pressured him into laying himself out to be trodden upon. To write it from gaol and that in the village of his origin, a few yards from his childhood home, knowing of the extreme embarrassment to the Rev. William Elias Scovil, the present incumbent, his esteemed brother, would rub salt into the wound of failure. A column in the December 5th edition of *The Morning Telegraph* comments as follows:

> From another quarter we have understood that Mr. Scovil was utterly ruined before he entered upon his heavy gold operations; he had met many serious business reverses, involving sums ranging in amount from $1,000 to $30,000 each. He is believed to have lost $6,000 at one time by the robbery of his safe, and large amounts, directly or indirectly, by McLean, Lingley, Gardner, Higgins (of Maine), Logan, the runaway, and a score of others. ... In another case, a vessel was taken in lieu of money for a debt (reported between $20,000 and $30,000) but the whole was lost by the failure of the Columbia Office in which she is insured.

The column continues:

> There can be no manner of doubt that besides his speculation in gold, Mr. Scovil experienced such

business losses as would have ruined any man or any institution not sustained as he was constantly by the contributions of confiding depositors. That he has saved anything for himself from the wreck is believed by well informed persons to be extremely doubtful, although on this point many of his depositors will scarcely be convinced until his books are made to prove that everything that went into the establishment is accounted for on their pages. It may be some time before this point in the investigation is reached.

Mr. Scovil's books were removed from his late Banking premises yesterday in charge of Mr. Wetmore (of Cudlip and Snider's office) for the purpose of being thoroughly investigated under the direction of the Creditors' Committee.

The "sorrow and shame" experienced by Samuel James and his family was prolonged by frequent and detailed newspaper reports. I have tried to imagine the immediate effect this would have had on his daughter, Bessie, old enough at nineteen to understand many of the ramifications. For her model of manhood to be considered to have lacked business acumen is one thing, but for some to imply that he had devious and dishonest intentions was another. I can picture her mother trying to make the best of a financial and social disaster, not wanting Bessie to lose faith in her father and yet not seeing any way around ruination, except depending on her own Robinson family, who had already tried to come to her husband's rescue.

The chatter at afternoon tea and dinner parties in Saint John and elsewhere must have concentrated on the scandal, compared investments lost, disobeying the Victorian dictum not to discuss money, politics, or religion at socially correct gatherings. Did Bessie and Mary Eliza give up attending? Did the invitations stop arriving? Perhaps the "failure" took on the qualities of a death in the family. In a sense it was. Samuel James' active life in business was over. Mother and daughter's withdrawal from social activities would have been understood and perhaps seen as a boon as it left the rest to discuss whatever aspect of the disaster they wished, without changing the subject whenever a Scovil joined the group.

In spite of the letter of remorse leading the article on Dec. 5th and a not unsympathetic account following, the latter part of the column contains an unpalatable inference—that S. J. Scovil was trying to slip out of responsibility for the failure, at least out of being arrested. I did not grow up with the knowledge that great Grandfather was a lawyer or attorney. That may have been because he did not practice, which seems to be the case, but the following quote, continuing from the previously cited *Morning Telegraph* of December 5th, 1868, is what is relevant to this story,

> It will interest the public to learn that the Chief Justice has dismissed Mr. Scovil's application to be allowed the privilege of an Attorney—freedom from arrest. The argument was resumed yesterday (Friday) afternoon before the Chief Justice of Quispamsis. Mr. Barker (of Wetmore and Barker) produced the affidavits of the defendant and his brother, W.E. Scovil, in answer to those on the part of the plaintiff. Mr. Crawford (of Crawford and Pugsley) was heard against the application, citing new authorities. His Honor gave Judgment immediately, dismissing the application, for discharge. The Chief Justice remarked that the parties who had now arrested Mr. Scovil had dealt with him in the capacity of a Banker and he felt that he would be doing grievous wrong to the commercial community of Saint John if he should decide that under the facts the privilege of freedom from arrest ought to be allowed in this case. He stated distinctly that this privilege is intended for the benefit of clients, and it did not appear that there was one to come forward to claim Mr. Scovil as his Attorney, and thus place him and his case in a better light.

It appeared that Mr. Scovil had been doing an extensive business as a Banker and Insurance Agent; had held himself out to the world in that capacity; had advertised his business as such; and had in no wise conducted himself as an Attorney; and while these facts might be only inferences against the defendant, yet coupled with the facts that last year he had only taken his certificate out on the 27th day of May when, it could be available for a few days only, that he had not taken out his certificate for this year until the 19th day of November when he had become insolvent and had actually been arrested, he must arrive at the conclusion that the certificate was taken out as a shield to prevent his arrest and not with the bona fide intention of resuming practice. He felt that he would be torturing the privileges of Attorneys and his own conscience should decide that upon the facts as they appeared from the affidavits before him, Mr. Scovil was entitled to his privilege. He should therefore dismiss the application. If the party was not satisfied, he could make an application to the Supreme Court next Hilary Term [beginning in January].

A small hope was gone. The would-be-registered-Attorney must have known, even before the hearing, that the possibility of being excused on the basis of his being accepted as an Attorney was as settled as a dry leaf on a windy day. Ripples shimmered throughout New Brunswick society from this business and private failure like those from a stone cast into a pond. Ecclesiastical life at the highest pinnacle was not immune. Again, the December 5th edition of the *Morning Telegraph* gives us a letter from Bishop Medley, the very one who officiated at S. J. Scovil's wedding:

As many of the members of the Diocesan Church Society may have apprehended that great loss would happen to the Society in consequence of the failure of its last Treasurer, S. J. Scovil, Esq., the Bishop of Fredericton, at the request of the Executive Committee begs to assure them that one of the bondsmen of the late Treasurer is prepared to meet the deficiency and the Committee confidently believe that no loss will eventually accrue. Prompt measures have been taken to investigate the affairs of the Society, in relation to its late Treasurer, and the salaries of the missionaries [clergy] will be paid as usual. A new Treasurer has been appointed, in whom general confidence is placed—H. W. Frith, Esq. of this City—and the monies of the Society will be lodged in the Bank of New Brunswick. No further apprehension therefore need be entertained.

John Fredericton
St. John, Dec. 4th 1868

This letter from Bishop Medley—signed in the manner of Anglican Bishops at the time—is hardly in keeping with the previously quoted comments by Juliana Ewing in her letter home to England on November 29th just a few days before the Bishop's letter to the press. To re-quote part of her letter: "The Bishop (Medley) is very full of all this and a good deal worried, as he has church money invested as well as money of his own…" The Bishop, ever mindful of the views of others, seems to have acted quickly to show that though he might not have chosen an entirely admirable man to be Diocesan Society Treasurer, he would be seen as producing one, "in whom general confidence is placed," thus spreading the blame if there should be another disaster. None of his personal worry shows in his letter, but as Juliana Ewing and her husband were close friends of the Medleys, they would know his real thoughts.

No matter how hot and embarrassing the gossip, no matter what arrows of criticism were aimed at Bessie's father, her uncle, William Elias Scovil, rector of Trinity at Kingston carried out his duties and met expectations of the greater community.

The Morning Telegraph of December 22, 1869 noted that he was one of five prominent Reverends to be present at the semi-annual Examination of the St. John Grammar School. Given the nature of the tests, it was necessary to have men educated in the classics as examiners. The *Telegraph* states: "The more advanced Classes were examined in Homer's Iliad, 1st book; Greek Testament; Aeneid of Virgil, 1st book; and Horace, 4th Book of the Odes. The first classes in Geography, History, and French completed exercises."

As Uncle William listened to nervous grammar school boys while they sweated the reciting of the Iliad, and as father Samuel James narrowly escaped a trial and endured a short incarceration, how was young Bessie able to face the world? I can imagine the weeks of newspaper accounts, the large numbers of investors affected, and general negative gossip in a relatively small community must have made life almost unbearable. Probably Bessie spent much of her time comforting her mother whose family name, Robinson, was prominently featured in the papers' accounts in the person of Major Robinson, her brother, and his "rescuing" the "culprit" and helping him to flee to Kingston. Supporting Mother was an urgent duty.

In the absence of definite facts there is always surmise, which keeps up interest in the story and sells papers. But it is also this type of reporting which would deepen both Scovil and Robinson humiliation. Did Samuel James' letter from the Kingston Gaol on November 28th help the family with their burden? It should have, at least to a small degree. References to his great personal loss would have indicated to newspaper readers that their own losses were unlikely the result of a scam, but as the letter stated, of poor judgment. Looking back from this distance, possibly unethical agents in New York or Boston contributed to the debacle. We will never know for what reason Samuel James bought gold on the New York and Boston markets on several occasions for more than he managed to sell it. Once should have been enough. Judging from his letter from gaol, poor judgment was chiefly to blame. Perhaps the New York agents were assuring that the price was going up; perhaps it did in the U.S. but not in Canada. A desperate man gambled on desperate action and lost.

As a great granddaughter of this humbled man, I cannot help but feel sorry for him. He had been conducting the business of a highly respected and flourishing lending bank, among other ventures, for many years. But now he had been having significant financial problems for several months and apparently lacked good business judgment in dealing with this crisis. Having a brother, a father, and a grandfather who were all clergymen would have added to his dependable, rock solid image. The Bishop would not have appointed a man with a shaky professional reputation to be the Diocesan Society Treasurer. All this meant he had farther to fall from his elevated pedestal, producing more shock to his family and to the affected investors.

If my great grandfather had practiced law only and not been seduced by the attractions of banking, how differently Bessie's life would have developed. As well as continuing to live in the city where she had grown up, able to look to her father as a generous provider for her, her three siblings, and her mother, she may not have felt so compelled to be educated for a profession, then in its infancy, but which would come to provide her with a steady income and financial independence. Looking at all the grief, embarrassment, and financial and professional ruin the failure brought on Bessie's father and his family, we might wish it had not occurred. However, it very likely played a role in Bessie's determination to become an independent, professional woman and to achieve all that she did.

Samuel James' productive life came to an abrupt end at only fifty-two. My mother said that for years afterward her grandmother attempted to pay creditors by selling family furniture and other possessions. This was not legally necessary but it shows how determined Mary Eliza was to do all she could to rescue the names of Scovil and Robinson.

* * * *

Just when Mary Eliza, Bessie, Jack, Morris and Barclay left Saint John for the Fredericton area is unknown, but it must have been as soon as arrangements could be made. Samuel James could not return to Saint John. He was still in Kingston, on February 4,

1869, according to the quotation from Juliana Ewing's letter in the book, *Canada Home*. He was presumably staying with his brother at the rectory after he left the Kingston gaol. The family would likely have remained in Saint John until they knew the decision of Judge Watters on February 4, 1869 that Kingston was out of his jurisdiction. Mary Eliza, perhaps with the help of her brother, William, would have then promptly made arrangements to dispose of their house and any possessions they would not take with them to Pine Grove.

Perhaps by the spring of 1869, when the ice was out and the river subsided from its usual flooding, the four Scovil children waved good-bye to the only place they had called home. With a heavy heart but a brave countenance, Mary Eliza and her children all boarded a riverboat for Fredericton. Samuel James would have remained in Kingston until he could join his family on one of the paddle-wheel steamboats bound for Fredericton that stopped at the Kingston Peninsula wharf.

Whichever riverboat they boarded, it would have landed on the South side of the St. John River at the Fredericton wharf. Perhaps one of Mary Eliza's brothers engaged a ferry to take them to the north side and the Parish of St. Mary's, later called Devon, where a servant would be waiting with a carriage and horses to transport the homeless family a few miles up river to Pine Grove, in Douglas, their mother's family home.

* * * *

The first Robinson in this part of the world was Mary Eliza's grandfather, Colonel Beverly Robinson, (1754-1815), sometimes called "the younger" as his father had the same name and rank. After his Loyalist regiment was disbanded, the officers and men were assigned land along the river, hoping for fertile soil. As the son of the original senior officer, and now in charge of the regiment, Bessie's great grandfather claimed prime land along the river, in what was called Nashwaaksis, a name he adopted for his extensive holding but which was often referred to as simply "The Farm."

John, the son of the young Colonel and his wife, Mary Simonds, was born in 1789 and was brought up in the surroundings of a prosperous farm. John eventually married Eliza Maria Allaire, the daughter of Major Anthony Allaire. Allarie, whose Huguenot ancestors arrived in New York in 1699 from Rochelle, France, was an officer of the Loyal American Regiment and a colleague of the young Colonel Robinson. Major Allaire built a large residence called Pine Grove in nearby Douglas. It was here that Mary Eliza, Bessie's mother, was born and grew up and to which she and her family now returned. Although a sense of shame persisted, she was glad to be away from the gossip and impossible atmosphere of Saint John, to be able to comfort her broken husband, and to bring up her still mostly young family.

In the late 1930s the house at Pine Grove was used as the Municipal Home. The York Manor Nursing Home was then constructed on the site and eventually numerous modern houses came to occupy the property. When the Scovil family arrived, Pine Grove was occupied by Delancy Robinson, grandson of Colonel Beverly Robinson the younger. According to newspaper clippings from the early 20th century found among the family papers, a fire later spread from burning grass and did major damage to barns, outbuildings and the residence. The newspaper account states that "Mr. Robinson was somewhat of an antiquarian and had a valuable collection of old books, manuscripts, Loyalist records etc. which were all lost." It was known in the family that among the losses were "love letters" from General George Washington to Mary Phillipse, who lived at Phillipse Manor, Yonkers, New York. However, she instead accepted the proposal of Roger Morris when the General was away soldiering. The elder Col. Beverly Robinson married Mary Phillipse's sister, Susanna, the richest woman in the colony. (A fictionalized version of this story is told in the book, *Dear George, Dear Mary,* by Mary Calvi, published in 2019.)

But in the spring of 1869, welcome fireplaces glowed with warmth for the unfortunate cousins from Saint John. Families and friends must support one another in times of need and in times of disgrace. Robinson family memory still recalled that first winter Fredericton in the 1780s, when friend Jonathan O'Dell offered hospitality to Colonel Beverley Robinson and his family before their home, The Nashwaaksis, was habitable. Occupancy was delayed by fire in the partially finished house that made it unusable for the winter. While it was being repaired and completed, O'Dell made room for them in his spacious home on the corner of Church and Brunswick Streets on the Fredericton side of the river. (More recently this house became the residence of the Bishop of Fredericton.)

Giving and accepting hospitality was essential to survival in those early days of Loyalist settlement. For Bessie and her family, it was still essential. It would be interesting to know what passed between the Saint John Scovils and the Pine Grove Robinsons regarding the duration of the former's need for shelter. Mary Eliza may have suggested a few months; her relatives may have answered, as long as necessary. Neither party could know the need would last for eleven years. Possibly Bessie was absent for short or long periods. My mother said that her Aunt Bessie often visited her Uncle William Elias and Aunt Frances and their six surviving children in Kingston. A sensible and resourceful young woman with a religious bent would be more than welcome in a child-filled rectory.

Bessie and her parents and younger brother Barclay were definitely in New York for the better part of a year, sometime during the eleven years of residence at Pine Grove. There is evidence that Samuel James tried to find employment in New York, presumably in finance. The family probably stayed with relatives. His attempt was not successful so the family returned to Douglas. The last two years of their stay (1878-1880) coincided with Bessie's studying nursing in Boston at the Massachusetts's General Hospital. She did not return to live at Pine Grove, her family home having switched in 1880 to The Farm at Scovil Point, across the river from Gagetown, which she soon named Meadowlands.

There is no record of whether the boys, Jack, age 13 and Morris, age 9, were pleased by the relative freedom of rural Douglas or if they missed their friends and more sophisticated lives in Saint

John. Little Barclay, only 2 years old, would have enjoyed the excitement of the riverboat trip and playing with his cousins. After a few days for settling in, the extreme tension that had permeated the family for the past few months must have started to recede, which would have been a relief as they made the uncomfortable transition from past affluence to being the poor relations.

Of all the children, the change of dwelling place must have been most disruptive for Bessie, just going into her 20th year. We know from a long letter she wrote to her mother while, at one point, in Saint John, that Bessie had enjoyed a lengthy visit with New York relatives the year before, probably with her mother's brother, Henry Barclay Robinson, his wife Caroline Betts and their numerous children. Clearly, she was capable of travelling independently and making her own decisions. Although her formal schooling extended only to age sixteen that was sufficient for her to take up teaching in Fredericton in the period before she made up her mind to train for a career in professional nursing. When he was in his 70s, her youngest brother, Barclay wrote to his great nephew, Roger Scovil, three years after Bessie died, that she had taught school in Fredericton during her 20s. Her teaching would have brought in a little money for the family and allowed Bessie to meet Frederictonians from a variety of social and economic backgrounds. Otherwise her social contacts would have been confined to family and their friends and to their association with Christ Church Cathedral, which they attended.

Gossip and ill will toward the Scovil family considerably diluted as the years passed, although the stain of Samuel James's financial dealings left its mark on his name as the man responsible for the financial losses of those who trusted him with their investments. The Scovil name would have been rarely mentioned without some reference to the disaster. The loss, the scandal, the failure as the bankruptcy was variously called, was firmly stuck in the family psyche as something that no one wanted to discuss. Very few details were ever aired, especially in front of my mother's generation. She was not aware of the facts of the case revealed by my research in the newspapers of the time and elsewhere.

* * * *

Trying to put the disagreeable past behind her, Bessie settled into the routine of her new home. With how many Robinsons did Bessie and her family share Pine Grove? Census reports in 1861 and in 1871 did not include addresses, only the name of the Parish. There were two households of Bessie's Robinson relatives in the Parish of Douglas. The home of Colonel Beverly Robinson, called The Farm or The Nashwaaksis, which was situated just past the present Stone Bridge down Burpee Street toward the Saint John River, and Pine Grove built by Major Anthony Allaire, a few miles along the road in Douglas.

In the 1861 census, John Robinson Esq., Farmer, 74 was listed as head of the Pine Grove household (died 1866, age 78) with Eliza Maria, wife, age 67 (later died 1874, age 79), T. Barclay, son, age 22 (died 1914, age 75), J. Delancey, son, age 20 (died 1913, age 72), and Ellen Turner, an Irish servant, age 18.

When John Robinson, son of the Colonel, married Eliza Maria Allaire, they set up their home at Pine Grove after her parents died. From several clues in letters, mostly written by Samuel James from Pine Grove to his son Jack in New York, where he settled in his early 20s, we can come to the conclusion, adding and subtracting from the 1861 and 1871 census information, that the following Robinsons greeted the Scovil family in 1869: Delancey (farmer), his wife Susan (Hubbard), his mother Eliza Maria (Bessie's grandmother), and his children Fanny, age 4 and Mary, age 2.

Delancey, Mary Eliza Scovil's youngest brother, remained in the family home, marrying young and taking over the farm a year or so before their father died, which was three years before the Scovil family arrived. Mary Eliza Scovil's mother, Eliza Maria, with five more years to live must have been delighted to have her own daughter, and 19 year-old granddaughter, Bessie, unexpectedly added to her household. Susan, Delancey's wife, well embarked on frequent pregnancies would have appreciated the arrival of more women, especially Bessie, who was only two years her junior. Susan and Delancey's children, Fanny and Mary, would have their boy cousin, Barclay, approaching 3, as a playmate. Jack at 13 and

Morris, not quite 9, would find life on the farm far less restricted than the one they had known in the city. The total came to ten living under the same roof until Frances Delancey was born to Susan, but dropping back to ten again in 1874 on the death of Eliza Maria at age 79.

Bessie left for Boston and her training in 1878 and Jack for New York, sometime between 1876 and 1878. He was still in Douglas in the spring of 1876. A certificate found among family papers and dated April 5, 1876, states that 20 year-old Jack was "Cadet No. 30," graduated from the "School of Military Instruction in the Reserve Militia of the Dominion of Canada, able to command a company at Battalion level." Samuel James made reference in a letter written from Pine Grove that Jack took excellent references with him to New York for finding work as an accountant so presumably he had also been employed in an office in Fredericton, as an accountant. Jack probably left Douglas for New York when he was 21.

Though reduced from six to four with the departure of the two eldest children, the remaining Scovil family wanted their own home. Mary Eliza mentions in a letter to Jack, now settled in New York, that they are happy at Pine Grove but his father would like to be settled in a place he could call his own. Samuel James must have known that his Uncle Samuel Scovil, before he had died in 1856, bequeathed to him two properties including a property in Saint John and the nine hundred acres of interval and forest land at Scovil Point on the St. John River four miles from the small village of Jemseg. Scovil Point was on the east side of the river directly across from the larger village of Gagetown, and about half way between Fredericton and Saint John. The term "interval land" generally means low lying valleys between hills, but in New Brunswick is widely used to designate the flat land along the courses of rivers likely to be flooded by high water during spring run-offs from melting ice and snow. Interval land is the deepest, richest, most naturally fertile soil in the Maritime region. It is prized for growing farm crops and especially for producing lush crops of hay. The Scovil farm property at Scovil Point was a prime agricultural asset.

Although Uncle Samuel's will left the Scovil Point farm to his nephew, he put in a clause that allowed his second wife, Mary Smith, to live in the house until her death. His first wife, Deborah Gilbert, had no children and neither did his second. Had there been children from either marriage, The Farm at Scovil Point would not have been acquired by Bessie's family. Her life would have been decidedly different, especially from 1903 on, when she retired from her nursing career in the U.S. and came to live at the farm. Uncle Samuel's gravestone, a prominent obelisk in the Jemseg Anglican Church graveyard, describes him as;

> Samuel Scovil, JCP, 4th son of the late James Scovil, who for 88 years resided in this parish and was repeatedly a consistent churchman, of sterling integrity and unaffected piety, born Oct. 9, 1768, died Nov. 30, 1856.

The name Deborah Gilbert, his first wife, is not on his stone. The name of his second wife, Mary Smith, appears without any dates. Church records, however, show that Mary Scovil was buried in the St. James churchyard in Jemseg on January 19, 1874, aged 81 years.

When Uncle Samuel made his will, he could not have imagined that his chosen up-and-coming nephew would have been so in need in 1869. Had he known, he might have worded his will differently. As it was, Mary Smith Scovil was free to live in the homestead-house on the farm or in the Smith house, likely her family home in Jemseg that would have belonged to her husband by marriage. She preferred the former and remained on the Scovil Point farm until her death in 1874. Why did Samuel James and family not move to the farm at that time, especially as it was clearly left to him by his uncle twenty-three years earlier. Why did it take another six years before they made the move? My mother said there was a foreclosure situation that had to be resolved before the family moved. Although not mentioned in any letters or in the will, it's possible this was the cause of the delay.

There is evidence in Mary Eliza's letters that she and her husband were quite close to Uncle Samuel, probably the closest of his nephews, which is presumably the reason for choosing Samuel James as his chief beneficiary. In their early married life the Saint John Scovils visited Scovil Point so frequently that three of their ten children were born, baptized, or died there.

Sophia Allaire, their third child, "born in St. John 1850…died 1854 at Cambridge Queen's County (Scovil Pt./Jemseg)"; the fourth, Samuel, "born in St. John 16 February 1852, baptized in St. James Church, Cambridge…6th June 1852; the fifth, Samuel John, "born at Cambridge 2 June 1856, baptized in St. James Church, Cambridge 27 July 1856. This information was copied by Samuel James Scovil from the family bible for his eldest surviving son Samuel John (Jack). The original is in a scrapbook of family history prepared by Jack and handed down to his grandson, Rev. Charles Karsten.

The property to which Samuel James, Mary Eliza, and their two sons—Morris and Barclay—moved in 1880 had a strong element of familiarity to the adults. But what did Samuel James know about farming? He had been brought up in a rectory. He would have absorbed something of farming techniques from living for the better part of eleven years at Pine Grove, a large farm and his wife's family home. When the family moved to Scovil Point, Samuel James became a gentleman farmer overnight, essentially taking charge of activities and telling others what to do. His son, Morris, now 20 years-old, had to grow up quickly becoming a knowledgeable and capable farm manager. The young farmer appears to have been naturally adept at the vocation and the farm flourished.

The three years left to his father were a steadying and encouraging influence for Morris. Samuel James was educated to be an attorney and had taken up a career in finance and investment banking. Although he would not have been knowledgeable about the fine points of animal husbandry and agriculture, his experience with financial accounting would have been an asset. He had a witty, active mind and was keenly interested in national and international politics. His physical health had never been strong and with the devastating failure of his career was probably in decline even before the move from Pine Grove to the farm at Scovil Point. Had his public reputation been less blemished and his health better, Samuel James might well have enjoyed a career in politics, representing the Union Party (Conservatives), of which he was a sincere supporter. But that could not be. In those days it was extremely difficult to re-create yourself as trustworthy once your business reputation had been blackened.

Bessie's mother prepared for the move to Scovil Point several months before the event. In a letter dated 11 Feb. 1880, she wrote to her son in New York:

> Dearest Jack,
> I am getting things together by degrees for the farm and expect to be very happy here and then from May to July will only seem a short time till you and dearest Bessie will walk in. We get on very well here but your Father will be glad to have a home of his own to live in. How soon the time will come…for moving. Canon S. (Scovil) is just as anxious as ever that your Father and I should have a home and speaks…on the subject.

The Scovil family moved in May but July is the month to which Mary Eliza is really looking forward. Bessie graduated from her two years of nurse's training in 1880. Jack, still unmarried, must have planned his summer holidays to fit in with an inspection of his new family home at Scovil Point. Bessie was now in her early 30s, of independent mind, and would have happily travelled alone but would now be accompanied by her brother on this homecoming visit to New Brunswick.

Rather than being just a cousin who was concerned about Samuel James and Mary Eliza and their family having a home, Canon William Scovil appears to have had a financial interest in the farm. In the same letter quoted above, Mary Eliza writes that:

> "Mod [nick name for son Morris] has written that Ned [DuVernet, brother of Harriet, Morris's future wife] intends having an auction in the spring which will enable…to buy in what I…want and also put Ned in funds to pay us $200 in cash, one of which goes to pay the Canon's interest & the other we will.…to him when we can sell the hay next summer.

It's unlikely that "interest" refers to interest on a loan, but rather some financial claim on the property. There is no evidence that he lent money or paid for repairs or partial building of his uncle's house, although something like this may explain "the Canon's interest." Canon Scovil distinguished himself in ecclesiastical matters, having been the Canon of the Cathedral in Fredericton.

Certainly Canon Scovil kept an eye on the family's progress, in particular Bessie's accomplishments, even after he moved to Brighton, England in 1877. In the same letter to son, Jack, quoted above, Mary Eliza mentions the Canon's recent comments, suggesting that he could be anything but charming:

> We have lately had a letter from Bessie. She has had letters from Canon Scovil and his wife. They are in Cannes, South of France, he writes very civilly and complementary, begins his letter, "My dear coz." quite a difference from his first studied production of last summer.

Although any but very close relatives were often referred to as "cousin," the family connection goes like this: The Rev. James Scovil (1732-1808), first Rector of Trinity Church, Kingston, had six sons—three of whom were William Scovil (1766-1851) (father of Canon William Scovil), Rev. Elias Scovil (1771-1841) Second Rector of Trinity, and (Uncle) Samuel Scovil (1773-1856) original resident and owner of the farm property at Scovil Point. These three brothers—William, Elias and Samuel—were uncles of Bessie's father, making them her great uncles and Canon Scovil, the child of William, her first cousin once removed.

*   *   *   *

By 1880, Bessie age 31, had already successfully launched herself into the world of nursing, having completed her two-year course at Massachusetts General Hospital and quickly obtaining a position at St. Paul's School in Concord, New Hampshire, where she was in charge of the infirmary. Jack, 24, was settled in New York working as an accountant. A letter from their father, written at "Pine Grove, Douglas, N.B., Ash Wednesday, 11 Feb. 1880" to Jack establishes that Bessie was indeed settled and Jack was finding his feet in the big city, although his father still seemed to think he needed advice. Jack was always addressed as "John" by his father, although by no one else.

> My Dear John,
> Yes! Bessie has certainly made a grand hit of it in her Concord engagement. It seems every thing she could wish except that it is out in a country town instead of either New York or Boston. ...
>
> And now here is another triumph for Bessie. She has received a most affectionate letter from Canon Scovil and also one from his wife [Sophia Simonds Gilbert] who hasten to do homage to her pluck and perseverance.
>
> Altogether the lines have fallen to both of you and her in pleasant places. The wheel of fortune is again turning in our favor. Is it not glorious living in New York with all its privileges and advantages? So much to see and hear every day something new. It is such a fast age...
>
> I want you to do the best you can for yourself—to make the most of your life—of course business first then recreation. Bev [cousin Beverly Robinson, son of Mary Eliza's brother] seems such a good companion.

But you must keep a steady hand and a pure heart. Don't throw away a moment of your precious time in idleness or dissipation. ...

Take as much exercise as you can — when not hurried walk instead of riding to the office — health before everything.

He continues, mentioning a Mr. Ellis, Editor of the *Saint John Globe*, who, "they say," lost his position as Post-Master at Saint John, worth $2,500 a year, because of the attacks of his paper on the Dominion government.

He belongs to the Liberal or Mckenzie party whereas the Conservative McDonald and Tilley party is now in. Such are the ups and downs of Political life. ...

How much better off are you than those who hold their positions under our present system of responsible government — a very precarious tenure. As long as you do your duty no doubt you will be all right — and if the Company does not fail may hold your place for years.

Along with the advice of father to son, and praise for his accomplishment, there is more than a small amount of envy for Jack's life in New York, a city for which Samuel James obviously had affection. After several pages of witty gossip, political comment, references to religion and death, both sudden and expected, the tedium of life at Pine Grove, which Jack knew well, creeps into his father's musings:

At Pine Grove there is no fear of our ever loosing, for one moment, sight of the long line of illustrious ancestors: Robinsons, Streets, and last not least Hubbards whose ghosts are sprung upon us at every turn almost in conversation and I suppose you hear enough about the Robinsons at all events in your social chats with Bev. and the Rev.'d Bev.

A little more than a year and a half later Jack discovered more to like about New York than convivial time spent with Cousin Bev. and his father. On the 13th of October, 1881, Bessie writes from her employment at St. Paul's School in Concord to Adeline Barker in New York, now engaged to her brother Jack, to welcome her into the family fold.

> We do not seem quite like strangers, though I hope we shall know one another very much better in the future, so I can tell you how glad we all are that you are to be one of us and how sincerely we hope that you will be happy amongst us.

With Bessie a professional nurse and Jack working as an accountant and engaged to be married, that left only Morris and Barclay and their parents to make a life for themselves at the Scovil Point farm. It also provided a stable home for Bessie to which she would return every year for her long summer holidays and whenever else she could from St. Paul's School and later from other employment.

By the 10th of April 1882, nearly two years after their occupation of the farm began, Mary Eliza writes to "My dear Addie" preparing her for her September visit, which will be her honeymoon with Jack.

> We are very isolated, & see few people in winter. You will find us very quiet I am afraid. Because it is Jack's home, he of course thinks it lovely & I am afraid you will be quite misled by his appreciation of it, & what you will find it to be, a small, small cottage on the bank of the river, everything very plain but comfortable and much love enclosed within its walls—which we

lavish on our children & we shall be proud to include you in the number when you come in the Autumn. ...

This early description of the house is calculated to downplay its size compared with New York dwellings with which Mary Eliza was familiar from her visits with her brother and his family. In the same envelope is a letter, also written on April 10th, to "My dear Addie" from her future father-in-law. There is less detail than in his wife's warning, but a general comment that was aimed in the same direction, lowering Addie's expectations of what she might find at the farm. "No doubt you will be pleased with the novelty of the change from gay, busy N. York and enjoy the comforts of your happy home all the more after roughing it a little in New Brunswick."

It's certain that Samuel James and Mary Eliza discussed their approach to communicating with their future daughter-in-law, very much hoping to avoid her disappointment with anything connected with Jack. Judging by various comments made in his fatherly letters to Jack about the need for a balanced life, outdoor exercise every day if at all possible, avoiding frivolous friends and relations including "Bev.'s amours" and the need for frugality, Samuel James appears to have harboured some concerns about his son being an acceptable match. A year earlier, on October 18th, 1881 Mary Eliza writes to "My dear Addie":

> I am delighted to hear from Jack that you have made him the happiest man in the world by consenting to become his wife. He has from childhood up been an excellent son, & by his steady good conduct repaid all my love and care of him. This is the best guarantee that he will make a kind, good husband. ...
>
> I thank God that Jack has been guided safely through many temptations and set his heart on one so entirely worthy. With love and esteem founded on religious principle there seems a bright future before you.

Reference to "many temptations" is probably nothing more than general ones connected with moving to a big city from a small community, but possibly also included the particular delights presented by Jack's cousin Bev and his friends and parties given by fun-loving Aunt Carrie Robinson for her young adult children.

Adeline Barker, with a doctor for a father and a maternal grandfather who was a clergyman (Rev. Gilbert Hunt Sayers, 1787-1874) in the early days of the Episcopal church in Jamaica, Long Island, could not have been bettered as a suitable consort. No wonder every effort was being made to welcome this pretty young woman into the Scovil family, anchoring Jack to a respectable and apparently affluent family. However, he was to discover much later that the widower Dr. Barker, although highly thought of in his community and with pre-Loyalist family ties in the Maugerville/Sheffield/Barker's Point area along the St. John River in New Brunswick, lived in a way that fully used up his New York income. When he died there was no appreciable inheritance coming to Adeline, his only surviving child. The unlikely possibility of being financially propped up by Bessie, his unmarried sister, eventually became a reality. But in 1881 all Jack's prospects looked rosy.

The future, however, was not all that encouraging for his father. A year and a half after taking up residence at Meadowlands, he wrote in a letter dated 17 Nov. 1881, from "The Farm, near Gagetown" to "My dear Dr. Barker" to say how pleased he is that their children have become engaged. (Samuel James never used "Meadowlands" as a name for The Farm. This was the name given it by Bessie and was not in general use until after her father's death. Perhaps he thought his daughter had chosen a too flowery name for a serious endeavour.)

> I have not been at all well this fall and wished to write before to tell you how much pleased Mrs. Scovil and I are with John's engagement having heard of the careful training your daughter has received, her sound religious principles and sweet, amiable disposition. . . .

John has always been an active, industrious fellow
and took very satisfactory testimonials with him from
the Province. Naturally of a kind and affectionate
disposition he ought to make a good husband & I
trust they will be very happy together.

This letter to Dr. Barker is doubly useful. First, it proves
that Jack did not travel to New York without prospects. While
living in Douglas at Pine Grove, he must have been working in
Fredericton, perhaps as an assistant to an accountant. Since he
presumably remained at school until sixteen, the usual age, and
he was definitely over twenty when he went to New York, he had
a few years to earn his "very satisfactory testimonials" on which
his job offer in New York was based. From one of Bessie's letters,
we learn that she asked Mr. Kingsbury, President of the Scovil
Manufacturing Co. in Waterbury, Connecticut, whose wife was a
Scovil, to help find a position for Jack, which he did. He probably
could have found one in his own company but must have thought
it prudent not to employ his wife's relatives.

Second, this is the first mention that Samuel James is not in
good health. He lived only another year and a half so the illness
must have been of a serious and progressive nature. Oddly, neither
Bessie nor her mother ever refer to his specific sickness in their
letters, although there are general comments about his not being
well. The tragedy of Samuel James's decline in health, just after
nicely settling into his own property after eleven years in his wife's
old home, caused Bessie and all the family a great deal of sadness
and regret.

In 1881, Mary Eliza and Samuel James were looking forward
to welcoming son Jack and his bride in the fall, encouraging
second son, Morris, in his efforts to learn the art of managing a
nine-hundred acre hay and livestock farm and their youngest son,
Barclay, to continue attending school across the river at Gagetown.
Morris remained at Meadowlands for the rest of his working life.
Barclay, like Jack, gravitated to New York where he worked for
seventeen years in an import business on Broadway, probably as

an accountant. His position was obtained, as was Jack's, through the good offices of the President of the Scovil Manufacturing Co.

Barclay, remained single and eventually moved to Alberta where he became a Canadian Government agent hired to deliver treaty money to the remote Indigenous communities, employment that required extensive wilderness travel on horseback. In later years, letters to Bessie indicate how well he took to this rugged, outdoor life even though a mishap cost him an eye. According to an undated newspaper clipping in the family papers, "B. A. Scovil, an old St. John boy, has been elected overseer of the recently incorporated village of Bawlf, Alberta." When this came to light I thought it must be a misprint and should read "Banff." However, an Internet search tells me that Bawlf, Alberta was established in 1905 when the Canadian Pacific Railway went through this particular part of the prairie. Although it did not prosper in a spectacular way, it has endured and has a current population of close to four hundred. Barclay spent his last few years in an impecunious state in Calgary. He had a fine inquiring mind, wrote beautifully, and contributed considerably to the Brainard book on the Scovils, published in 1915.

* * * *

Of all the influences on Bessie that combined to make her take up an independent and unusual mode of life, her father's professional failure was certainly of uppermost significance. During her years at Pine Grove, from 1869 to 1878, Bessie would have been constantly reminded of her father's inability to engage in an occupation that would provide an income and a home for his family and free them of the stamp of "poor relations." It seems likely that Samuel James suffered from clinical depression and may quite early have shown signs of his final illness, perhaps heart trouble, aggravated by the stress of his bankruptcy and un-employability.

Looking back over her young life, Bessie must have been sharply aware of the impermanence of affluence, and all that goes with it, if extreme caution is not used. She dared to think that the only way for a woman to be certain of economic stability is to be in charge of her own life. If she depended on another, especially a man who does not share his business dealings with her, she could be in for a nasty and disastrous surprise through no fault of her own, no matter how supportive she had been as a wife. Her mother was a perfect example of such helplessness. What could she do that would make her financially secure so she would not have to suffer the need to lean on relations, to be humiliated, and to forgo the amenities, intellectual stimulation, and social life of her native city?

The few references to Bessie's early life indicate she was educated privately in Saint John. This means that either she attended a small, private school for young ladies, which is most likely, or someone came into her home to teach her, or she with other girls of her age and social standing gathered in one of their homes for lessons. It is improbable there was a live-in governess. I imagine Bessie's mother taught her the 3 R's while waiting for babies who did not live long. By the time Jack arrived, the first baby after Bess to bless her parents with survival, and was of a teachable age, she would have been far beyond struggling with the basics and too old for a family classroom. In Victorian times girls were given much less formal and shorter education than boys. Domestic arts were paramount, although reading, writing, and enough arithmetic to enable them to eventually run a household was considered sufficient, and of course Scripture learning for all.

As early as November 12, 1853, the *St. John Courier* carried an advertisement for a school which may be similar to one attended by Bessie:

Select Boarding and Day School for Young Ladies
Conducted by Miss Thompson
Assisted by her Father, Elder Thompson, AM.
The course of Tuition pursued embraces the entire
routine of
Thorough English education –
the Continental Languages and if required
Greek and Latin – Drawing, Painting, Music and
Singing, together with Natural and Moral Philosophy

and the general range of Polite Literature.
Two classes of Day Pupils consisting of 12 only.
The Domestic Department is under
the supervision of Mrs. Thompson.

The books, articles and speeches Bessie subsequently wrote suggest an advanced grasp of the English language, a deep knowledge of the Bible and a wide familiarity with American and British authors. Bessie obviously followed whatever formal schooling she experienced with continued informal self-study and independent, ongoing learning. It's also evident from the way she quoted appropriate sources in her mature books that she read widely in contemporary literature and in the classics along with the Bible. In a letter to her mother regarding brother Barclay's future and possible need for further education, Bessie wrote that leaving school at sixteen had not been a hindrance to her, implying that it need not be so for her brother

Bessie had a gift for teaching and enjoyed it. When she spent extended periods of time at the Kingston Rectory with her Uncle William Elias and Aunt Eliza Scovil, along with their six children, she would have read to the young ones and quite possibly have taught them to read. Had she pursued teaching as a career, however, she knew she would never be in a position of influence. Head teachers were always men, except in ladies' private schools. Women teachers were paid about half as much as men and on marriage their contracts were terminated. Bessie knew that if she married, all her possessions would legally belong to her husband, and so, literately, would she. It's likely all this was a strong influence on Bessie and her decision to take up a career other than teaching.

Although she turned her back on teaching, Bessie retained a professional interest in childhood learning and development into her advanced years. Her 1920 and 1921 book publications were aimed at enabling small children to read Bible stories. *Wee Folks Stories from the Old Testament in Words of One Syllable* was followed by a book of New Testament stories composed in the same way. She also wrote a dozen one-page short stories for her young English nieces and nephew a year before she died, all with a moral teaching. They were unpublished, preserved in her distinctive Victorian, slanted hand.

There is no reference in her writings, including personal letters, that gives any clue regarding her never marrying. The young men she met may not have had the right combination of qualities that she thought necessary in a husband. Even if they appeared to have them, they may also have a hidden weakness, like her father, that would destroy her economic wellbeing. How could she be sure they did not? Was marriage worth the gamble? Did she want to produce a baby every year or so, like her cousin at Pine Grove just to see them perish when still infants, as they had for her mother? Was marriage worth the risk?

Bessie was an attractive young woman. The studio photograph taken of her when she was nineteen proves that. The frontispiece photograph in her book, *Morning Strength*, probably taken when she was about 43, shows her still beautiful eyes without glasses, full lips and a roundness of cheek, which softened her determined chin, more obvious in her later pictures.

For whatever combination of reasons, Bessie did not marry. She was not an ordinary woman and may have sensed she was called on to accomplish out-of-the-ordinary feats—as did Florence Nightingale—that would have been impossible with a husband, children and domestic responsibilities. A woman was depicted in the 1860s, and much afterward, as chiefly the emotional and social supporter of a man from whom she was to derive her sense of identity and purpose in life, and of course her name. In return, the man provided the woman with frequent pregnancies, the financial resources to rear those who survived, as well as enough to run the home and entertain to the standard that her husband's position in society required. If neither the vision of being a school teacher under the supervision of a man was appealing, nor the role of wife to a possibly unreliable husband who might give her a multitude of children but little else, what was she to do with her life other than just being "at home"?

Bessie was a confirmed Christian in both senses. She delighted in spending extended periods of time with her ordained uncle and his family at the rectory on the Kingston Peninsula. Years later, she would make use of her religious knowledge in her many books. There was no profession within the Anglican Church open to women at the time and over one hundred fifty years later there is just the beginning of one. Her youngest brother, Barclay, after Bessie died, wrote fourteen pages in close long hand titled, "Notes On The Scovil Family." In a special section on his only sister he wrote: "She was a sincerely religious woman without parading her Christianity." This is a fair summary. Her writings show a wide knowledge of religious subjects, but she makes no reference to God or the Bible in any of her over thirty surviving letters, although frequent mention of attending church and inviting rectors to tea at Meadowlands.

According to my mother, Aunt Bessie bowed her head at the name of Jesus in church, which indicates caring about the niceties of high church ritual. (My mother maintained with glee that her aunt was once three bows behind at a Sunday service.) There was a strong Anglican high church movement in New Brunswick in the latter half of the nineteenth century that penetrated Saint John and Gagetown. The late Betty (DuVernet) Hamilton of Gagetown told me in 2004 that she and her five sisters were all brought up to bow their heads at the name of Jesus when attending their Anglican Church in Gagetown. She thought this was the influence of a high church rector from the 1920s to 1940.

Bessie embraced a practical religion. Even in the matter of writing religious books, the outcome was often extremely practical—needing the income to pay for a new barn door or money in the bank for essential bills or for assisting family members. Much of her eventual wealth, before the stock market crash of 1929, was spent on Christian charity, notably to the needy in her extended family but also to such worthy causes as a perpetual fund that supplies monies for renewing the roof on the St. James Church in Jemseg and to the Pickett-Scovil Memorial Fund for assisting sick clergymen and their families. After the death of the originator of this fund, her friend and fellow graduate of the Massachusetts General Hospital, Lucy Pickett, Bessie served as its Secretary and her name later added to the honour role.

The standard of health care in the mid to late Victorian period was appalling, women frequently dying of septicaemia (blood poisoning), often called "child bed fever," within a few days or weeks of giving birth. This is what happened to my paternal grandmother as late as 1894, ten days after my father was born. My grandfather, a qualified medical doctor, not only delivered his wife but three of her friends within a few days of one another. All four young women died of "child bed fever." This was a sad loss to the small town of Amherst, Nova Scotia, but not unusual for the time.

Louis Pasteur, in France in 1862, announced his theory of fermentation and putrefaction. Joseph Lister (1827-1912), later Lord Lister, applied Pasteur's theory to surgery, realizing that the formation of pus was due to bacteria. In 1865 he made the discovery that complications after surgery were the result of germs so he used carbolic acid spray to kill them in the air surrounding the operating table. The improvement was immediate. Later it was understood that preventing germs from getting into the air, or near the patient was even more effective, so boiling instruments, scrubbing hands, wearing sterile clothing were all introduced. It must have taken some time for this information to filter down to general practitioners in the young Dominion, to medical schools, and schools of nursing. Bessie mentions in a speech she gave in the spring of 1934 in Greenville, South Carolina, that when she was a nursing student in 1878-1880 "we had no knowledge of microbes." This was because the medical and nursing professions did not immediately embrace Lister's discovery in 1865.

We don't know for sure if the often unfortunate level of medical care at the time influenced Bessie's decision to take up nursing, but it does give some idea of the challenges she met after her decision. Her plan to study nursing, to improve health and to decrease suffering and pre-mature death was certainly formed with the awareness that in her own family six siblings had died in babyhood. She was also undoubtedly motivated by her family's tradition of service.

Her uncle, grandfather, great-grandfather, and others had been clergymen. Many other relatives had taken up leading political, military, and legal roles. Contrary to usual expectation, she must have had a strong desire not to be dependent on her family for financial security and, perhaps be of some small financial help to family members as needed. At age twenty-nine, whether by preference or not, Bessie was likely to remain as an unmarried woman. Although her father had a legacy of property, he was not able to access it until 1880, and when she entered nursing she may not have been certain he ever would.

It's fair to assume that because she was not a stranger to caring for others, Bessie's decision to become a professional nurse had been brewing for many years. With younger siblings to care for through childhood ailments, a less than robust father, and her experiences with the child-filled home of her uncle in Kingston, she already had been exposed to the challenges and satisfactions of practical nursing.

Bessie enrolled in the Nursing School of the Massachusetts General Hospital in Boston in 1878, graduating from the prescribed two-year course. No great outlay in the way of funds was needed for this education. Nurses in training were expected to pay for their instruction and room and board by time spent working on the wards. It's likely any monies needed came from the Robinsons at Pine Grove, who, by now, were well aware of Bessie's intellectual and organizing abilities. We know for sure that her mother did not immediately embrace her plan.

An interview published in *Canadian Nurse* in 1924 provides evidence for the reluctance of her dear mother.

> Miss Scovil told, with a little smile, of her mother's horror when she went to be interviewed by the secretary of the committee of ladies, who then selected the candidates for hospital training, and was asked by the maid to sit down in the hall to wait! "My mother said she would prefer me to become a housemaid. But after I graduated I wrote an article for the Youths'

Companion which brought, it was estimated, over a thousand applications for admission to the training school, and which brought me the thanks of the committee, so I was able to assure my mother she was quite avenged[1] for having sat in Miss W.'s hall."

For a gentlewoman to take up any profession at this time was highly unusual, and those involving hard work and physical contact with others were usually reserved for the uneducated and illiterate. The knowledge of Florence Nightingale's accomplishments likely removed this taboo for Bessie. This great innovator and reformer of the nursing profession provided the perfect model for Elizabeth Robinson Scovil, when, at twenty-nine, she decided to follow in her footsteps.

Miss Nightingale's contribution to lessening suffering in the Crimea War had made her famous. The war began in 1854 and ended in 1856 when Bessie was only seven, but by the time the accomplishments of "Lady of the Lamp" filtered out to the general population, the little girl in Saint John was old enough to be affected by her example.

When the heroine of the Crimea was only seventeen, in 1837, she wrote on a scrap of paper, "God spoke to me and called me to his service." Miss Nightingale spent many frustrating years not knowing exactly to what she was being called. She had a strong desire to learn all she could about nursing but her family objected so she had to do it surreptitiously. Eventually, at age 31, she finally broke the chains of conventional life and entered a convent in Germany for her first experience of actual training. She then studied hospital organization in London, Edinburgh, and Paris.

In 1853 she took the position of Superintendent of the Institution for the care of Sick Gentlewomen. The Crimean War broke out the next year. When grim reports of dreadful conditions and terrible suffering reached England, Florence wrote to a friend, Sidney Herbert, who was the Secretary for War and offered her

---

1   "Avenged" is the rare instance of Bessie using the wrong word. She probably meant, "compensated".

services. A letter from Herbert, asking her to take charge of the nurses and the organization of the military hospital at Scutari was in the return post. She left a week later with thirty-eight nurses and a shipload of supplies, just in time to receive the wounded from the battle at Balaclava. "The Lady of the Lamp," as she was called because of her checking the wards at night when soldiers would kiss her shadow as it was thrown on to their bedding, became a legend of service to the suffering. Her dedication, innovation, and determination to improve health standards proved to be a unique and revolutionary contribution to the nursing profession.

Before the reforms of Miss Nightingale in Crimea, and in the world of nursing in general, "nurses" had minimal if any training and were often impoverished women, prone to drunkenness and prostitution. Ladies or gentlewomen, as they were called did not flock to become nurses even after the reforms to the profession initiated by Florence Nightingale. The work was extremely hard and unless they had a strong urge to serve humanity by doing something useful rather than being social butterflies, they resisted Miss Nightingale's encouragement. However, in England, a few ladies from privileged backgrounds did enter the profession, usually in a supervisory capacity, which began to improve the image of nursing.

A low view of nurses never held sway in North America the way it did in Great Britain, partly because those in charge of training were determined to prevent the uneducated, the impoverished, and those with loose morals from entering the profession. However, this is not to say that a version of this "nursing problem" did not exist in North America and had to be overcome when training was established. But nursing was professionalized relatively early in North America. Being much younger countries, the United States, and later Canada, learned to prevent many of the problems with nursing that had to be overcome in Great Britain.

It was not until Miss Nightingale established a nurses' training school at St. Thomas Hospital in London in 1860, which she oversaw in minute detail, including interviewing young women who applied for training, did the low image of nursing begin to change. That she did this mostly from an invalid's bed where she often reclined while suffering from brucellosis is even more amazing.

The model of the great Miss Nightingale was undoubtedly the strongest influence in Bessie's decision to take up nursing. This influence, combined with her desire to be financially and intellectually independent, kept her motivation on track through training and for the rest of her professional life. Although it meant remaining single, Bessie had many child-filled years, as we shall see, and the great satisfaction of wide influence through her writings on the care of children and the improvement of family life. Perhaps unexpectedly, her best selling books brought in substantial income and made her a wealthy woman, a circumstance she regularly channelled into the generous support of family members in need of assistance.

Chapter Three

Nurse

The calendar had scarcely turned to June in 1878 when Elizabeth Scovil and her mother, Mary Eliza, travelled overnight by train to a destination that changed both their lives. For the daughter, it opened a world of service, fame, and prosperity, but it robbed the mother of her only daughter's companionship. The journey from Fredericton to Boston was one they had made before, sometimes going on to New York to visit family.

As their journey began, Bessie and her mother were both preoccupied with the reason for this trip—an interview with the head of the Ladies' Committee of the Massachusetts General Hospital in Boston to determine whether Bessie was a suitable nursing student. The train rocked and whistled its way along the line, clicking the miles away, flanked on both sides by quiet lakes, tall, dark pines, spruce, and pointed firs, lightened by occasional clumps of fully leafed white birch. After a stop at the railroad junction village of McAdam, New Brunswick, the grandeur of the wilderness was interspersed by views of hamlets and lonely farms as they passed into Maine. Later, the views would include villages and small towns as they entered the region called the "Boston States."

Both mother and daughter made an effort toward amiable conversation. Mary Eliza had been partially deaf since adolescence and was in the habit of speaking loudly when in noisy environments. But after she settled in the comfortably upholstered train seat, she tried to remember to speak in a well-modulated voice to Bessie who was sitting opposite her. Her cardinal rules for public travel, which she was fond of stating in appropriate circumstances, were to keep conversation private and not disturb the other passengers.

Dining cars were not yet a feature of train travel, so an extended trip meant taking along enough food for at least one meal. The Scovil ladies came prepared to be well nourished with egg and parsley sandwiches, plus generous squares of moist sour cream gingerbread—always in the pantry at home as it was a favourite of Bessie's father and the whole family—topped off with a bottle of raspberry cordial made from last summer's Pine Grove crop. As the train crossed the border into Maine, the travellers enjoyed the freshness of their picnic lunch.

With white damask napkins spread over their black serge travelling skirts, they discussed non-controversial subjects, which was a family rule when eating, though not always followed. They pronounced the sandwiches to be delicious, though Mary Eliza thought a little more salt would have improved them. When they came to the gingerbread, they talked of Father and the probability of his eating the same, likely with a large portion of whipped cream.

Though the weather of early June remained cool, the afternoon sun warmed their side of the train to the extent that both mother and daughter removed their long jackets. Bessie's jacket had intricately covered buttons and the suggestion of a belt; Mary Eliza's was trimmed with a black velvet collar with insets running the full length of the front. Their white blouses, with slim sleeves, were decorated with lace at the collars. Mary Eliza wore a cameo broach at her neck. Bessie wore an intricate silver broach given to her by her father when affluence was taken for granted before his bankruptcy in 1868.

Their clothes were the product of an exceptionally capable seamstress in Douglas who based her designs on pictures in New York magazines, though the Scovils did not choose the most dramatic fashions. They were both wearing bustles, of course—kapok pads tied around the middle that required a special way of sitting, quite difficult on a long journey when one needed to rest one's back. Mary Eliza wore her favourite black straw hat, sitting at a sensible angle, but recently augmented with a fresh, wide grosgrain bow, tied at the front, which replaced the previous one that had become somewhat limp. Bessie, because of the importance of this trip, had been encouraged to visit the local milliner. She had chosen a pillbox style hat in black felt with a blue taffeta bow at the back. She wore it slightly tipped toward the left eyebrow, covering the middle parting of her hair but showing off her nicely braided chignon at the back.

When the remains of the picnic were put away, and they were again enjoying the fleeting scenery, Mary Eliza could not resist suggesting what had been on her mind all along; it was not too late for Bessie to withdraw her application for nurse's training. They could go on to New York, spend the week with her younger brother Henry, his wife Caroline and their considerable family, then return to Pine Grove where Bessie could continue occasional teaching in Fredericton without any of this degrading and messy need for a nursing career. At this suggestion, Bessie sat up a little straighter, adjusted her hat, and trying to keep the required well-modulated voice, said, for the umpteenth time that she had firmly made up her mind; nursing was the career she wanted — not marriage, not teaching, not just living at home and passing cucumber sandwiches at church teas. She said she realized it was a bitter pill for her mother to swallow, but she greatly appreciated her coming with her on this trip and believed her mother was aware, deep down, how much she wanted to be a qualified nurse. Mary Eliza, of course, understood that at twenty-nine Bessie was no child and should be free to make her own decisions, though not until repeated large servings of parental advice were offered.

The two had always been very close. Bessie was her first child to live past the age of four. When Bessie was eleven, Jack was born, followed by Morris and Barclay. Bessie, at age nineteen, had been a particular comfort to her mother during the time of her husband's failure and financial ruin in the banking business. It was hard for Mary Eliza to accept that she was apparently loosing all influence over her determined daughter.

There was a silence between the two for a time while they continued to digest their picnic and the other's point of view. While each was trying to think of something placating to say to the other, along came the porter who said he would be making up their beds within the hour, if that would suit them. They agreed that it would. This meant spending a little time in the general sitting area, as their compartment seats would be swivelled around and made into an upper and lower bunk, with individual curtains providing privacy from anyone walking in the aisle. Bessie announced she was happy to take the upper bunk, which was expected. On previous journeys she always accommodated her elders in this way.

With a change of seating came a change of topic—what they might expect from their visit with Uncle Henry and Aunt Carrie and their multitude of Bessie's cousins. They gave polite smiles to other travellers, also waiting for their berths to be set up. Both mother and daughter took small leather bound books of Bible quotations with helpful interpretations from their handbags for a time of reading. Before long the porter had completed his job and all was in place for the climb into their berths. Bessie kissed her mother on the cheek and they both stowed their valuables under their pillows. The excitement of the day and the swaying of the train soon lulled the two women into an unexpected deep sleep.

The porter awakened everyone when morning came, announcing they would be making a half hour stop for a trackside breakfast at 8 A.M., while the train was being refilled with water. While all the passengers were eating breakfast in a rustic establishment that served hot acceptable food, the porter swiftly changed their sleeping berths to seats for daytime travel.

Before long the familiar outskirts of Boston appeared and soon they were in the city's crowded station. A carriage took them to the Massachusetts General Hospital where they arrived a half-hour early for Bessie's interview. They were shown to a long, well polished wooden bench in the hall outside the office of the Chair of the Ladies' Committee. Like Florence Nightingale before her, who personally selected candidates for the first training school for nurses, she had the power of accepting or rejecting applicants. Neither would accept a candidate unless she was seen to be a gentlewoman of Christian education who would not disgrace the newly established nursing profession with inappropriate behaviour while on duty in the hospital or outside during her leisure time.

Bessie was the perfect candidate. After an hour answering questions, she was told by an efficient, but surprisingly charming presiding lady, that the training school would be pleased to accept her, and an official letter would be sent to her in due course.

As planned, Mary Eliza and Bessie then caught a train to New York and later in the day were met at Grand Central Station by Bessie's Uncle Harry. He made a great deal of his niece's triumph in the "lion's den" and hoped she would soon qualify to wave her magic wand and make everyone in the family "as healthy as fighting cocks." The week went too quickly for Bessie, but Mary Eliza was quite pleased to be back at Pine Grove, away from the busy city life, which, in only two months time, would consume her only daughter for at least two years. By late August, Bessie had packed her trunks and was again making the trip from Fredericton to Boston, this time, at her insistence, by herself. She reasoned with her parents that if she were going to lead an independent life away from family for the next two years, she should be allowed to start now. They accepted the reasonableness of their daughter's argument.

All went according to plan, not unlike the previous trip with her mother, but with more conversation with other travellers, especially with a young woman and her daughter, who were planning to visit relatives in Boston. Bessie had much to occupy her thoughts. She knew the next two years would not be a bed of roses. She was a realist and was aware the journey toward independence and service would not be easy, but she was no flighty girl wanting to leave home at all costs. She had taken much time to think about her choice of career and her life in a bustling city instead of the hamlet of Douglas where she had spent nearly ten years of her early adult life.

Though Fredericton, across the river from Douglas, had been established in 1785 and was a thriving industrial centre, as well as the seat of the provincial government, by 1878 the population was only slightly over six thousand. Bessie was making a much larger city her home for the next two years. Boston, established in 1630, boasted a population of approximately three hundred and fifty thousand when she arrived.

* * * *

Unfortunately, we have none of the letters Bessie undoubtedly wrote to members of her family during her two years in nurses training at Massachusetts General Hospital. The program must have entailed concentrated study and long periods of work on the hospital wards, both of which would have demanded energy and determination to sustain. We gain a particular appreciation of Bessie's determination when we realize that she succeeded despite being forced to cope with two personal conditions that, from time to time, were somewhat disabling—severe headaches and eyestrain.

We learn about these conditions from later correspondence. Without specifically mentioning these afflictions, Bessie's mother, Mary Eliza, writes the following in a letter on January 16th, 1882 to Adeline Barker, her future daughter-in-law.

> I have wanted to write you ever since Christmas but had been much occupied with Bessie and Mr. Scovil…She has never been quite strong since she had measles when quite grown up…I do not think she could remain at St. Paul's very long, she had a very trying time last winter, but they hope to have less severe illness this [year]. [Bessie's first employment after graduation was as a nurse at St. Paul's School in Concord, New Hampshire.]

Bessie confirms her mother's views in a letter to Addie from St. Paul's two months later, March 2, 1882:

> If my father continues as well as he is now, I hope to be able to go to England in June. I suppose it is the effect of the year's work teaching and nursing but whatever the cause I am decidedly breaking down and must do something desperate if I do not want to become that most to be pitied person, an invalid.

Even before Christmas in 1881, Bessie wrote from the school to her future sister-in-law, Adeline Barker: "My eyes are troublesome today and Dr. Williams warned me so expressly against using them when they pained me that I dare not disobey much." On April 15, 1882 Bessie also reported to Addie; "My head aches a good deal but not violently. I have not had to give up to it yet this spring."

A year after graduation she writes the following to Addie: "I can not use my eyes at all in the evening, which is my leisure, and am obliged now to spare them even the daylight, therefore I cannot write long letters…" Bessie, at this time, is employed at St. Paul's School in Concord, New Hampshire where she is in charge of the infirmary. In a letter to Addie on June 2, 1882 from St. Paul's, she writes:

> Yesterday was the School Anniversary and a time of great excitement here. There were about two hundred visitors, a small luncheon in the gymnasium, games and a concert in the evening besides private theatricals in the afternoon. I had one of my worst headaches and could go to nothing. I did struggle out to the concert but had to leave before it was half over. The doctor talks encouragingly about 'sea air, changes, etc., and I try to believe they will affect a cure for I feel it is almost impossible to bear these much longer. I always do recuperate quickly when I begin to mend.

During the summer of 1882, Bessie sailed for England in early June and did not board her returning ship from Ireland until September 22nd. In a letter from London to her brother, Jack, on August 30th she writes: "Though my head is in a perfect whirl and I was very tired after doing St. Paul's from the crypt to the bell I must send a line to tell you about the bridesmaids' presents." After two paragraphs she stopped and did not continue until the following day.

"Thursday. I was so tired last night I had to stop writing and have now only a few minutes to scribble an ending." She mentions

that the Ketchums, a New Brunswick family, and Judge Duff, were
going to dine with her hosts that evening, and that William and
Sophie Robinson, Bessie's maternal uncle and his wife, took her
to Windsor and Eton. The letter continues:

> I came back here and Charters [Sir Charters
> Symonds, a leading surgeon connected by marriage
> with the Scovils] took me to the Savoy theatre to
> see 'Patience'. I went over the Bank of England on
> Monday. I shall be glad of a few quiet days in Ireland
> to get my thoughts straight.

In a later letter to "My Dear Addie," she adds other London
activities: "Mrs. Symonds had a little dinner party one night.
I went over Guy's Hospital and the Evelinen, a childrens' hospital,
to St. Albans, a very high church, to Kensington Gardens and
the Albert Memorial." From previous references, it is clear Bessie
suffered from migraine headaches that sometime became more
frequent and severe when she is under stress. But now, on this
extended holiday, and in spite of such a busy schedule and clearly
being very tired, she mentions nothing about her eyes hurting or
having a "bad head." The holiday cure seems to be working.

Relaxed and away from professional responsibilities, thirty-
three year old Bessie was clearly enjoying her holiday and the
association with her various hosts. As often happens when visiting,
others make most decisions. Bessie did not have to find her way
around London. She mentions Charter's wife taking her to a
wholesale jewellers so, at half retail price, she could buy bracelets
for her brother, Jack, to give to the bridesmaids at his forthcoming
marriage to Addie.

Later, when visiting the H. J. Robinsons, relatives of her mother,
at Portrush, County Antrim, Ireland, Bessie writes to "My Dear
Addie" on September 10th:

> I am staying with very kind friends and the sea air
> has already had one good affect in making me sleep

well, better than I did in England. Indeed my visit
has cured my headaches and done me an immense
amount of good.

Unfortunately, she was too optimistic. Her headaches returned and
the eyestrain continued.

Bessie's references to having eyes sensitive to the light, suggests
she may have suffered eye damage from red measles as an adult.
Her Mother wrote about Bessie not being "strong" after having
measles when "quite grown," but did not elaborate on any
particular complications. On checking with medical professionals,
I have learned that encephalitis (swelling of the brain) is one of
the complications of measles, especially in that era. Encephalitis
may include damage to the optic nerve, causing "photophobia" or
sensitivity to bright light. I can scarcely imagine how migraine
headaches, plus painful eyes, affected Bessie when she was in nurses'
training. Suffering from these disabilities undoubtedly made her
acutely aware of the overly stressful conditions encountered by
nurses in training and in subsequent employment.

* * * *

Bessie entered nurses' training at nearly thirty years of age
with a fully formed judgment of ethical behaviour, a sharp eye
for inequities, and a keen sense of fairness. While she obviously
appreciated and valued the opportunities the program of training
afforded, she was also quick to see that nurses' training was a
relatively new effort in the field of healthcare and, along with the
conditions of employment, needed to be significantly improved to
achieve the full potential of the profession. Elizabeth Robinson
Scovil brought a strong, analytical mind and the skill of rational
critique to the nursing profession; it became a lifelong mission for
her to unhesitatingly apply both these talents to nursing education
and to the conditions of nurses' employment.

In a 1931 article about her early days of nursing, Bessie states
she was the head nurse on a ward for five months during her two
years of training. Even with her disabilities, Bessie showed superior

skills. Her article on training for a career in nursing, published in *The Youth's Companion* shortly after she graduated, added to her stature in the field. It brought in a flood of applications to the School of Nursing at Massachusetts General Hospital. Clearly, her skill as a writer, which she later employed as a medical journalist and as a lecturer, was already well developed.

In 1914, Elizabeth Robinson Scovil made a major presentation titled "The Care of Nurses" to the Canadian Society of Superintendents of Training Schools for Nurses at their annual conference in Toronto, which was subsequently published in the November 1914 issue of *Canadian Nurse*. There is much to be learned from this speech about her experience of nurses' training and her ongoing mission for its reform. She was completely candid. After a brief sketch of some of her professional accomplishments, including her experience as the Superintendent of the Newport Hospital in Rhode Island, which equipped her to be "familiar with at least some of the problems which present themselves to the members of this Society" (meaning her audience), she said, "There are three things which are obviously necessary to the proper organization of a hospital, yes, even to its very existence: the patients, the buildings and the staff."

She briefly touches on patients and buildings before moving on to her main concern — staff:

> An enormous medical literature is directed to the analysis, classification and treatment of their [the patient] diseases. The staff exists for their service. The buildings are erected with special reference to their needs. These buildings are carefully planned with regard to heating, lighting, ventilation and sanitation. A large number of books have been written on hospital construction and able architects have made a special study of the subject. The buildings have not been neglected. We have some in Canada which are second to none. The new Toronto General Hospital, for example, and the Nurses' Residence at

the Children's Hospital in the same city, which is one of the most beautiful and convenient I have ever seen.

She then moves on to the staff. "Now as to the third hospital necessity, the staff. This may also be divided into three parts." She lists the trustees, setting out their duties, and the doctors on which she elaborates slightly. She then turns to the nurses:

> Last, as becomes the importance of the subject to us, giving us time to think upon it more at length, come the nurses. Without efficient nursing service a condition would prevail in all hospitals similar to that which Florence Nightingale found in the military hospitals when she went to the Crimea.

Miss Scovil lists some of the difficulties experienced there. For example, no physician could order a stimulant to be given to a patient; he was obliged to administer it himself. She continued, "The nursing problem would be comparatively an easy one if we had to consider only the relation of the nurse to the hospital." She suggests there is "little left to be said on that side," as so many books and lectures have been produced on that topic. She continues:

> We are only gradually awakening to the fact that hospitals have very important and very urgent duties towards their nurses, which in the past have been sadly and shamefully neglected. Who is to speak for these nurses? They cannot speak for themselves. Who, but we, their Superintendents. We understand the conditions thoroughly, we have trod the whole long and difficult way, have been probationers, pupils, head nurses, graduates, we know by personal experience the hardships of the road and we are they who should be foremost in suggesting means to lighten them.

A very wise observer, Dr. Hurd, of the Johns Hopkins staff, has said that unless the hours on duty of nurses are shortened and better food is served to them, the standard of nurses will continue to lower. Miss Adelaide Nutting, who is the Director of the course in Nursing and Health in Teachers' College, New York, in connection with Columbia University, in enumerating the causes which make it difficult to attract suitable applicants to training schools says: "First, there is a decided and almost universal objection to the long hours of hard work, especially to the twelve hours of night work." Thus, trained observers see that there are abuses to be remedied. Why do pupils enter a training school for nurses? It is that they may acquire a profession and be thoroughly fitted both by practical and theoretical training for all the duties which it may demand of them.

Here, Bessie has given, at least partially, the reason she took up nursing thirty-six years before.

Does it so fit them? Which comes first in planning the daily round of work and instruction, the needs of the hospital or the requirements of the nurse? Is it just to take the hard service, the great expenditure of bodily strength which the care of the sick requires, and give in return to the nurse a preparation which does not fully prepare her for the emergencies she may have to meet after she graduates?

There are drawbacks to the most perfect hospital training which are inherent in the very nature of the case and cannot be overcome. For example, implicit obedience to orders, which is absolutely necessary if discipline is to be maintained, is not conducive to quickness of resource, the ability to meet a condition that may arise in the absence of the doctor and require to be dealt with at once for the benefit of the patient.

Here is an indication of the impositions of nurse's training at Massachusetts General Hospital on the opinionated and frustrated Bessie. We do not need to guess her response to the following issues.

Apart from this, is the attitude of the hospital towards its pupil nurses, that of a teacher, willing and anxious to place all its powers of instruction at their service and to use the material which it possesses in such abundance to further in every way her advancement in the knowledge of her art! You know Florence Nightingale said: "Nursing is an art. I had almost called it the finest of the fine arts." I do not think we can truly say that the hospital does this, at least in the great majority of cases. The nurse is used for the benefit of the hospital, as a means of having its sick carefully cared for. The long hours of exhausting work in the wards so overtax her strength that it is difficult for her to study and so master the theoretical part of her profession.

While practical instruction is most necessary and nothing can teach nursing but the actual doing of it, the constant repetition of all the numberless things that must be done for the comfort and welfare of the patient, yet this is not all.

We must delve far below these to the foundations, the reason why these things are required, else we are only craftsmen and not artists. Such a simple matter as the avoidance of a wrinkle in a draw sheet leads to a consideration of bed sores, questions of tissue changes, anatomy, and physiology. When a nurse comes off duty too tired to think she cannot follow this, or any other point, into text books, or hope to elucidate by study any subject that is not clear to her. When the body is over fatigued the mind is not alert, or at its best. A nurse cannot assimilate a lecture, or profit by a demonstration when her attention is distracted by aching feet, or her nerves quivering from more demands upon her than she has been able to meet.

What a condemnation of nurse's training! How Bessie must have suffered as a student to write with such passion so many years later.

Her lecture continues with several paragraphs on the subject of teaching. With the professional experience of several decades and her reflection on what might have been, she had this to say when speaking to her fellow Superintendents in 1914.

The quality of instruction given has improved immensely during late years. Many admirable textbooks have been written for the use of classes. Lecturers take their duties more seriously than in the early days of training schools, and some of the courses given are most useful for the purpose of information and instruction.

These statements imply the reverse was true in 1878-1880, when Bessie was involved in the early days of a training school—in the fourth and fifth years of its existence. There were few patterns to follow other than those from the Nightingale School in London and in the three other embryonic schools in the United States that were all struggling to develop credible nurse training programs.

Canadian schools of nursing were established later. The first graduates of the Western Hospital School of Nursing, in Montreal, are listed as having completed training in 1889 and the first class of the Montreal General Hospital's School of Nursing did not receive their diplomas until 1891.

As early as 1875 the Montreal General asked St. Thomas Hospital in London to send Miss Maria Machin as Lady Superintendent together with several trained nurses from the Nightingale Training School. Only one trained nurse arrived with Miss Machin. Gradually, more came until there were thirty trained nurses and assistants from London, which made one nurse or assistant for an average of one hundred and forty patients. A special committee dealing chiefly with the cost of nursing in the hospital in 1877 reports:

> The trained nurses brought from England have been of very great service and the retention of a certain number of these is most desirable. They should take a lead in various wards, and be able accordingly to train up nurses in this country, whose services would prove of very great advantage in future. (H. E. MacDermot. *History of the School of Nursing of the Montreal General Hospital.* Montreal General Hospital, 1950.)

Some of the superintendents in Bessie's audience in 1914 might well have experienced being trained by one or more of these efficient British nurses at the Montreal General Hospital. They heard her speak with enthusiasm about the three-month's course of preliminary training given by a few hospitals to nursing student before they enter the wards:

> Before being called upon to do anything for a patient, she is taught by a competent instructor exactly how it should be done and receives an elementary training in anatomy, physiology and materia medica. She thus enters the wards with a certain amount of confidence, which enables her to make the best use of her opportunities for observation and to begin her work intelligently, without waste of time.

In 1914 there was no alternative to two-year training. Miss Scovil's underlining the need for a graduate nurse to be in charge of every ward suggests that it was not always so. She writes; "No undergraduate should be entrusted with the teaching of pupil nurses."

> The Superintendent should arrange a plan of teaching for each ward, such and such subjects to be especially emphasized there, and she should satisfy herself that no pupil leaves a ward without understanding them and having mastered them. You will perceive that this would prevent a nurse from being hastily moved from ward to ward, according to the exigencies of hospital emergencies. If a hospital is a school for nurses it should conform to the needs of the pupils, they should not be exploited to serve the requirements of the hospital.

This would have been seen as an impossible luxury back in 1878, which is no doubt why Bessie made such a point of it to her Toronto audience in 1914. She goes on to discuss another controversial subject, the payment of nurses, which she describes as "already pressing, and will be increasingly until it is settled." From her experience as a nursing student, practicing nurse, and as a superintendent nurse, she was equipped to propose a logical solution:

> If a nurse receives any form of money compensation from a hospital for her services therein, she is bound to render them to the fullest extent demanded. She gives them at a much lower rate than she would receive for them elsewhere because in addition to the money paid her she has certain instruction, formal and incidental, which she accepts as part of her compensation. Her education in her profession is not the chief end in view, as it is in a medical school.

Her last statement contains an element from the past, before the establishment of nurses' training schools, when the chief undertaking of a nurse was to make the patient comfortable, relieve pain if possible, give nourishment and bandage wounds, without much thought to learning techniques for future use that advance nursing skills. It is true that medical students are allowed less of a hands-on connection with patients and even in their final year are closely supervised. However, it is surprising she saw nursing education as not "the chief end in view" for a woman working toward becoming a professional nurse. However, Bessie's point gains more credence with the proposal she then offers. Continuing on the subject of payment, she writes:

> The hospital is bound to provide for the care of its sick; it is for this purpose that it exists. This service it attains from its pupil nurses for a comparatively small sum. It is, therefore, under the deepest obligation to supplement this inadequate compensation.
>
> Does it do so? Would it not be better for the training school to say frankly to the hospital: "We need the education in nursing we can only acquire by the personal care of the sick who are in your charge. We do not wish to be paid while we are learning to nurse. We will freely give the service, which your patients cannot do without. We require that you maintain a sufficiently large staff to prevent us from being overworked. That you have ward maids in sufficient numbers to relieve us from the housework, which, after it is once mastered, is not a necessary part of a nurse's daily training. That you give us enough time for the classes, lectures and demonstrations by means of which we must be properly grounded in the theoretical part of our profession."

The ordinary hospital board would probably say at once, "Impossible, we could not afford it." Take the case of a hospital with 40 nurses, to whom is paid $10 a month cash, $4,800 a year. If they give their services gratuitously, this sum would provide maintenance for a larger staff, more ward maids, paid lecturers and a better classroom equipment.

Would the greater number of hospital trustees expend the money saved in this way? Would they not probably enlarge the buildings and take in more patients? Before this step is taken by any training school it should be distinctly understood that the money saved is to be expended for the benefit of the pupils and not added to the income of the hospital.

For this point to be made so passionately suggests that Bessie may have crossed swords with the Board of Governors at Newport General Hospital on this subject. To expand their quantity of service, rather than quality of teaching student nurses, which is not immediately noticeable in the community could be a difficult decision by blinkered members of hospital boards. Communities may think they are justified in criticizing boards that do not have a policy of constantly increasing bed numbers through erecting timber and bricks.

Next comes the subject of payment:

Personally I do not think that nurses should ever be obliged to pay for their training, as is advocated by some enthusiasts. A nurse during her hospital life performs many hundred acts of service for the benefit of her patients which when once learned are not necessary for the perfecting of her own technique. When she has made 6 poultices she has mastered the composition of poultice, she may make 60 during her training by the order of the physician, and this extra service should be accepted by the hospital as full compensation for the knowledge she has obtained. The parallel between the nurse in training and the college student is not a just one, because the latter renders no personal service for the education received.

Bessie's thoughts were never far from careful expenditure. She would not have accumulated the fortune she did had this not been her practice. On the subject of food and the student nurse, she makes some concrete financial comparisons and suggestions. She had already written extensively about food in *Preparation for Motherhood* and in *Care of Children*, and in numerous monthly articles for mothers of growing children in *The Ladies Home Journal* from 1890 until 1901 when she was an Associate Editor and occasionally thereafter until 1906.

The audience of Nurse Superintendents is then given Miss Scovil's strong message on food and diet:

> Efficiency is the ideal of the nurse. In connection with labor one hears of nothing but the conservation of energy, the coordination of effort, that every movement may yield the maximum of result with the minimum of expenditure of power.
>
> Is the hospital obtaining from its nurses the best that they can give, and if not, why not? I have no hesitation in saying that one very potent reason is because it does not feed them properly. No engine can do its work well without proper and sufficient food, adapted to its needs. The human machine is no exception to this rule.
>
> I have in mind one hospital where the nurses are obliged to supplement the fare provided for them by purchasing biscuits, chocolate, etc., to be eaten in their rooms. The food is unappetizing, badly cooked and badly served. In another [training hospital] pork frequently

appears on the table during the summer months, when it is surely out of place as an article of food.

No one expects luxurious diet in a hospital, but the meals provided for the nurses should be palatable, abundant and nourishing. There should be no just ground for complaint, either as to cooking or serving. It is not easy to eat when one is tired; the appetite flags. Nurses are usually tired and food should be presented to them in such a form as to be tempting and not disgusting. At once we hear the objection from those in control of the finances: "We cannot afford the expense of better fare." Is it necessarily more expensive? One concrete example is worth a hundred vague statements.

The University of Valparaiso, [in] Indiana, gives a student an abundant, well cooked and well served dinner for 10 cents, a supper of the same order for 4 cents, and breakfast for the same sum. Out of the profits the authorities have built up a university, which has an annual revenue of $200,000 and has been in existence about 35 years.

In the dining hall at Yale a plate of buttered toast costs 10 cents, at Valparaiso a comfortable dinner is provided for that amount. Everything is as good as it would be in a well-managed private household. What is the secret of the difference?

Brains applied to the problem: careful buying, good management and the elimination of waste.

A competent person should be in charge of the kitchen of every hospital, not necessarily as cook, but as overseer and manager. She would save her salary many times over. Waste is one of the principal factors in increasing hospital expenditure.

We can see Bessie spending a week in a hospital kitchen — making lists, requesting storage to be reorganized, finding new wholesalers, planning menus to dovetail so today's stew will be tomorrow's soup, and arranging to sell non-edible kitchen residue plus food served to patients but not eaten to a local pig farm, thus securing a small stream of new income for the hospital. Unable to do this in person at all the institutions represented in her audience, she lights a fire of enthusiasm for good management among her listeners and hopes for results:

> The bill of fare for the nurses should receive as much attention as that of the private patients. While luxuries are unnecessary, food values should be carefully studied and it should be seen that efficiency is kept at the highest standard by means of sufficient and suitable nourishment. It is useless to purchase the best provisions the market affords if they are spoiled in the cooking and serving. If food that should be hot is half cold when it reaches the nurses, they cannot eat it with relish. A little money expended in modern appliances for keeping it hot would double its value. Night nurses should have a digestible and appetizing midnight meal, and time to eat it, outside the wards. Their breakfast should be substantial, as many sleep little during the day and require food to sustain them.

No doubt, many superintendents were inwardly squirming thinking of the dry, curled edged, cold sandwiches their nurses eat whenever there is a lull in the night's demands. Bessie concludes the section on food with this:

> This whole question of feeding the nurse is one that should be re-adjusted by the light of modern ideas.

Bricks cannot be made without straw, and nerves and muscles exhausted by responsibility and hard work can be recuperated in no other way than by an ample supply of nourishing food. If you carry nothing else away from this Convention of Superintendents take with you the determination to fight the battle of your nurses for ample, satisfying and attractive meals.

I can imagine a brief pause for a sip of water, a quick hand up to her substantial hat to check that its sensible angle has not altered, and then onward:

Next to food as a means of preserving the health of the nurse is rest. The pupils who come to us are usually young; they cannot endure a prolonged strain without injury. Rest is necessary to keep them in the highest state of efficiency.

When I began my hospital training we worked for 14 hours every other day, from a quarter to seven in the morning to a quarter of nine at night, with a short interval for dinner and tea. The alternative days we got off duty about two o'clock. The nurse who was left in the ward had to do all the work with very little assistance from the head nurse.

It may not be possible to establish the 8-hour system in hospitals. If the nursing staff were increased, as it should be, nurses could have shorter hours of duty in the wards and more time for study outside them.

If Bessie could have looked into the future she would have seen that her hope for an eight-hour work shift was eventually realized.

It is the habit to advise nurses to walk in the fresh air during their hour off duty. A far more sensible plan is for them to spend the time sitting, or lying in a hammock in summer and lying down near an open window, warmly wrapped up, in winter. Their duties in the wards give them sufficient exercise and in their hours of rest they should keep off their feet.

No doubt her memories of her own aching feet dominate this advice. She continues:

The time may come when hospital wards will be built with some regard to the needs of the nurses as well as of the patients. Economy of effort would be promoted by the use of square wards instead of the long corridor-like rooms when the farthest beds are a long distance from the bathroom and service room. The distance has to be traversed many times a day to wait on the patients, with great unnecessary expenditure of strength.

It is [now] a fixed principle in the arrangement of a ward that everything connected with the care of a patient must be kept out of sight, usually as far from the bed as possible. Whatever appliance is required must be brought from a distance to the bedside and hurried away again as if its presence there were a disgrace. These unnecessary exertions would not be tolerated by the director of an efficiency squad. He makes every movement tell and not one useless one is permitted.

Why should not small articles be kept in the lockers close at hand? Why should not screens, when not in immediate use, stand folded against the wall nearby? Bed rests and bed tables slide into grooves at the head of the bed instead of being carried away and brought back each time? The conservative head nurse cries out aghast because these devices for the easement of the nurse would interfere with the uniformity of the ward. They need not necessarily do so, they may even add to it. And if they destroyed it, which is the more important, uniformity or increased efficiency? Regularity in the appearance of the ward or more time and strength to devote to the care of the patient? We are too much the slaves of convention. Let us think for ourselves and not be afraid to step outside the grooves of habit if by so doing we can accomplish results that are worthwhile.

These reforms are the outpourings of a student nurse, a graduate nurse, superintendent of nurses, and a nursing educator. They have been accumulated over the years from nurse Scovil's experiences. It is improbable many were implemented during her years as Superintendent of Nursing at the Newport Hospital, but, if they were, student nurses and graduates there would have been extremely fortunate. If their adoption meant extra expenditure or radical changes, the Hospital Board, normally very conservative, would become involved.

If any of the superintendents to whom Bessie was speaking were still feeling at all smug, it is unlikely they remained so for long. She goes on to expose another part of the nursing profession that needs their immediate attention:

There is no part of the nursing service that requires more thought and care on the part of the Superintendent than the night duty. Some nursing authorities think that this work should only be performed by graduate nurses. It is an enormous responsibility for a pupil even when there is a night Superintendent, which, of course, is not the case in the smaller hospitals.

The nurse on night duty leads an unnatural life. There is a certain strain on the nerves, even under the most favorable conditions. When to this is added the sense of responsibility, the meeting of emergencies, the possibility of accidents occurring for which she is not directly responsible, and yet for which she must bear the blame, as in the case of a patient escaping from the ward, she is kept in a state of perpetual tension. There are hospitals where a nurse is kept on night duty for six months at a time. This is worse than wicked, it is stupid — a stupid lowering of the whole tone of the nurse, which should be carefully conserved as the best asset in the hospital. Stupidity is the one sin that this age of efficiency cannot forgive in Superintendents.

How many superintendents are again squirming inwardly at this old woman's all-knowing remarks? Miss Scovil's position as one of the most, if not the most, senior Superintendent in North America makes her unassailable and she no doubt knows it. It frees her to be entirely truthful and not worry about stepping on sensitive toes. Her aim is to improve the conditions of nurses and by so doing to raise the standard of the whole profession, which will attract women of ability, who will improve, further, the condition of nurses.

Elizabeth Scovil does not just criticize whatever she sees as less than satisfactory in the nursing world, she offers answers and realistic compromises.

> One month at a time, except under very exceptional circumstances, when it may be prolonged for a week or two, should be the limit of the term of night duty.

> Many nurses cannot sleep well during the day; want of sleep lowers the vitality and overtaxes the nerves. The victim of insufficient sleep is so weary that it is hard for her to get through the early morning work and sometimes most difficult to keep awake during those hours on duty when sleep is a crime.

> The Superintendent should insist that the night
> nurse's quarters be in the quietest part of the nurse's
> home and that no day nurse is allowed to share her
> room and disturb her.

It is not difficult to read into this an abysmal arrangement
for night nurses back in 1878. Did the student Bessie manage to
prevent herself from committing the "crime" of falling asleep while
on duty. Perhaps she did not. It sounds like the voice of experience.
How many nurses of Bessie's generation tried any of the following
practices to help their bodies believe that day was night? Other
than opiates, there was not much available to medicate a restless
body. Over the counter sleeping pills did not become available until
after World War II:

> She [the Superintendent] should know whether her
> night nurses sleep or not. There are simple means to
> induce it which she can recommend them to try if
> they do not sleep; such as an ice bag at the back of
> neck and a hot water bag at the feet, a glass of hot milk
> immediately before getting into bed, a few biscuits, or
> a sandwich, or a slice of meadow butter, to be eaten
> about 10 o'clock, if sleep does not come, a warm bath
> on coming off duty. A night nurse who sleeps badly
> during the day is on the way to become a nervous
> wreck. Many nurses feel very much the isolation of
> night duty and this is an added reason why it should
> be made as short as possible that they may not lose
> touch with the various activities and opportunities of
> the daily routine in the wards.

> In what condition is a nurse who has just come off
> six months night duty to undertake the day duty in a
> hard ward? This lengthened night duty is an economic
> waste, a relic of less scientific methods and should be
> relegated to the dark ages where it belongs. It is the

bounden duty of the hospital to see that the pupils who come to it for training do not suffer in health during their sojourn there. It is the height of absurdity to make well people sick to make sick people well. Yet this is what a hospital does when it overworks and underfeeds its nurses.

These thoughts must have crossed Bessie's mind as a student nurse when her feet were tired and her eyes could not support all the demands on them and she longed for leisure to sit and enjoy a good New Brunswick meal prepared from fresh produce, including "meadow butter" prepared by her loving mother. Her last paragraph on the subject of night nurses has an almost suffragette fervour. Women still did not have the vote in 1914 but it was not long before Bessie helped to get the women voters of Gagetown, New Brunswick to the polls when that historic day finally arrived in 1917:

> Is it not high time that we Superintendents, who stand between the hospital authorities on one side and our nurses on the other, rise and demand better working conditions for them in order, if for no other lesser reason, that they may give the best that is in them to their patients?

Unfortunately Bessie did not see much rising and demanding of these improvements by superintendents during the next twenty years remaining to her. She lifted a banner and handed it to the superintendents in 1914. They may have held it, but not high enough. Many years were to pass before working conditions for nurses were measurably improved.

The modern ideas of this elderly veteran of the beginning of the nursing profession are truly amazing. Her ideas in the section of her lecture on discipline are in keeping with those of the 21st century:

One of the most difficult problems that confronts the Superintendent of Nurses is the matter of discipline. It is hard to draw the line between liberty and license. The pupils who come to us are not children, they are young women, accustomed to order their own lives and decide questions of right and wrong for themselves. It is not easy for them to submit to arbitrary regulations, often about subjects which seem to them of little importance one way or another.

As a nursing student Bessie was a decade older than those usually beginning their training. She must have been particularly annoyed at petty regulations:

There are certain points which must be enforced — punctuality, neatness, thoroughness, are cardinal virtues in hospital work. It is part of the nurse's training to weave them as may be into the very character itself. Honesty and truthfulness are pre-requisites in a nurse. If these are lacking there is no foundation to build upon, no technical instruction can supply their place, or make a reliable nurse without them. These, of course, are truisms, hardly worth mentioning because everyone knows them. It is in the borderland outside that a Superintendent's troubles begin.

Why not follow the example of many colleges and large schools and place the discipline, or rather its enforcement, in the hands of the nurses themselves? How many of the Superintendents listening would be willing to give up their power and authority to this extent, I wonder?!

Nurses as a body are as jealous of the honour and reputation of their training school as students are of that of their college. Many little restrictions which are very irritating when imposed from without, become bearable and reasonable when they are the result of internal discussion and decision. The Superintendent, while very careful not to interfere in the workings of the council, remains the final court of appeal.

It is possible, too, that the common sense of the whole body of nurses may be wiser than her…judgment. When a nurse graduates she is obliged to become the arbiter of her own actions, why not give her practice beforehand in the training school? Would there be as many infringements of professional etiquette after graduation if a nurse were called upon more often during her training to consider and decide what is and what is not conduct becoming to one of that high calling?

Superintendent Scovil knew the problems of discipline. Too much or too little make the problems worse. We don't know if she is speaking from her success as Superintendent of Nursing at the Newport Hospital in encouraging councils of nursing students or if she is wishing she had found that solution?

The penultimate subject of this 1914 address is "out duty" for nurses, to which Bessie strongly objects. She feels so passionate about the subject and is so logical it deserves a full quotation:

There is one point on which Superintendents should be especially firm in defence of their pupil nurses. They should not permit them to be sent to private cases, outside the hospital, during their training.

The stock argument in its favor is that they are thus better fitted for private duty after they graduate. If they could be under constant supervision during this time, as they are in the wards, this might be so, but, as we all know, exactly the opposite is the truth. The average employer hesitates to report back to the hospital the faults and mistakes of the nurse, unless they are very glaring ones, and so they are unknown and uncorrected.

In this day of widening opportunities for nurses, many of them after graduation go at once into institution work, or do other outside duty, and do not take up private nursing, so that the plea of preparing them for it, even if it were a good one, loses its value. The injustice to the pupil in training is great. She loses lessons and lectures, besides the indirect teaching, which she can never regain.

It is an injustice to the nurses remaining in the hospital, lessening the number, probably already too scanty, available for the care of the sick in its charge. It interferes with the regular routine of duty, which should be sacredly observed for the benefit of the nurse, and adds greatly to the Superintendent's cares and perplexities.

The hospital receives a certain monetary return, but nurses are not in the school to add to the income of the hospital, and when there is a question as to the advantage to one or the other, the nurses should have the benefit of the doubt. In this case their interests are the first to be considered. Let justice be done if the heavens fall!

There have been many opportunities in her address to the Superintendents for Miss Scovil to inject her meetings with Florence Nightingale, but she holds that sweet tidbit, until her last topic, "The Superintendent's Influence."

In one of the interviews that I had the great honor of having with Florence Nightingale, she picked up a little book on the care of children that had been sent her, which was lying beside her on the bed and said: "I'm so glad that this book has not a skeleton in front." Afterwards, in speaking of a certain training school, she said: "The Superintendent is just a book with a skeleton in front. She has no sympathy with her nurses. The last one was a mother to them."

Do we fully realize the enormous and far-reaching influence that our personality has over our nurses? I was much struck by a statement made by the director of the course in nursing at Teachers' College, Columbia University, in a conversation that we had a few weeks ago. We were speaking of the frigid, not to say disagreeable, attitude which some head nurses seem to consider the proper one towards the assistant nurses in their wards. Miss Nutting said that this spirit could always be traced directly back to the school in which the head nurse had been trained. If she had been treated kindly and considerately, she behaved in the same way to her nurses. If she had been the victim of rude reprimands, discourteous innuendoes, or withering, sarcastic remarks when she had made a mistake, or failed in some detail of duty, she passed it on with interest to those under her command.

If this assessment is accurate, and it seems likely to be the case, then perhaps Bessie's superintendent at the Massachusetts General Hospital Nurses' Training School treated her in a considerate way. With her Victorian view of strict discipline producing good results, Bessie may have been in no need of harsh correction. Yet, she writes so fulsomely and in detail about such negative behaviour, she must have been somewhat subject to it, or at least seen less than kind and considerate treatment administered to others.

Being more mature than many other students when she began to train as a nurse, Bessie probably would have been better able to contend with harshness from her superiors than would the others. Lest the audience of superintendents think that in her old age Miss Scovil had lost her determination to reform the culture of nurses' training, she continues with her theme.

> The tone of our schools depends upon us. Gentleness and courtesy towards our pupils are no bar to the insistence on the strictest performance of duty. It is rather a great incentive to its performance. I remember a not particularly impressible young woman, inclined to be indifferent, who, having been rather severely reproved for some neglect, was found weeping over the sink where she was polishing a basin. Oh, yes," said the weeper, "I shouldn't mind that, but she was so kind I couldn't stand it." More flies are caught with honey than with vinegar.

> If we can first of all obtain the respect of our nurses by our own uprightness and impartiality, for nothing appeals to the average person like perfect fairness, we can secure their regard. It is so easy by the exercise of the courtesy, which a gentlewoman should show to everyone with whom she comes in contact, and by a real interest and sympathy in their problems, to win the affection of our nurses. They are ready to give it to us if we will have it. Without it we cannot lead them towards those high ideals, which it is our privilege to present to them.

With so many Anglican clergy in her family background, her long visits to the Kingston Rectory, and her many books on religious subjects, it is not surprising she ended her lecture with reference to scripture. This closing likely gave Bessie's pleas extra power and authority in the minds and hearts of her listeners.

The Bible says, "Where there is no vision the people perish." A modern writer has said, "Ideals are realities. They are not a creation of the human brain, they are not conceptions we have imagined; they are realities we have discovered."

With our 21st century sophistication from decades of world travel and familiarity with other cultures, we may see this view as out of date. Though Bessie had by now travelled widely for the times, including visiting the Italian Lakes and Alaska, and was well read, her accepting the view that ideals are realities fit nicely into the psychology of World War I and the best of the Biblical ethos. She concludes her address:

> What would our great profession be but mere drudgery without its high ideals of service, of self-sacrifice, of unselfish devotion to the good of others? Somewhere perfection exists. We shall not reach it in this world, but we can struggle towards it, gaining strength in the pursuit.

> Love is the fulfilling of the law. It floods its bare facts with life as the brown mud flats of the tidal waves are filled by the inrush of the shining water when the tide comes in. It is love and the faith that is born of love that can move mountains. It is this that we can teach our nurses, by example, by suggestion, by the spoken word, as occasion offers.

> It is this knowledge that will make them faithful nurses in small things as in great, that will urge them to high endeavor when duty points to some difficult task, that will enable them to accomplish it. My sister Superintendents, this is our opportunity. Shall we not rise to it?

Whatever we think of the origin of ideals, Miss Scovil finished on an unarguable theme — unselfish devotion for the good of others and love as the motivating force is the power that stands behind the profession of nursing. Is it not likely her sister superintendents rose to applaud Senior Superintendent Scovil, with enthusiasm? It is also likely the development of nursing in Canada moved forward in many positive directions as a result of this forthright address to those with the power to make progressive and lasting reforms a reality in the culture of nurses' training.

* * * *

Of the three lectures given in 1914, 1917 and 1918, respectively, all published in *Canadian Nurse*, "The Care of Nurses," which I have just examined, probably reflects most accurately Bessie's experiences as a student nurse. However, we also find direct references to those days at the beginning of her 1917 paper entitled "The Ethics of Nursing":

> It is a source of great pleasure to me that you should have so kindly asked me to address this meeting of the Canadian National Association of Trained Nurses. When I look at this assembly and consider that it represents the trained nurses of Canada, my thoughts go back to the day, now nearly forty years ago, when I entered the Massachusetts General Hospital in Boston, to begin my training as a nurse.
>
> There were then but few of us, and we strangers in the land, for at that time there was still a part of the hospital not under the care of the training school. This was the private ward where patients were too precious to be nursed by an experiment. An "experienced nurse," who lived outside in the city, came every night as she had done for many years, to care for the patients, who had their own permanent staff of day nurses. We pupil nurses looked at them with some

respect and wondered if we should ever be as efficient, hardly knowing that we were seeing the last relics of the old system which we were supplanting.

Members of the Association must have listened intently to this straight-backed, be-hatted legend as living history, as indeed she was. They would have been aware that the "experienced nurse" whom Miss Scovil and her fellow pupils looked at with "some respect" would not have graduated from a nursing school, but would have acquired all her knowledge of nursing from observing other nurses and on the job. All members of the Association, by definition, had come through training schools, an experience they shared with the speaker, but in her day as a student, an innovation and a novelty.

There were at that time only three training schools for nurses in the United States — New England Hospital in Boston, Bellevue Hospital in New York, and our own at the Massachusetts General Hospital also in Boston. Canada, of course, as yet had none. I have not the exact figures in my possession, but apart from statistics you can see for yourselves how the profession has grown in our own land. It is no longer necessary for Canadians to go abroad to prepare themselves for the work of nursing. I am told one large Canadian hospital had more than 1,200 applications from would-be pupils last year. We are very proud that trained nursing has attained the status of a profession. Exactly what does that imply? The dictionary says a profession is "any business or calling, engaged in for subsistence, not being mechanical." In those last words seem to me to lie the gist of the whole matter, the reason why trained nursing is superlatively entitled to be considered a profession and not a trade. It has to do not only with the bodies of suffering mankind but with the spirit as well.

Anyone who has investigated the beliefs of Christian Science[2] knows that there is a modicum of truth under-lying its assumptions—if it were not so the system never would have attained the proportions that it has achieved. The mind does have an enormous influence over the body, and no nurse can afford to disregard its influence if she wishes to secure the best results for her patients and acquire the utmost skill herself.

Bessie was convinced of this mind/body relationship from her own experience and offered a persuasive example for her listeners:

I remember a patient who was being treated for the morphia habit. It was being broken off by degrees; she withstood the desire for the drug as long as it seemed humanely possible to her, and, when she felt the necessity was too imperious to be resisted longer was given a hypodermic of sterile water, believing that she was having her accustomed dose. She slept late that next morning, soothed, as she thought, by the opiate. Every nurse knows of many such instances in her own experience. The whole use of placeboes is founded on this trait in human nature.

A nurse's duties are not purely mechanical. They cannot be done by machinery nor by a machine. They do not end with giving intelligent assistance to the physician, nor putting on a perfect bandage, not even with devising means to nurse critical cases comfortably in uncomfortable surroundings and supplementing the doctor's vague directions as to food and feeding with a well-balanced diet and the

---

2   Christian Science is based on the writings of Mary Baker Eddy (1812-1910) that relate all the teachings of the New Testament to the curing of health problems through the application of mental exercises.

proper administration of suitable nourishment. They include very often the ministering to a mind diseased, of which Shakespeare speaks, "when think-coming fancies keep her from her rest." A physician, writing of his own experience in his serious illness, said the thing that he craved most from his doctors and nurses was the assurance that he would recover. Although he knew his own state to be almost hopeless, the fact that they seemed determined to pull him through and the thought that he would live gave him courage to exert all his powers to struggle back to life, and he succeeded.

This is an inspiring introduction to a paper on ethics. Bessie describes the term in the next paragraph dealing with "the realm of the spirit, where realities live." She wants to be certain that those practicing her beloved profession are aware of and take account of all aspects of their patients in order to hasten their recovery and to be seen to be more than just mechanics:

What, then, do we mean by the ETHICS of nursing? The word comes from the Greek, through the Latin "ethicus," and means manners, usage, the science that treats of morality; that which relates to human actions, their motives and tendencies. Deep-reaching and far-searching you see, not to be disposed of by any surface conformity to the customs of civility nor the exercise of any merely technical skill. It pertains to that high region, the realm of the spirit, where realities live. It has been well said that ideals are realities; they are not a creation of the human brain. What we call ideals are not conceptions we have imagined, they are realities we have discovered. Somewhere there exists that absolute fidelity, that unselfishness, that tenderness, that forbearance, that gentleness and strength, that courage and wisdom that united in one would make the perfect nurse. Even if we cannot individually attain to it, that is our ideal towards which, perhaps with many falterings and failings, we can still strive.

It would be interesting if Bessie had named the "modern writer" she referred to three years earlier in her speech to the Superintendents of schools of nursing in Canada who said "ideals are realities," and to whom she again refers in the previous quotation. This "idealism" would be more readily understood by our contemporary, multicultural worldview if it had been contextualized within the particular culture of the speaker. But that was not yet the perspective of Bessie's era so, of course, that was not a nuance that would have occurred to her. Almost all else she says stands up a century later, and even her idealism still has its appeal for many folks. It is a small bone to pick, considering the still digestible feast of ideas she gives us from a world so different from present times. She continues:

> Every profession has its own body of rules and laws and a spirit which animates it. The Medical profession has a high standard of honour; there are certain things which no reputable medical man will do, such as advertising himself or violating professional confidences.

Other than to announce the commencement of practice or a change in address, this custom of not advertising still exists, except in subtle ways. For Bessie to give "advertising himself" the same weight as "violating professional confidences" shows how abhorrent such behaviour was in 1917:

> The law has its own conventions—an honourable judge does not take bribes to influence his decisions; a lawyer is supposed to hold the interests of his clients sacred, though it might be to his own advantage to disregard them.

Our profession is the youngest of all, and it is we who are setting the standards and establishing its customs. Let us see to it that they are worthy ones. Our sense of honour should be at least as keen as that of the medical profession, with which we are so closely associated. "As trustworthy as a nurse" should be a proverb, a standard of comparison that would carry instant conviction.

It is the custom in some training schools to administer to the graduating pupils a modification of the Hippocratic oath. The original form was used in Greece several centuries before the Christian era, and was named after Hippocrates who was born 460 B.C. and was the most celebrated physician of antiquity. The modified version adopted for nurses is as follows:

"You do solemnly swear—each one by whatever she holds most sacred—that you will be loyal to the physicians under whom you shall serve, as a good soldier is loyal to his officers;

"That you will be just and generous to all worthy members of your profession, aiding them when it shall be in your power to do so;

"That you will lead your lives and practice your profession in uprightness and honour;

"That into whatsoever home you shall enter it shall be for the good of the sick to the utmost of your power, and that you will hold yourself aloof from all temptations;

"That whatsoever you shall see or hear of the lives of men and women, whether they be of your patients or members of their households, you will keep inviolably secret, whether you are in other households or among your friends;

"If you accept these obligations let each one bow the head in sign of acquiescence.

"If you shall be true to your word, may prosperity and good repute ever be yours; the opposite if you shall prove yourselves foresworn."

This is strong stuff. The oath is not far off saying, if, as graduate nurse, you are not close to being a perfect nurse and human being, you will deserve to languish and suffer a bad reputation. However, at this emotional time in a young nurse's life, when idealism is still to the fore, perhaps it is appropriate to connect graduation into the profession with an expectation of excellence and ethical behaviour. This would have been especially desirable in Bessie's mind, as she was among the pioneers—the "guinea pigs"—to learn the art and science of nursing through a rigorous course of study in nursing schools rather than just in the hospital wards. It was especially important for those early, professionally trained nurses to be seen as "perfect" in order to erase the taint of unqualified, poor women, mixing prostitution, alcoholism, and theft along with "nursing" in order earn a living. The experiences of Florence Nightingale in the Crimea, trying to bring discipline to her mostly unruly crew of nurses, and the description of her struggle back in England to do the same, underline the distance already travelled by the nursing profession. The need for constant vigilance and maintenance of high ideals is central to Miss Scovil's advocacy of the nursing profession. She continues:

If this oath were taken by each graduating nurse, what a high standard would at once be established for our profession to live up to. What is it that we, each one for herself, would promise to practice?—Loyalty, justice, generosity, uprightness, honour, fidelity. These are great words, the symbols of great virtues. If we are to do our duty in this responsible work to which we have given ourselves, we must acquire these virtues if we do not already possess them, or fall short of our high calling.

Let us examine them a little in detail: Loyalty to the doctor in charge of our patient is not always easy. We come, perhaps, from a large hospital where the treatment is up to date and the most modern appliances are at hand to be used as a matter of course. We find the family physician, as we think, very much behind the times in his methods and not at all realizing how much might be done for the sufferer if he only were more wide awake.

Let us remember, for our comfort, that in very many cases, nature, if left to herself and only assisted by rest, warmth, and proper food, will effect a cure, in spite of what seems to us culpable negligence. Let us beware of criticizing and above all, of weakening the confidence of the patient in his physician; it may be a serious hindrance to his recovery.

In some cases nursing is more than half the battle, and we can redouble our own efforts that the patient may have every advantage that skilled care can give. If the doctor makes a mistake and, much as we hate to admit it, doctors are fallible and do this occasionally, the nurse should call his attention to it as tactfully as possible but on no account mention it to the family, nor to anyone else. The loyal cooperation of the nurse with the doctor is essential to the best conduct of the case. His orders she has been taught to obey, but loyalty means more than this. Soldiers follow their officers unquestioningly; they may grumble a little privately, under their breath as it were, but they do not hang back in face of the enemy, for that would mean disaster. So the nurse tries to carry out the spirit as well as the letter of the treatment, and, knowing that the responsibility rests on the physician, gives him all the help that is in her power.

How practical! A nurse must be loyal to the doctor, but what should she do if he is incompetent? Bessie does not dance around the problem. Tell him, but keep it a secret between the two of you. She is quite aware that the nurse's reputation as an efficient professional is on the line, almost as much as the doctor's. If a well-liked doctor with a charming bedside manner and his nurse are seen to be ineffective, their patients rarely recovering when the expectation is that they will, nursing care is apt to be seen at fault; how much better to seek correction by gently pointing out his errors, and look for a new position if necessary.

Throughout her writings and in spite of her being born during the first half of the Victorian era, Bessie shows strong leanings toward feminism. Considering the quotation below was written well before any women in Canada could vote, it gives more than a subtle nudge to women reluctant to take power.

Justice is not popularly supposed to be a feminine virtue. Is it not rather a question of individuals than of sex? There are some women who have the breadth of vision and clearness of mind that enables them to see both sides of a case and to decide between them, and there are some men who do NOT have it. There always are two sides to a question and if we are to be just we must remember this, even when we are most aggrievedly and determinedly sure that ours is the right side. The ability to see the opposite side and give it due weight is the foundation of justice. Those who have not this power should cultivate it as one requisite in performing their duties.

This is the first time I have noticed Bessie use block capitals to emphasize a point. Could she, in her many years of being connected with the medical profession, possibly have met "some men who do NOT have it"? We can imagine scenes of the young nurse having to swallow hard to keep from contradicting an esteemed doctor who put two and two together and got six. When the Superintendent of Nursing and head of the nurses' training school at Newport, R. I. General Hospital, how many times did Bessie have to remind herself that the doctor must be seen as a god and she as never more than a ministering angel? However, she may well have taken the advice she was giving in this paper in 1917, and tactfully told doctors when they were wrong. It's not clear at what stage in her development she felt confident enough to do this, but she must always have wanted to, especially when she was "most aggrievedly and determinedly sure" she was right. In this 1917 address to the Canadian National Association of Trained Nurses she is certainly speaking from experience and ready to advise her sister nurses accordingly.

After justice comes generosity. Here Bessie takes a more conventional line, especially in her second sentence, which was more or less the norm until the 1960s when the Women's Liberation Movement gave women a different view of themselves:

> Generosity, ah! that is another matter. Woman is created to give, and she usually does give most lavishly—her time, her means, herself to any object that especially appeals to her, be it friend, lover, husband, children or profession. A selfish woman seems an anomaly, a departure from the common rule, an offence against nature. But who is it to whom we are to be especially just and generous?—the worthy members of our own profession. Those of us who have done much private nursing know there are times when the temptation to break this promise is very strong indeed. When one succeeds a nurse at a case, for instance, or when one hears tales of a

predecessor that make one feel she has forgotten the high principles in which she was trained, though she has not committed any very heinous sin. Whenever two nurses work together, this requirement should be borne in mind by both.

Though I have almost no particulars of Bessie's career in private nursing, we know from general references that she was employed in this field, and she writes with familiarity on this aspect of her profession. Reputation was hugely important in the days when women's choice of occupation was so limited. In the decades preceding 1917 and through the middle of the 20th century being nursed at home was common practice. A nurse's reputation went ahead of her. It would not take many snippets of gossip, based on no "very heinous sin," for a woman to look for a different nurse than the one who, for example, had cared for a friend or her friend's husband. Reputations can be damaged by careless talk for no good reason. Miss Scovil counsels her audience of nurses to avoid such talk and support each other:

> We should cultivate, too, that "esprit de corps," literally the spirit of the body, which should animate and bind together our whole profession. One does not criticize the members of one's family to strangers, and the fact that the person under discussion is a nurse, a member of our professional family, should incline us to take her part and suspend judgment until the defence can be heard.

> As to material help in service, or money, most nurses are ready and willing to render it to one another when the occasion arises.

She then turns to the all-important theme for the nurse of properly caring for her own health:

Amongst the multiplicity of duties that a nurse owes to everyone, there is one she is very apt to overlook—her duty to herself. A nurse should do all in her power to preserve her own health and strength. Without it she is useless in her profession, her training is thrown away, and she becomes a care instead of being able to lift the burdens of others. We are in the world not for what we can get out of it, but for what we can give to it. There are occasions of emergency when a patient's life hangs in the balance, and a nurse is more than justified in putting aside all thought of self, just as she would try to snatch a child from danger, even at peril of life and limb. These do not come very often and if in her daily routine she has been careful to care for her own health she is ready to meet the strain without permanent harm. It is generosity run mad to destroy her own usefulness, which properly husbanded, might have proved a blessing to others during a long lifetime.

Generosity of service is Bessie's theme, but also that it should not be taken to such extremes that it threatens the health of the nurse, as she will then lose her usefulness, her reason for existence. Bessie knew from her experience with her "bad heads" the need for a nurse to look after her own health:

Uprightness and honour: Do these words seem almost synonymous, to mean the same thing? They do, and yet there is a shade of difference which makes it well to include both in this Hippocratic oath, the keeping of which by the whole body of nurses would go far to establish the ethics of nursing on a firm foundation. Uprightness is absolute honesty, the inability to say or do an underhanded, mean thing, integrity that cannot be corrupted by self-interest. Honour is dignity, the result of self-respect, a scorn of meanness, whether in one's self or another. Uprightness is an ingredient of character, something in the warp and woof of one's innermost being. Honour governs one's conduct to others; it is a rule of life. It is on this high plane that we are to lead our lives. These virtues are not a professional uniform to be worn only when on duty and cast aside as soon as we have finished a case. They are to animate our every action, public and private, in all our relations to others. If we are tempted sometimes to swerve from this high standard, let us remember how far-reaching the effect of example is. We are all bound together by innumerable ties. One cannot do wrong without affecting the whole body. Our firm stand in some matter of principle may help in ways we shall never know—a sister who otherwise would have fallen, and hurt not only herself, but the profession we love.

Imagine the audience at that conference of Canadian National Association of Trained Nurses, whether just recently graduated or well experienced. How could those in attendance not have resolved to live more closely to the distinguished speaker's expectations, based on a type of Hippocratic Oath? There is no possible reproach to be made against the ethic for nursing being advanced. All Miss Scovil's life's teachings are rolled into this paragraph. This philosophy unfolds from her Victorian upbringing in Saint John, the influence of her ordained uncle and grandfather in Kingston, her two years of nurse training in Boston, and her many decades as nurse, superintendent, journalist, author and public speaker.

Many times, in her writings, she returns to the theme of the need for those in the profession of nursing to be above reproach in all aspects of their lives. Unlike many in her audience in 1917, she can remember when a "nurse" could be a woman of doubtful character, doubtful training, and doubtful honesty, far removed from uprightness and honour. But she is likely not the only one in the room who knows from experience how disastrous a blow to the profession of nursing one unsuitable practitioner can be. It is likely that in her conversations with Florence Nightingale they talked about the need to be ever vigilant in the selection of student nurses, a topic of supreme importance to them both.

Continuing to look at Bessie's speech, we see she elaborates on the importance of standing firm "in some matter of principle"; otherwise many could be hurt in the profession of nursing:

> Does this seem to you a truism? It is, and yet a truism is only a fact that has been so often proved true it has become tiresomely familiar. The fact remains true, like "the commonplace sun in the commonplace sky makes the commonplace day" [Susan Coolidge], and it does us no harm to be reminded of it occasionally, lest we accept it and do not act upon it. A nurse's word should be sacred; as binding as any legal obligation that can possibly be written. A promise must be kept unless illness makes it impossible to do so; an engagement should never be broken without consent of the prospective patient, except for the same reason. You remember that in that ancient Book, which in spite of all Higher Criticism is still our best guide to conduct, the Psalmist honours the man who "sweareth to his own hurt and changeth not," or as the Prayer Book version has it, perhaps more appropriately for us, "who sweareth unto his neighbor and disappointeth him not, though it were to his own hindrance" [Psalm 15 v. 5]. Any material benefit one may gain does not count a feather's weight in comparison with the loss of honour that comes with breaking one's word.

It may be that when Bessie was writing this paper, her mind took her back to 1868 when, in the financial collapse of St. Stephen Bank, her father lost his honour among his colleagues and the general population of New Brunswick causing hundreds to see their life's savings vanish. Though the havoc he caused was not deliberate, but rather the result of poor judgment and bad luck, he was a broken man, never working again, leaning on his wife's family for hospitality—an unforgettable blow to his nineteen year old daughter. The lecture continues with more obligations, this time to patients:

> The last two clauses of this obligation [in the previously quoted oath] refer especially to our duties to our patients. I think most of us, whether in hospital or private house, try to render service that shall be for the good of the sick to the utmost of our power. There may be times when negligence or ignorance hinder us, the weakness of our mortal nature getting in the way, but there are few of us who do not try conscientiously to give our best skill to relieve the sufferers in our care. If there are any who do not, this part of the Hippocratic oath may cause them to realize that they have mistaken their vocation and had better seek some other calling, if there is any such, where faithfulness is not an essential.

In 1917, news travelled quickly through conversation and gossip. With almost no cars during WW I, and many without horse drawn carriages, walking to nearby destinations was common. And what happened on the way? With others doing the same, people often stopped and chatted, exchanging news and gossip. Bessie warns nurses against this kind of casual conversation.

> The mischief that can be done by indiscriminate talking can hardly be exaggerated. It is not peculiar to nurses, but is emphasized here because of their special opportunities to do harm. In time of illness, not only the patient but the whole household is off guard. Secrets that at other times are closely kept are laid bare to the eyes of the nurse. Shall she betray them? You say, instinctively: "No, of course not." Yet, a careless word to someone in conversation may give the clue that spreads a scandal.

Could Bessie ever speak or write the word "scandal" without the painful memory of the years of suffering and shame after her dear father's economic ruin was made worse by gossip and exaggeration on the street and in newspapers? No wonder she writes so precisely about the importance for nurses to avoid speaking about the circumstances, and perhaps secrets—in whole or in part—of families they serve.

> We all take a healthy interest in each other's affairs. Personalities are to many of us the most interesting form of conversation, and this is perfectly natural, because, as a rule, persons are more interesting than things. Are we, then, to be prohibited from talking about them altogether? Do you know the derivation of [the word] gossip? It comes from the Anglo-Saxon "Godsibb," related in God, as a sponsor in baptism. Has it not fallen from its high estate? If we restore it to where it came from, and when we gossip about our patients, say only those things that one member of God's great family should say about another, we shall be safe. Those of us who cannot trust ourselves to discriminate must be silent about our former patients, lest we injure them and discredit ourselves.

The primary importance for nurses, and the profession as a whole, to be above reproach is never far from Bessie's thoughts. Not only is this important for erasing the memories of the unsavoury activities of so-called "nurses" in the previous century, but also to now attract young women of high moral standards who will honour and advance the profession while in nursing schools and in their careers.

> Make it a positive rule always to believe the best. Do not condemn hastily, and if your best judgment is a severe one, keep it most scrupulously to yourself. You will never be called to account for the harsh word you have not said. Sometimes when you are engaged on a

long case you become very tired of monotony; crises of the patient are tiresome, the peculiarities of the friends are annoying, and yet your dissatisfaction is not great enough to make you wish to give up the case. Is there a remedy? Yes, but it lies with yourself. You are out of correspondence with your environment; there is constant jarring, and friction wears out machinery running. If you cannot change your environment change your outlook.

When I read this last sentence, I felt more than usually connected with my great Aunt Bessie. Years ago, when I was studying for a degree in Social Work, I read somewhere, "If you cannot change your life, change the way you look at it." I wrote it out and propped it up on my desk; I tried to put it into practice and to help my eventual clients do the same. Though nearly seventy years separated Bessie's advice and my discovery, the truth of it makes it universal in time and place. She continues:

Resolve to see these petty annoyances in their true proportions, not as mountains, but as molehills. Bring your sense of humour to bear on the situation and try to salve these daily irritations with a little kindly tolerance. It is not the thing itself that matters — ever — it is our attitude towards it, and that is in our own power.

Had Bessie spoken to this group a dozen or so years later, when the subject was more in vogue, she would have done justice to an address titled "The Psychology of Being a Nurse":

The remedy acts as well in the hospital and the training school as in the private household. Try it, those of you who are in charge of wards and have assistants and probationers to deal with who, you think, would make Job lose his halo.

They are really only girls trying, each in her measure,
to acquire the skill that is now second nature to you.
Alter your point of view and your eyes will be opened.

I wonder how many Ward Sisters heeded these words from the
nursing legend before them? I like to think the martinets among
them allowed her wisdom, achieved from decades pondering the
ideal approach, to lodge firmly in their brains and be accessed
when confronted with unruly or inappropriate behaviour from
their subordinates:

> We are very slowly learning to treat in a more ethical
> manner the problem of the education of our nurses.
> For many years the training that a pupil received in
> a hospital was entirely secondary to the requirements
> of the hospital. She was there apparently for the sole
> purpose of nursing the sick; incidentally she acquired
> skill in so doing and received a certain amount of
> instruction to render her more efficient. The duty to
> which she was assigned was considered principally
> from the standpoint of the necessities of the service,
> with little reference as to whether she required that
> particular experience to round out her training. Of
> course the sick must be nursed excellently, superlatively
> well; that is the end and object of our training, but
> in order to attain it the pupil must have a well-
> balanced curriculum in clinical as well as in theoretical
> instruction. Those in authority are beginning to feel
> that a young woman who offers herself for a three
> years' course in hospital work has rights akin to those
> of a student in a college, and that these should be taken
> into consideration in utilizing her services.

There can hardly be a single nurse, no matter where she was
trained who would disagree with a word of the above paragraph.
Those who heard Miss Elizabeth Scovil, R. N. on that warm

Montreal day in June 1917 at the Canadian National Association of Trained Nurses Convention, or those who later read her words in *Canadian Nurse*, would have had no difficulty in remembering their own early years and their less than ethical treatment:

> Fine sentiments are noble and inspiring, eloquent words tell of what we hope to do and would like to do. Has our profession any concrete evidence of deeds done to show that our ethical standard is high and that we do try to live up to our ideals?

In Canada, in the early part of the 21st Century, we are apt to quote *The Globe and Mail* or possibly *The New York Times* when backing up our points in a speech. But in 1917, most of Canada was still very British and Britain was thought of as the "mother country," as I remember it being called during WWII. Bringing a London paper's comments into her speech to boost her views was natural to Bessie and to her audience:

> Hear what *The London Daily Telegraph* has to say on the subject: "The story of the nurses' part in the war constitutes a fresh page in the annals of a race which is not without its glorious memories. This war has submitted British womanhood to the test of a storm of fury unparalleled in the history of the world. How magnificently the nurses have stood up against this blizzard of hatred, the fruit of increasing despair, the official records of the Matron-in-Chief of Queen Alexandra's Imperial Military Service could reveal. But the organization maintains a silence comparable with that which the Navy has relentlessly imposed upon itself, only very occasionally and partially is the veil lifted to reveal a little group of nameless heroines, pathetic and yet majestic figures, confronting, unmoved by personal fears, horrors calculated to make strong men blench."

Bessie continues:

> I can give you an even more intimate glimpse than this from a private letter from a nurse who has done strenuous work from almost the beginning of the war in a large base hospital. "You can't imagine what an absolute happiness it is to work for those sweet, patient boys. Such courage and thoughtfulness for others as they almost invariably show when suffering indescribable tortures. It is almost super-human their endurance, and to work for them is just a privilege. As for honours, it is awfully nice of you to wish me to have mention, but we sisters don't think much of them over here. Of course, it is nice for one's people, but unless you have done something deserving of them one would rather not have them, and for me I would be ashamed to receive anything of that kind when so many who have done such wonderful work have not been recognized; many of them giving their health and some their lives. Our hospital has been mentioned several times in dispatches for its good work, and that is the best honour of all." As for the work done, she says: "We had 1,400 beds last summer and only 73 nurses, and some ill always. In the operating room sometimes as many as 80 major operations in one day, four tables going all the time, and only four sisters. Once in 48 hours we admitted 1,200 patients. Death is so close to life, only the essentials of life seem to matter now." Does not that simple heroism in the face of daily unremitting toil and danger, stir one like a call to battle?

In 1917, when Miss Scovil was speaking these words, World War I (1914-1918) had produced horrendous casualties. Though the Allies were quite successful in halting the German advance in various battles in 1914, by 1915 when the Second Battle of Ypres (or the Second Battle of Flanders) took place on April 22-26th, poison gas (chlorine) was released from pipes and bombs with many casualties resulting. In 1916, from February 21st to November 5th, the Battle of Verdun resulted in over three hundred thousand French casualties and more than that for the Germans, who were unable to prevent the Allies from taking the city. From July 1st to November 20th the First Battle of the Somme, in northern France, was fought with enormous losses on both sides, resulting in a small gain for the Allies. The British used tanks for the first time in military history. In 1917, from July 31st to November 6th, shortly after Bessie spoke at this Convention, the Third Battle of Ypres (or the Battle of Passchendaele) raged, with a slight gain for the Allies. However, it was fought in mud, and the tanks were useless. The mood of the time was sacrifice for the noble cause, the ethical cause, when noble and ethical behaviour was required, especially for all nurses. Nurse Scovil then goes into details:

> A vivid illustration of what would be the result of the loss of ideals and the discarding of the ethics of nursing as a useless encumbrance may be found in the behaviour of certain of the German Red Cross nurses towards the British wounded. The Swiss correspondent of *The London Times*, writing from Berne, is responsible for the statement, made, it is said by scores of British soldiers of all ranks released from German prison camps. On the long journey of the wounded through Germany it was common for these women to tempt the men, in the last extremity of hunger and thirst, by holding out food to them and then snatching it away. Many of the wounded begging for water, had coffee, water and soup tendered to them, and at the last moment the nurse would spit in the cup or glass; or a glass of water, after being offered, would be poured slowly on the ground. The nurses not only refused to attend the British wounded, but insulted them and spat on them. Frequently they even struck, or kicked a bandaged limb in order to give

pain. It is earnestly to be hoped that these women were not trained nurses. Surely they cannot represent the spirit of the whole body of German nurses.

Underlining the undesirable background of German nurses, Bessie quotes, Florence Nightingale and her impressions of Kaiserwerth, though at the time, Miss Nightingale was delighted to escape from her conventional and restricting family and at least make a start on her nursing career:

> It was Germany that gave to Florence Nightingale the early instruction that she could not obtain at home, although her biographer tells us that she objected strongly in later years to the current statements that her own training was confined to Kaiserwerth. "The nursing there," she wrote, "was NIL. The hygiene horrible. The hospital was certainly the worst part of Kaisewerth. I took all the training there was to be had—there was none to be had in England, but Kaiserwerth was far from having trained me." She really served her apprenticeship in Paris, at the Maison de la Providence, managed by Sisters of Charity, to which was attached a hospital for aged and sick women.

So Miss Nightingale's training was not corrupted by the horrible conditions at Kaiserwerth and unacceptable practices of German nursing. It was obviously important for Bessie to see and portray her heroine as having been unblemished by her early training at the institution of a now reviled enemy:

> Our profession has its saints and martyrs—black letter saints, perhaps even those who have never been canonized by the Church but none the less saints. We are too near them to see them in their true proportions, for their human weaknesses have not faded out of sight and been obscured by their shining

virtues, as is the case with the olden saints whom we gaze on from afar. If we had lived with those, or even in their day, we should have known of many flaws which have been mercifully hidden from us by the splendor of their characters.

What is Bessie getting at here? I think she is not referring to the Great One, Miss Nightingale, but preparing us for the following paragraphs:

This frightful war has given us our opportunity of transcendent service, and we as a body, have risen to it. Think of the nurses on the British hospital ship Anglia who, when the ship was torpedoed, refused to enter the lifeboats until their patients were safely boarded, one of them saying, "No, Tommy, wounded first." Only one nurse was officially reported lost, but all were ready to sacrifice their lives and nearly lost them.

She then added more reports of dedicated and selfless nursing:

Lady Ralph Paget, who had been nursing in the Red Cross Hospital at Uskub, Serbia, rather than desert the wounded in her care, refused the opportunity to escape from the city before its capture by the Bulgarians. Her husband came from Nish in a motorcar and implored her to return with him to safety. She remained behind and was taken prisoner.

A party of British nurses retreated from Serbia with the Serbian army across the snow-covered mountains of Albania. They encountered a blizzard while crossing a mountain 8,000 feet high and endured great hardships from cold and hunger, nearly losing their lives.

What a contrast to the balmy June day in Montreal when Miss Scovil's audience, safe and secure, heard these stories of their sister's extraordinary bravery and determination, wondering, perhaps, whether they would be so heroic in similar circumstances:

> There are thousands of unrecorded instances of superhuman sacrifice and selfless devotion that will never be known. Long hours of tendance on sick and wounded and dying amidst many unavoidable privations. The courage, the resourcefulness, the unwearying watchfulness, when fatigue taxed human nature to its utmost; all this, and much more that cannot be told, stands to the credit of our nurses in this terrible struggle between despotism and liberty.

Bessie, in keeping with her theme, then quotes this excerpt from a poem by Frederich Schiller (1755-1805):

> What shall I do to be forever known?
> Thy duty ever.
> This did full many who yet sleep, unknown,
> Oh, never, never!
> Think'st thou, perchance, that they remain unknown
> Whom thou know'st not?
> By angel trumps in Heaven their praise is blown,
> Divine their lot.

> You all know of the order of the Royal Red Cross that King George instituted for the decoration of nurses, to be awarded for special service to the sick and wounded of the army and navy. The nurses receiving the Red Enamel Cross of the first class are entitled to use the letters "R.R.C." after their names. On the arms of the cross are the words "Faith, Hope, Charity," in the centre a portrait of the King, on the reverse side the royal cipher and crown. The nurses

to whom the second class decoration is awarded are known as Associates of the Royal Red Cross. Their badge is of frosted silver with a Maltese Cross of red enamel in the centre. Many nurses have received these decorations, but there are many more, who perhaps deserved them equally, whose work being unnoticed, did not obtain this recognition. It may be said of our great army of war nurses, as was said of the Canadians at Vimy Ridge, each one deserved a Victoria Cross.

Vimy Ridge, for those readers not familiar with World War I history, was an escarpment five miles northeast of Arras, France and was a strongly held part of the German defence. It was stormed successfully during the Battle of Arras by the Canadian Corps of the British 1st Army in April 1917. It is generally considered that the Canadians' involvement in Vimy Ridge had great symbolic significance, establishing Canada as an independent nation. Bessie then turns to the story of Edith Cavell:

When we speak of heroic nurses, our thoughts turn instinctively to that noble woman, Edith Cavell, who, on October 13, 1915 was executed at Brussels by the order of the German Government. What was her crime? She was charged with harboring British and French soldiers and Belgians of military age, and assisting them to escape to join their colours. The American Ambassador urged in her behalf that she had nursed the German soldiers as well as those of the Allies, showing no difference between them. An Amsterdam correspondent said she had long been suspected by the Germans, but had refused to leave the city as long as there was a single wounded man left in Brussels, saying that duty compelled her to remain where there was suffering. A Dutch newspaper said: "She was one of the great martyrs of the centuries."

Edith Cavell (1865-1915) was an English nurse, born in Swardseston, Norfolk, who was appointed the first Matron of the Berkendael Medical Institute in Brussels in 1907. During World War I, it became a Red Cross hospital. In August 1915, before a German military court, she was charged with helping approximately two hundred Allied soldiers escape to the Netherlands. Her execution produced condemnation from many quarters and she became famous as a heroine of the Allied cause:

> In her last interview with the clergyman who attended her a few hours before her death, she said; "I wish my friends to know that I willingly give my life for my country. I have no fear or shrinking. I have seen death so often it is not strange or fearful to me." When the clergyman said good-bye to her she smiled and said, "We shall meet again."

The example of Edith Cavell gives Bessie's last paragraphs heightened vigour. Miss Cavell's execution occurred less than two years previously so the circumstances would be fresh in the minds of all those in her audience:

> It is not given to all of us to be martyrs, but is it not the serene courage of this great soul in the presence of death an inspiration to us who, in the course of our daily duty, are so often brought face to face with it? How shall we regard it? How shall we bear ourselves towards it when, as so often happens, we see it approaching the patient we are striving to hold back from it?

> We must apprehend its true nature before we can determine our attitude towards it. Death is only an incident in life. It is not the end of all things, but the beginning of a fresh phase of existence. Never mind theological dogmas, or ecclesiastical pronouncements

about things which no mortal knows, or can know, until he, too, has passed beyond the veil. Let us reason from analogy. We know the familiar examples of the butterfly emerging from the chrysalis, the leaves from the dry twig, the green shoots from the hard seed—all miracles, but so common we have ceased to look upon them with awe. Throughout nature the germ of a new life is in everything that has once lived, and why should man be the exception? He is not. With us the body drops away, leaving the spirit (the germ of a new life) to pursue its course, free at last to develop, under changed conditions, into the perfection it could not attain here.

Perhaps by this stage in her life Bessie had become impatient of Anglican Church dogma and was happier to consider general truths. She knew her audience was of mixed denominational conviction like any other collection of Canadians. There had been immigration of families from trouble spots in Russia and parts of Europe during the late 19th and early 20th Centuries, and many of their daughters would still be attached to the land in 1917. Otherwise, immigration was mostly from Great Britain. From 1890 to 1930, this included over one hundred thousand children, mostly from the streets of large cities in England and some orphans from Barnardo's Homes. The boys and girls were sent to farms throughout Canada. The couple that owned the farm often adopted the children under five years old. Some were treated like slaves or worse, beaten, made to eat with the dogs, deprived of attending school. Others were loved liked members of the family, attended university and developed their potential. These "farm children" would have taken on the religion of the family with whom they resided so the status quo of religious observance was not disturbed by this influx. It is possible some members of Bessie's audience had been "farm children."

Considerable immigration took place after World War I, again, mostly from Britain. It was not until after World War II that a greater complexity of immigrants from many ethnic regions really began. In the late 1940s, with the welcoming of talented "displaced persons" from Europe, Canada became a more culturally rich country.

However, in 1917 the religious makeup of Bessie's audience was probably similar to Canada in general, which was not far off the findings of the 1921 census: Roman Catholic 38.6%, Anglican 16%, Presbyterian 16%, Methodists 13.2%, United Church of Canada 1%, and no religion 2%. (Methodists combined with some Presbyterians in 1925 to form the United Church of Canada, which had already started by 1921. In the 1931 census, Methodists were no longer listed).

Bessie, being closely connected with the Anglican Church, was fully aware of resistance to ideas expressed by someone parading denominational views that may be contrary to those of her listeners. She was on firm footing eliminating "theological dogmas or ecclesiastical pronouncements" as a basis for her remarks. Bessie brings her 1917 address to a close with three paragraphs that reach deeply into a philosophy of life and view of death that undergirds her focus on the ethics of nursing.

> When the violinist breaks his bow we do not say the musician is dead. We know that, given a new instrument, he can again bring forth the strains that speak to us of love and parting and sorrow, of reunion and joy and conquest, and make our heart strings vibrate with his melody.

> In death we lay aside this outworn instrument, the body, that can no longer answer to the needs of the spirit within and go on, in the words of the Apostle, "to be clothed upon with immortality."

> Keeping this high conception before us, need we fear death for ourselves, or others? The one thing that concerns us is to see that no base action, no willful

> departure from duty, no selfishness, no unkindness
> shall mar the character that we are to take with us.
> We shall not then fail either in our duty to ourselves,
> or others. Our profession calls for the best that is in
> us. Shall we not give it ungrudgingly? As we do so,
> we keep alive in it that ethical spirit without which it
> would degenerate into soulless drudgery.

Considering the prolonged impact of World War I, Bessie no doubt realized that many of those listening to her, and many of her eventual readers, would have recently experienced the death of a brother, a father, a husband, a sweetheart, or friends. Through invoking the nurse's attitude to their patients, she has seamlessly enlarged her theme. Addressing the difficult subject of death makes a powerful ending to this well-constructed paper.

Bessie's writings on the nursing profession do not provide us with precise references to her early experiences in nurse's training and employment from which she developed her views on the need for reform. However, reading and reflecting on these quotations from her mature addresses to professional audiences provides us with a comprehensive overview of the concerns and themes to which she repeatedly returned. Over the course of her long life, she continued her determined effort to transform nursing from a vernacular vocation into a medically sophisticated profession. She was sought out to address nursing conferences and given regular publication in U.S. and Canadian nursing journals. Clearly, this record of activism on behalf of the nursing profession is solid evidence that her efforts were appreciated and successful.

Chapter Four

Author

Although Elizabeth Robinson Scovil authored numerous articles, through many decades for magazines, periodicals and journals, I am making a distinction between her career in journalism and her achievement as the author of published books.

As a journalist she played a significant part in improving the health, nutrition, comfort, and happiness of children and their mothers, chiefly in the United States and Canada. This widespread influence was the result of her monthly articles in *The Ladies' Home Journal*, of which she was a founding associate editor. Starting in 1890, it quickly came to have the largest circulation of any magazine in the world.

She was also involved in the founding of *The American Journal of Nursing* for which she was an Associate Editor for twenty-one years. Her monthly column, "Notes From the Medical Press," kept nurses in the U.S. informed of contemporary views and developments in the medical world. Even before she graduated from nursing school, Bessie had articles accepted for publication in various periodicals. She was a supporter and early contributor to *Canadian Nurse* when it was founded. Many of her inspiring speeches given to conferences, annual meetings, and various gatherings of graduate nurses and superintendents were published in *The American Journal of Nursing* and *Canadian Nurse* and so reached minds and hearts of thousands of nurses.

However, if she had been asked at the end of her life, Bessie would probably have put a greater value on her published books, partly because they are in a more durable form of publication and partly because many of them address religious themes and spiritual development, which became a strong focus in her later years. My mother said that whenever they needed to make an investment on the farm, for example, a new barn door or similar expensive improvement, Aunt Bessie would come up with a new book knowing her publisher would accept it and her loyal readers would eagerly purchase it. If it had a religious theme, so much the better, as she had no problem giving her religion a practical application.

Elizabeth Robinson Scovil wrote twenty-one or twenty-three books, depending on which count we accept. I have collected or seen in library archives only seventeen of them and cannot prove either number correct. Henry Altemus of Philadelphia published a book of Bessie's poetry in the early 1890's, the period in which she launched her book writing career. This book has not been found. My mother told me Bessie wrote a children's book around this time called *The Littlest Loyalist*. I have also seen references to a book by Bessie, titled *History of the Kingston Peninsula*. Copies of these books have not come to light in the course of my research.

As an associate editor of *The Ladies' Home Journal* starting in 1890, and author of a monthly column on advice to mothers, Elizabeth Scovil was repeatedly asked by expectant or new, inexperienced mothers about suitable food, clothing, and, in general, the care of infants. It must have become quickly obvious after a few months that a great number of mothers and mothers-to-be were looking for the same information. We don't know if it was Bessie approaching Curtis Publishing Company with the idea for a book, or Curtis approaching Bessie—Curtis was the publisher of *The Ladies' Home Journal*. But we do know that the book Bessie produced and Curtis published became a best seller and launched her on a major book writing and publishing career.

In the May 1892 issue of *The Ladies' Home Journal*, the following notice appeared at the bottom of the "Mother's Corner" page written by Bessie:

> In response to the many inquiries, the editor of the "Mothers' Corner" prepared a little book called

A Baby's Requirements giving practical advice as to the first wardrobe: the necessary toilet articles, the preparations needed for the mother's comfort, the food and general care of the baby. It can be obtained from the Curtis Publishing Company for twenty cents.

In September of the same year this testimonial appears as the last paragraph of the "Mothers' Corner" column:

A Baby's Requirements. I found in this little book, which I got from the "Journal" office, all the help I needed in preparing for my baby, for I am utterly inexperienced, but I should like to know the exact proportions of the tannin and glycerine lotion mentioned on page 45. C.M.C.

Author Scovil provides the answer: "Two teaspoons of powdered tannin to one teaspoon of glycerine."

Over the years there were bags full of letters bursting with readers' gratitude. Bessie makes many references to the book in a new question and answer column. In the May 1893 issue, following a question entitled "Weaning Baby" signed "Young Mother," Bessie, offers several recommendations. She then adds, "You will find some hints on weaning a baby in *A Baby's Requirements* which will be sent to you from the *Journal* office for twenty-five cents."

Bessie must have been pleased with the response to her book. Clearly, the information provided was of great assistance to new mothers. Complimentary references to the book continued to appear in letters to the magazine. Bessie's question and answer column was titled "Suggestions for Mothers."

One recipient of her book, however, gave her something of a backhanded compliment. Shortly before one of Bessie's visits to England, she sent one of her books to Florence Nightingale.

Miss Nightingale replied on May 28, 1897 with a spirited and somewhat critical letter. "Thank you very much for your book which is admirable for lady-mothers. But what do you do for poor mothers who have hardly one, if one, of those conveniences and arrangements which you so justly advocate?" Florence Nightingale was deeply involved with improving conditions of poor mothers at the time, so the slant to her praise is not surprising and would have been readily appreciated by Bessie.

I assume *A Baby's Requirements* was the book that gave rise to Miss Nightingale's remarks, though I may be wrong. The Henry Altemus Company of Philadelphia published Bessie's *Care of Children* in 1894 and her *Preparation for Motherhood* in 1896, so the gift could have been either of those, especially the latter, as its contents fit more appropriately with Miss Nightingales's remark. These three books were the beginning of Bessie's work as a serious author, separate from that of journalist.

Though *Care of Children* was copyrighted in 1894, by 1896 the Henry Altemus Company was advertising a revised edition. The following promotion appears on the flyleaf of *Preparation for Motherhood*:

In Uniform Style by the Same Author
THE CARE OF CHILDREN
New and Revised Edition
With a practical and copious index
360 pages cloth $1.00

When *Preparation for Motherhood* appeared in book shops in 1896, the title page stated that Elizabeth Robinson Scovil was "Late Superintendent of the Newport Hospital, and is Associate Editor of *The Ladies' Home Journal* and author of *The Care of Children*." For bookshop owners and for potential buyers and readers the fact that the author had been a superintendent of a prestigious hospital and is an associate editor of a magazine held in high repute would be an assurance of her ability to deal with pregnancy, a delicate and rarely spoken of subject.

Having the two books in "uniform style" suggests that the second is equally as good as the first and they were, in a sense, a pair. In hindsight Bessie may have wished she had written them in reverse order, which would have been more logical, but perhaps she was testing the waters before taking up the more delicate and normally hidden subject. The significance and impact of *Preparation for Motherhood* can be judged by the fact that it appears to have been the first book of its kind in the English language—further evidence that Elizabeth Scovil was on the frontlines of the early feminist movement.

Her niece—my mother—could not fathom how a childless spinster, no matter how well qualified otherwise, could possibly write a book on preparing for motherhood. At the height of her teenage impertinence, about fifteen years after publication, little Mary said as much to her Aunt Bessie, who defended her qualification with a simple, yet deeply thoughtful, reply; "The watchers see most of the game."

Neither *A Baby's Requirements* or *The Care of Children* were available to me until recently. A cousin in England, Joanna Wootten, Aunt Bessie's great, great niece lent me her grandmother's (Elisabeth Scovil Villiers) well-used copies until my next visit when they will be replaced on her bookshelf. Having these books at hand has been of enormous value in assessing the significance of Elizabeth Scovil as an author.

* * * *

It makes sense to look at these books, published two years apart, in chronological order. The best way to place *A Baby's Requirements* in the context of the time is to quote the short preamble:

> This little book is written in response to more than twelve hundred letters to me, as one of the Associate Editors of *The Ladies' Home Journal*, appealing for information on subjects connected with the care of infants. It has been prepared under the pressure of duties incident to the position of Superintendent of a

hospital. If the mothers who have asked for assistance find it here, it will have amply fulfilled its object.

E.R.S.

The table of contents must have immediately assured the new or expectant mother that this book would meet her need for specific information: "Clothing, Food, Nursing, Feeding, Amount of Food, Interval of Feeding, The Nursing-Bottle, Weaning, The Bath, The Basket, The Bed, The Mother's Comfort, Ailments."

Nicely anticipating that a grandmother or grandmother-in-law might sneer at some of the ideas in this book, the author deals with the possibility in the introduction, enabling the new mother to have confidence in the suggestions that follow.

> During the last few years, a revolution has taken place in the manner of feeding and clothing babies. In all the wonderful progress of this age of miracles, it would be singular if there were no improvement in the methods of caring for the infant scions of the human race, the lord and master of all.

> These modern ideas seem strange to the elders who have never practiced them. There will be plenty of wise women to say to a young mother: "I brought up my children before these new-fangled notions were heard of. They always wore bands, and had soothing syrup, and were fed when they cried; and I should like to know how much worse they are for it?" The point is, would they not have had a more comfortable childhood, better digestions, and stronger nerves, if they had been treated more in accordance with the laws of Nature?

> The world moves, in spite of the assertions of incredulous persons to the contrary. Infant mortality is steadily decreasing under a more enlightened

management of young children, and it is foolish not to avail one's self of the results of the best scientific thought and experiment in this direction.

Bessie may have arranged the chapters according to the frequency with which questions were asked of her as columnist in *The Ladies Home Journal*. Having read her columns, I notice that queries about clothing out-numbered all others. The choice of the first wardrobe appears to cause a lot of uncertainty. The number of garments, the material of which to make them, and the proper shape for them are puzzling matters to an inexperienced person. Bessie acknowledges this in the first paragraph, thus making readers feel comfortable in their ignorance and ready for the coming information and advice. It is likely *A Baby's Requirements* was so popular because the author acknowledged all women of varying abilities and incomes:

> There are some points that each person must decide for herself. If you can sew neatly, and are well enough to work with ease, it is slightly less expensive and more satisfactory to make the things yourself. If you have to pay a seamstress, it is better to buy them ready made from some reliable house. In this case do not purchase a layette, as this includes some articles that can well be dispensed with; but buy the garments singly, getting only those you really require.
>
> It need not be a drawback, if you live far from a large city, catalogues are readily sent upon application. ... If you desire to make the clothes at home, send to the Butterwick Company or the Domestic Company, New York, for catalogues.

Then follows an extensive list of specific clothing items illustrating how practical and detailed the advice:

bands[3] (needed only for the first week or two);

shirts (ribbed cotton and wool cashmere, high necked and long-sleeved, open all the way down the front);

petticoats (of cotton-and-wool flannel, like a sleeveless slip, opening at the back, four are necessary, twenty-eight inches in length—while the baby is little the bottom can be turned up and fastened together with safety-pins to keep the feet warm);

napkins [diapers] (four dozen are necessary of Canton flannel sometimes called cotton flannel, preferred over cotton and linen which is too cold—keep a square of soft, old linen in the napkin, to be burned, instead of washed—a square of thick flannel at night protects clothing—never use a rubber diaper, sure to injure delicate skin);

slips (six are sufficient);

dresses (nainsook[4] muslin, costing from 50 to 75 cents a yard, is the prettiest, Butterwick pattern No. 3643, for the first style—hemstitching, feather-stitching and tucks are most appropriate trimming with a narrow Hamburg edging or Valenciennes lace as a finish—elaborate embroideries are no longer considered in good taste—the yokes can be purchased ready made from Best and Co, New York and the skirts added at home— six dresses are enough);

wrappers (useful to put on early in the morning or over the dress when the room is cool, silk-and-wool

---

3   Bandages wrapped around the baby's middle quite snugly, often for three months, to keep the navel from protruding.

4   From Hindi, meaning eye pleasure.

flannel, Scotch flannel, cashmere, decorate with feather stitching or lace);

socks (if you can crochet or knit, or they cost 25 cents a pair ready made, at least six or eight pairs);

blankets (silk-and-wool flannel with an inch hem and a spray embroidered in one corner, but the most useful ones are knitted from single ribbon of the desired color which can be taken out before it is put in water);

bibs (linen lined with Germantown wool, in plain knitting on large bone or rubber needles, pale pink or blue stripes near the ends are pretty at first but lose their beauty when washed, better to run six or eight rows of baby ribbon of the desired color which can be taken out before it is put in water);

bibs (linen lined with cotton flannel, shrunk before using—white table oilcloth makes a convenient feeding-bib for older children);

cloak and bonnet (usually cashmere or silk-and-wool flannel for cloak and silk for the hood—troublesome for unaccustomed fingers and costs nearly as much to make as to buy—make sure the hood or parasol of the carriage is arranged to shade the eyes—do not trust with a young child or a careless servant);

short clothes (shorten them when a healthy baby is four months old or put aside for the next baby).

Two pages then follow detailing changes in growing baby's wardrobe, how long black stockings should come above the knees, which ought to be cashmere in winter, "delicate tints and small patterns" for summer dresses, and in winter eider-down flannel for the cloak and velvet and cashmere for the bonnet.

The final paragraph of this chapter on clothing is perhaps the most useful. It describes in detail how to wash flannels or worsted baby clothes, including the use of Ivory Soap, hand washing and rinse in water of the same temperature, wringing knitted things in a towel before reshaping and laying them flat in a warm place to dry. The care of baby clothes was a time consuming business for which *A Baby's Requirements* provided complete instructions.

Suitable food for babies ranks second in the count of most frequently asked question. *A Baby's Requirements* provides an exhaustive eleven pages on all possible combinations and permutations of infant nourishment, starting naturally, with nursing and what should be done if mother's milk is not tolerated. A large intake of liquid is recommended for nursing mothers, milk being the best. Bessie anticipates a dislike of ordinary milk by some of her readers so she suggests a dozen ways of giving it character, including "shake it in a glass jar with the white of an egg to each half pint, a pinch of salt and cracked ice." She also advocates nourishing, solid food for the mother and the avoidance of acid foods that "may disagree with the baby, but only experience can teach you what these are."

According to Bessie, "Cow's milk, properly prepared and diluted, is the best substitute for the mother's milk." She describes various methods of preparing, including mixing with cream, barley water, and limewater, or using Peptogenic Milk Powder.

Bessie includes a section on the appropriate amount of food required, according to the weight of the baby and how "vigorous" it is. Another section is devoted to the frequency of feeding. The author is very definite on this matter:

> A baby's stomach requires rest, just as its other organs do. To feed it every time it cries is as absurd as it would be to poke food down the throats of grown persons every time they yawned, or groaned. Many lives are sacrificed to over-feeding. Do not sacrifice your baby.

She then gives specific directions — feed every two hours until a baby is two months (twice at night if necessary). After that, "gradually lengthen the interval of feeding, a few minutes each day, until it has food every three hours" (and perhaps once at night). The remainder of the chapter on food is taken up with the selection and cleaning of the nursing bottle and with detailed instructions on weaning.

Further advice on advancing a baby's diet follows:

> By the time a child is a year old a lightly boiled egg every other day, the juice from rare roast beef or mutton on bread and the soft part of a well-baked apple, and a little vegetable is appropriate, along with little or no meat, unless cut in tiny pieces, until the double teeth are through.

This highly informative chapter on food and feeding is easy to read and must have allowed many a prospective mother to relax a little.

The following chapter, "The Bath," is equally detailed, A tin foot-tub makes a good bath for the baby. When it is old enough to sit up and hold fast to the sides, it will have great fun kicking and splashing. Bessie covers the bath temperature, the avoidance of chills, thorough drying and powdering, changing clothes, prevention of "cradle cap," mouth washing, and lap protectors. She offers the reminder that dyes used to colour clothing are apt to run when wet. She recommends wearing a Lonsdale apron to prevent the dark dresses of the mother or nurse from staining the baby's white dresses after the bath.

The next chapter titled, "The Basket," describes "a pretty basket to hold the requisites for the baby's toilet."

> It is usual to purchase a wicker-basket about twenty-two inches long, square or oval and with sides three or four inches high, costing about a dollar. This is covered with silesia[5] or glazed cambric, pink or blue, and over

---

5   A smooth-finished, twilled cotton fabric originally made in Silesia,

this with plain or figured muslin, net, lace, or scrim[6] edged with narrow lace. Sometimes a delicate India, China or surrah slk is used for the outer covering. Two pincushions and two little bags of the same material are fastened to the sides, and the first effect is very fascinating.

This description is directed at engaging the prospective mother in making something useful, but also pretty, worthy of her pretty baby. The ever practical Bessie admits that "after two or three months' use the dainty decorations becomes sadly limp... and you awake to the fact that the basket must be renovated.... "After encouraging the reader to imagine this crafted creation, she then suggests a sensible alternative. "It is better to begin with something that will not require renewing so quickly. Choose a basket whose sides are woven in a fanciful pattern..." weave ribbons in and out, add bows, the color is a matter of taste.

All this might seem like a time consuming, dust collecting, unnecessary adjunct to preparing for a baby, but not if viewed from 1892 when most women's sense of fulfillment came chiefly from producing several children, caring for them, organizing their care, surrounding them with attractive clothes and paraphernalia, and raising them to adulthood. Bessie's then provides detailed recommendations on all the articles of baby care with which be-ribboned basket should be filled. She comments negatively on ready made and filled baskets, which cost at least $5.50.

She further recommends:

> ...a high bureau with lots of shallow drawers to contain baby's wardrobe. Its clothing cannot be too sweet...cut a piece of stiff brown paper exactly to fit the bottom of the drawer, tack on this a split sheet of white wadding thickly sprinkled with sachet-powder—a mixture of violet and powdered orrisroot

---

6   A cotton or linen fabric of open weave.

is pleasant — cover this with any pretty figured silk or other material preferred, and the contents of the drawer will always be fragrant. When the pennies have to be counted with care and there are not many to spare for luxuries, a trunk or large wooden box,… can be treated in the same way, lined neatly, the top stuffed and covered with chintz like an ottoman.

Surrounding the baby in a sweet smelling environment is certain to bolster the feeling of being a good mother. With a well looked after baby, natural smells being well masked, friends and family will feel the same way. The complimentary remarks from visitors will reward her for all her trouble, provide a sense of accomplishment, and make having more babies something she can look forward to.

Three pages on "The Bed" follow. Bessie begins her discussion with a surprising opinion; one that it is fair to say seems questionable.

If a child is never rocked, it cannot miss what it has not had. The cradle has been almost discarded, and we must find some other simile for a mother's influence than the old one — "The hand that rocks the cradle rules the world."

Some form of a rocking or swaying device has been used for centuries to lull fretful babies. Even strapped on a mother's back or carried in a sling on her hip while she moves about gives a baby the calming effect of constant motion. Bessie's dismissal of this tradition seems odd but perhaps her strong interest in the "modernization" of childcare prompted her to take this view. Modern designers have, however, now filled the gap caused by the demise of the cradle. Various alternatives, including a suspended seat on springs that responds to the baby's movements and portable beds that have the capacity to rock are readily available and widely used.

Bessie continues with advice to avoid the bassinette, which is soon outgrown and instead recommends the crib as "the most sensible purchase, for this can be used until the child is several years old." She is very particular about what is under baby. "The best foundation for the bed is a woven-wire mattress, and a soft hair one over it. On this lay a folded blanket, next a square of rubber-cloth, and over this the sheet." A soft blanket (no upper sheet) is recommended for warm weather and an eiderdown or wadded comforter is recommended for the winter. She further recommends a feather pillow but states it should be "thin [which] gives softness without over-heating the little head."

Bessie further advises:

> Never allow your baby to be wakened except for its food, unless it is in personal danger. To take it up from a sound sleep is a cruel invasion of its rights. You will be ready enough to complain, later, when the baby will not sleep in the morning, or refuses to take its nap when you are busy. Let it practice the good habits that it brought with it, and it will not learn the bad ones. Plenty of sleep means a healthy brain and tranquil nerves.

Part of a "baby's requirements" has to do with "The Mother's Comfort," which is the penultimate chapter of the book. Bessie writes: "It is the first duty of the expectant mother to keep mind and body in as tranquil and well-ordered a condition as possible." The seven pages that follow, elaborate on how to achieve and maintain this state. Mindful of her readers' awareness of the many deaths resulting directly or indirectly from childbirth, Bessie does her best to put that information in perspective:

> A celebrated obstetrical physician once said that if he were offered a thousand dollars to conduct a woman safely through an illness, and given his choice of ten ailments, he should choose a confinement, the number

of favourable recoveries was so large in proportion to the cases. While there is a risk, the danger is not as great as you imagine.

With both my grandmothers dying after childbirth ("child-bed fever" and pregnancy triggered diabetes in 1894 and 1903, and my mother only just surviving a four day labour with excessive albumin in 1924), I think this physician was a trifle optimistic for the time. However, Bessie was concerned to calm the novices' fears, and wisely details how to go about achieving a safe and successful outcome.

Avoid fatigue and excitement; take plenty of sleep; wear proper clothing; eat nourishing, easily digested food; take exercise in the open air as long as possible; do not work on a treadle sewing-machine more than you can help; have a sponge bath every morning or evening and you will have done all you can to keep yourself in good health.

Bessie briefly covers morning sickness. Her 1896 book, *Preparation for Motherhood*, which I will examine later, gives more elaborate suggestions for dealing with this difficultly. The remainder of the chapter details a variety of articles needed and preparations to make for giving birth, ending with the caution of using only washables on the confinement bed as "the danger of infection is too great."

Bessie takes aim at a custom of the Victorian period — rooms cluttered with every possession imaginable from stuffed birds, usually resting under glass domes, to collections of shells and trinkets from travels. In the interest of promoting hygienic conditions, she writes: "Do not have too many knick-knacks about to be dusted and kept clean." This is especially appropriate since the mother and her baby would not stray far from the bedroom for a month.

This little book is intended to deal with the basics and devotes only five pages to "Aliments." This final chapter deals only with colds, colic, constipation and diarrhea. Bessie justifies such a short list with her introductory statement: "When a baby is sick send for the doctor." She then equips the novice with enough information to confidently remedy the illnesses listed:

> There are, however, some slight ailments which may be treated without his advice, at least in the beginning, and some household remedies that it is safe to use without a prescription. If a baby is kept in an over-heated room, it is very apt to take cold. The temperature of the nursery should not be above seventy degrees during the day and sixty to sixty-five degrees [Fahrenheit] at night.

Fresh air is the next important element that must be provided, if necessary through complicated arrangements of anti-draught boards and/or blankets guarding the open window. If an open window is ruled out because the stove or furnace is not generating enough heat to keep the room warm, the baby must be taken into another room and the nursery windows opened wide for airing twice a day, then re-warmed:

> After its morning bath, rub the back and chest with a little alcohol and water. This decreases the liability to take cold. If…in spite of your care…[baby takes cold] rub the chest with warm oil and pin a square of flannel inside the little shirt.

> Colic is usually caused by over-feeding… Sometimes, however, a malicious colic fiend seems to pursue the baby, torturing it without apparent cause. In this case, the mother can only try to circumvent it by special care in keeping the baby warm.

Bessie then gives detailed instruction in how to do this including putting peppermint essence in warm water for a bath, warmer than for usual baths, and stomach massage. Knowing that colic can nearly drive parents to the edge, she warns against taking extreme measures.

> Never, as you value your child's life and health, give soothing syrup [usually laced with alcohol], paregoric [a camphorated tincture of opium] or any nostrum [a medicine made by the person who recommends it] whatever.

In the sections on constipation and diarrhoea, Bessie suggests precise and simple cures. With constipation, a suppository of glycerine or white soap "an inch long and about as thick as a lead pencil" is usually effective when other methods fail. With diarrhoea, make sure any milk is sterilized "or if you are already doing this, stop giving milk altogether, and try barley or rice-water for a day. If there is no improvement, speak to the doctor." Though colic is still a problem, it is now well known that when nursing mothers avoid consuming all milk products their infant's colic often disappears. Bessie was ahead of her time.

A strong and succinct clincher sentence usually finishes Elizabeth Robinson Scovil's chapters and her books. *A Baby's Requirements* is no exception:

> A cheery, tranquil mother makes a happy, contented baby, and is worth more to it than the exact fulfillment of the best theories by a careworn individual who has let her anxieties quench her sunshine.

At twenty-five cents a copy, this little gem found its way into the uncertain hands of thousands of soon-to-be mothers, who, with great relief, turned to relevant chapters as they progressed toward and into parenthood. Most copies would likely have turned to ashes or been crushed in landfills by now, having long fulfilled their purpose. But I can imagine a few copies are still waiting in attics to be re-discovered by the smiling descendants of the original purchaser. Others may be on musty shelves of second hand bookstores. I like to think that the preservation of the books themselves is not as important as the information they provided to the original readers and the confidence they gave to those mothers, and which continues to be passed along from generation to generation. I am forever grateful, however, that a copy of my Great Aunt's first book was retained in our family and came into my hands for study through my generous cousin.

*　*　*　*

Following the success of *A Baby's Requirements*, Bessie saw the need for a sequel which she entitled, *The Care of Children*, which was published in 1894 with the price of $1.00. The copy in front of me states that it is a "Revised Edition with a Copious Index"—indeed, with a twelve-page index. An excerpt from the introduction explains why there was a need for her second book. After making reference to *A Baby's Requirements*, she writes:

> This little book brought forth so many inquiries as to the care of children after babyhood that it was determined to expand it into a larger volume, containing beside the greater part of the original matter, the information desired.

In case any of her readers believe that only a doctor, therefore a man, should advise on her child's illnesses, Bessie brings out her credentials:

> An experience of many years in hospital work has given a familiarity with the details of nursing that it is hoped will render the chapters on the care in illness especially useful. It is then that the inexperienced mother most feels her helplessness and welcomes friendly aid. An effort has been made in *The Care of Children* to answer in a plain and practical manner the

questions that are most likely to arise to puzzle those
to whom this charge is entrusted, whether in sickness
or in health

This five by seven inch book of three hundred and forty-eight pages with a linen, cream coloured hard cover is divided into eighteen sections and twenty-five chapters, several sections having more than one chapter. As stated in the introduction, this book is an expansion of *A Baby's Requirements* covering the same information in more detail but then extending her discussion to needs and concerns for children as they grow toward adulthood. The following excerpts show Bessie's understanding and thinking to be highly advanced for her time and how she was especially sensitive to her readers' needs.

Ever a master of introductory sentences that entice the reader to continue, Bessie produces a gem for the chapter on "The Food of School Children":

It has been well said that "children in school are more or less like animals in captivity." They are existing under artificial conditions of cramped position, enforced stillness of body, and stimulation of mind, and too often deprived by bad ventilation of a fair share of oxygen that is necessary to maintain vitality.

Under these circumstances their diet becomes a matter of increased importance. Reading this substantial chapter reminds me that in the 1890's very little was known in the general population about the need for a balanced diet and for more or for less of a particular food in special situations. To rectify this, Bessie's sub-heading under "The Purpose of Food" is followed by information that was only beginning to be understood at this time. Once again, we see her forte as a writer was to pick up on the advances in scientific information, along with health and medical practices, and present them for general understanding.

Food serves two great purposes: to build up flesh and bones, nerves and blood; to furnish heat and power to the body. The first end is accomplished by protein, a substance found abundantly in lean meat, fish, eggs, milk, cheese, and in some vegetables and meals, as peas, beans, oatmeal, wheat flour, rye and corn meal. Heat and energy are furnished partly by fats, as cream, oil, butter, and the fat of meat; and partly by starch contained in potatoes, many of the cereals, rice, tapioca etc. and by sugar.

Children, from their ceaseless activity, require a large amount, proportionately, of the latter class of food. Fortunately, many articles of diet contain both classes of food materials, as wheat bread, Indian meal, oatmeal, peas, beans etc.

Always mindful of the less than wealthy, the author affirms that all mothers "may give her child the substances necessary to develop their body" as it is "not the most expensive that is most nourishing."

Bessie is determined her readers' school age children will be well fed. She follows her general suggestions with those for breakfast, luncheon, dinner, supper, and at bedtime. This seems like an excessive number of meals, but luncheon appears to be a packed lunch when attending school, and dinner the noon meal, when not.

She is especially keen on a "substantial breakfast." A child in those days would usually walk to school so a substantial breakfast would be needed. Her menu includes "…porridge of some cereal and milk followed by fish or bacon with bread or toast and butter …and conclude with fruit if it is obtainable." For the drink, she suggests cocoa or hot or cold milk, "diluted with water if preferred." Fruit is not high on her list but she recognizes that as it is "very necessary in the animal economy its value must not be underrated."

In addressing lunch, Bessie starts with a progressive prophecy:

When parents recognize the importance of insisting that the bodies as well as the minds of their children shall be developed at school, food will be provided there as one of the means to the end. Until then the mother must furnish the lunch basket.

Sandwiches are the basis for a nourishing lunch for which she describes a variety of fillings including "minced or finely cut meat" and "delicately shredded fish sprinkled with salt" for a good source of protein. The sandwiches should be well wrapped in a napkin made from an old tablecloth. Nothing is without purpose in the education of a child. Bessie sees care in these details of packing a lunch as setting an example of how to do things correctly that will stay with the child for life. For desert, "Fresh fruit should be given whenever possible." Failing that, "a baked apple, stewed pear, prunes or any similar dainty" may be placed in "a jelly tumbler with a tin top."

The opening sentence of the paragraph under "Dinner" is no surprise. "A plate of hot soup should usher in the dinner." If the children cannot sip hot soup at school at least they can enjoy it when at home. "Nothing comes amiss to the soup pot; bread, cold vegetables, even fish, can be utilized, and their presence be unrecognized in the combination of flavours that renders the dish so acceptable." The soup is followed by meat prepared in any way but fried, though re-cooked with gravy (never greasy) is acceptable, with layers of tomato or sliced with mashed potato on top.

Rich gravies and highly seasoned dishes, as curries, should be avoided for children. With the meat there should be potatoes and one other vegetable; it matters little what so long as it is well cooked, neither over nor under done. ...The meal may be concluded by a simple pudding, fruit, or ice cream. Pastry should be given very sparingly, but a perfectly healthy child may eat it occasionally with impunity, if it is good.

Blanc mange, was the "simple pudding" the author had in mind. My mother remembers it frequently served in her childhood when her aunt was in charge of the household routine and meal preparation. She later names the bland concoction when describing a suitable supper menu for school children. "Eggs… the cereals, bread and butter, milk toast, blanc mange or custard and fruit (fresh or stewed), preserves, honey or syrup. Milk, hot or cold, and water are still the only liquids permissible." In other words, no tea or coffee and certainly no alcohol should be given to children. And finally, about the end of the day, Bessie has this to say:

> If a child plays hard and does not go to bed for two hours or more after supper, he may be hungry before he goes to sleep. In this case, it is wise to give a cracker and a glass of milk if they are desired.
>
> Sometimes, alas under our pernicious system of education, which obliges lessons to be learned at home, he, or more probably she, may be exhausted by an hour of study in the evening, and the tired brain will not easily quiet down to sleep. If this outrage on nature cannot be stopped, the evil effect may be a little modified by a glass of warm milk, which setting the digestive organs in action, will draw away the blood from the over-stimulated brain and render sleep possible.

This final paragraph in the chapter dealing with suitable food for school children says much about the author's progressive view of child development. Her pillorying of school required homework underscores the value she placed on the importance of free playtime at home. She also considered girls to be more easily tired by school homework than boys. In Bessie's day, the quality of girls' achievements was expected to be less than that of boys. In looking back in later years over how much she had accomplished in her life, Bessie must have seen the irony of her remark quoted above. She was the one who had accomplished so much compared to her presumably less easily exhausted brothers. There were very few women like Bessie in the 1890s, partly due to low expectations. With the writing and publication of each new book she raised the expectations for her own accomplishments and for women in general.

The section on ailments begins with a stimulating and challenging opening:

> Food plays a very important part in the treatment of disease, even more important than medicine. In serious cases it will be prescribed by the doctor in attendance, but there are many in which it is well for the mother to know what diet is most suitable for the time being.

For constipation in children, Bessie recommends a primarily vegetarian diet with lots of water plus, "a fig soaked overnight in a little water and given at breakfast before the other food." For diarrhea, change the food to "light and un-stimulating," no roughage, and give less. Arrowroot gruel is effective, "but not for very young babies." Food related causes take the blame for indigestion, as well. Starch given too early is often the culprit in babies. Eating too fast can be a problem in older children. She wisely writes: "When it is certain that any article of food disagrees with a child, its use should be forbidden. There should be as little discussion about the food as possible before the child."

Bessie advises that rickets, now almost non-existent except in countries were malnutrition is common, is caused by an "improper diet." "Earthy salts, or phosphates…contained abundantly in vegetables and grains" are the remedy, along with cod liver oil.

Bessie's approach to colds is time honoured; no food or very little, and only that which is easily digested, perhaps soup and lots of liquids. She assures young mothers that "starvation is a very slow process and a well-fed child may go without food for a day without suffering from the fast, if water is given as required."

For skin rashes, eliminate meat and oatmeal from the diet and allow very little sugar. Concentrate on milk in various forms. The ever-present blanc mange is mentioned by name, along with bread and crackers and an occasional egg, which should help treat everything from eczema to nettle rash. When a child's temperature is up, only liquids should be given, especially milk, sometimes shaken with the white or yolk of an egg.

Tuberculosis claimed the lives of many in the late 19th century. As this chapter concerns only dietary treatment, Bessie concentrates on the need for fat in the diet to aid in resisting TB. In particular, she encourages the eating of cream, butter, bacon and eggs, especially the yolk. She recommends soaking bread in bacon fat. In addition, she recommends the use of goat's milk which is known to be more easily digested and has a higher fat content than cow's milk.

The chapter, "Clothing After Babyhood," deserves special note. It illustrates how sensitive Bessie was to the aesthetics of child care, which, of course, was a benefit to both children and parents. Bessie begins with this firm proscription:

> It cannot be too earnestly impressed upon the mind of the mother that girls should never wear tight-fitting waists, nor corsets. No woman ever acknowledges that her corsets were tight, but no matter how loose they are, they interfere with the proper development of the growing girl, render her figure less pliant and graceful, and destroy the easy carriage that is such a charm.

> A comfortable waist with shoulder straps and buttons, on which the flannel petticoat, underskirt and drawers can be buttoned, does no harm and furnishes all the support that is necessary. If the muscles never have been weakened by the inaction that pressure maintains, they are abundantly able to support themselves and their owner, too.

If mothers only realized how important it is that the delicate organs should have free play, utterly untrammelled by pressure from without, and knew the disastrous consequences that must follow any infringement of nature's laws, they would be the very first to insist upon a rigid adherence to sensible methods of dress.

Leg covering has changed so completely that a look at the subject in the late Victoria period is of historic interest. Remembering that money was rarely abundant, especially for a woman to spend carelessly, Bessie assumes a need for frugality:

When economy is a necessity, a slight saving may be effected by purchasing stockings out of season, summer ones in the autumn and winter ones in the spring; they are often sold at a reduction to prevent the necessity of packing them away. Black is, on the whole, the most satisfactory, although navy blue and dark brown look well for boys with suits of the same colors. Those purchased for boys should be stout, cotton or woollen, according to the time of year; ribbed ones fit the leg better than plain. Knee pads are a great protection when short trousers are being worn. They are shaped to fit over the knee and made of leather, or thick felt, being worn under the trousers.

Though she suggests that "Little girls may wear hose to match their dresses in color," setting them apart from boys who only wear black, navy, or brown, she does not want the difference to go too far, especially when health could be damaged. "High French heels [in shoes] should not be tolerated for little girls." On the care of shoes, Bessie writes; "A little vaseline, well rubbed in before an ordinary dressing is applied prevents the leather from cracking." Bedroom slippers are essential as "running about in bare feet is a dangerous pastime."

Aprons, she observers, have gone out of fashion but are "too convenient not to be restored to favour, preferably high-necked, long sleeved aprons of striped gingham or blue and white cotton" or, "if fancied for school girls, black silk aprons, high-necked and with long sleeves."

"A girl always requires a wrapper [dressing gown].""Boys usually despise these, except in illness." Nightgowns should be flannel in winter with an underskirt of the same material or cotton flannel and "in the warmest weather, a single cotton garment." Touching on outdoor garments, she notes overcoats for boys, cloaks for girls, and a long rubber-cloth garment being "indispensable for rainy days for both."

Bessie advises that older children should be allowed some expression of their own choice in clothes particularly in the matter of head-covering. What seems a detail of perfect indifference to the mother may mean an agony of mortification to the sensitive boy or girl. In no case is it more necessary for us to be able to put ourselves in another's place than in dealing with the idiosyncrasies of children.

In selecting a hat for a girl, it is well to remember that it must be worn with several dresses and should not look out of place with any one of them. To accomplish this, it must be quiet in tone and not too conspicuous in shape. Ribbon or velvet or "ostrich tips" is a more appropriate trimming than artificial flowers. Bessie stresses that the cruelty of wearing the plumage of birds that must be killed to obtain their feathers should be early impressed on the childish mind. The lesson will then never be forgotten. In mentioning "ostrich tips" Bessie must not have known that ostriches do not molt and plucking causes great pain. Almost all ostrich feathers in the market at the time came from birds that had been killed.

The chapters on "Beds and Bedding" and "Baths" are chiefly extensions of material in *A Baby's Requirements,* with some additions for older children. For diseases of the skin, Bessie advises that rainwater should be used for bathing if available. She also recommends a "bran bath" treatment. Bran is a pleasant addition to bath water even when its use is not medicinal. It softens, and is said to whiten the skin. The procedure is to put a pound of bran in a bag and boil it in eight quarts of water, then using the water for the bath, diluting it if necessary.

Bessie did not look upon "open air bathing" with the enthusiasm of some Victorians. An hour and a half or two hours should elapse between a meal and a "plunge bath" in river or lake. The child should not be permitted to stay in the water more than fifteen minutes, and often "a shorter time is all that is permissible." The child should never be forced to go in the water because of the mistaken idea of making him hardy. A child frightened by the prospect of going in the water can usually be encouraged and persuaded to make the attempt, and ends up liking the fun. If it is impossible to reassure him, the plunge bath should be abandoned until he gains more confidence. (The Rev. Charles Karsten, grandson of Bessie's eldest brother Jack, told me that children were thrown into the Saint John River at Meadowlands and expected to learn to swim, quickly. No drownings were reported from this method as there was always a rope tied around their middles.)

"Care of the Teeth" contains simple, reassuring information. "Tooth powders are not necessary to keep the teeth in good order. Pure soft water and a brush are all sufficient if they are used with the necessary frequency (after eating). Many dentifrices do more harm than good."

The treatment for toothache when a cavity is present is a little alarming. "Oil of cloves, put on cotton-wool and pressed into the hole" is recommended when the dentist's office is closed, or "a drop of carbolic acid or creosote," which is drastic and can be dangerous, but was regularly recommended and practiced in the 1890s.

Bessie's knowledge of tooth straightening must not have been common at the time, but she is emphatic about the need for this treatment for young children.

> If the teeth are not perfectly even and regular the child ought to be taken to a dentist. Defects can often be remedied if attended to in time, which it is impossible to rectify after years of neglect. It is

comparatively easy to straighten teeth and put them in their proper relative position while the child is young and it is wrong to permit a deformity to exist which might have been prevented if proper means had been used.

Twelve pages are given over to the "Care of the Eyes," which is not surprising considering Bessie's eye problems and chronic headaches. She makes the connection between the two: "An undue strain upon the eyes is the cause of many ailments and diseases... headache is one of the most common and obvious." She covers everything from eye infections in the newborn, to pink eye, to colour blindness with succinct, sensible advice. She gives instructions for home testing of the eyes with regard to needing glasses.

After a detailed description of the construction of the ear, Bessie emphasizes its' sensitivity to injury, especially decrying the Victorian habit of boxing the ears. "It is criminal to strike a child a blow on the ear. The air is driven with such force against the membrane that it may rupture." Putting a plug of cotton in the opening to allow the injury to heal itself is the only permitted treatment. "Pulling the ears may cause serious inflammation, the impulse being transmitted from the outer ear to the more sensitive parts." This was a common humiliation in the classroom for bad behaviour in her time.

The gist of the chapter on "Care of the Hair" is that you inherit your type of hair and can only enhance its' good points and try to minimize the bad. "Nothing improves the hair more than systematic brushing" is Bessie's opener. Those who wash their hair daily will be shocked to know:

Too frequent washing of the head is injurious to the hair and tends to make it dry and harsh. Unless there is a special reason for its being done more frequently, once a month is sufficient, if it has daily a thorough brushing in the interval.

Every type of childhood hair problem is considered from curling to crimping, from nits (apply kerosene oil) to dandruff (use camphor liniment rubbed on the scalp plus butter and cream added to the diet). "Any attempt to alter the color of the hair by chemical means is sure to end disastrously. Nature tones it to suit the complexion and interference with her handiwork seldom results in improvement."

Bessie then includes a short chapter on the nails, which discourages biting them and thumb sucking:

> Thumb sucking presses the upper teeth out of place and injures the lower lip. When the tendency… is perceived in a baby, the sleeve should be pinned to the dress or the pillow so the hand cannot be raised to the mouth…. It is such a comfort to a baby to suck the thumb it seems a shame to put a stop to such an apparently innocent pleasure. It saves much future annoyance and disfigurement if the child is not allowed to form the habit, and present comfort must be sacrificed to future good.

If all else fails, bitter aloes or a paste of gum arabic and red pepper smeared on the nails will deter biting or on the thumbs to stop sucking. Gloves or bags on the hands may also be tried. A little bribery may "effect a cure" in the form of "a substantial reward in an older child" if "an appeal to pride or his affections" fail to get the desired result.

Bessie knew from first hand experience as a nurse how important care of the feet can be. She is definite in advising against urging babies to stand or walk before they discover the pleasures for themselves, as their soft bones are "especially liable to distortion." Most ailments of the feet are caused by improperly fitting shoes.

Damp feet are to be avoided. Children should be instructed not to sit in school with damp feet. If long rubber boots are worn, this accident cannot happen while the boots are whole.

Toes or fingers exposed to the cold may develop chilblains. If this occurs, Bessie suggests they may be "painted with iodine or rubbed with an ointment of one part of ground mustard mixed with three parts of lard."

She covers the subjects of "Ailments" thoroughly in the following thirty-two pages. She begins by carefully pointing out that "children need very little medicine," and that only the simplest remedies should be given them without the advice of a doctor. With this in mind, all her recommendations are made accordingly, plus basic information a young mother needs to know, such as: "A child's temperature rises very easily and an elevation does not mean as much as in an adult." In addition, a "disordered digestion" is the reason for many children's complaints. Often, one of several gentle laxatives "will often carry off the offending substance." "…a small dose of castor oil, citrate of magnesia, Rochelle salts, or spiced syrup of rhubarb may be ventured on with perfect safety." Exposure to plenty of fresh air, along with a laxative can be helpful in these cases.

Many childhood disturbances can be successfully treated with these simple medicines, including sleeplessness, growing pains, chills, and stiff neck. For "night terrors," a lighter evening meal along with a warm bath before bedtime can be tried. Bessie advises the mother first make sure the nurse or other servants have not frightened the child with alarming stories. For general health maintenance, she emphasizes the need for nutritious food. For skin rashes, she recommends trying the elimination of meat, sugar, or oatmeal along with frequent cleansing of the affected area.

In order to be prepared in advance, Bessie suggests the mother should equip a medicine box with the following items and keep it safely stored on a closet shelf:

> Compound of liquorice root powder, spiced syrup of rhubarb, castor oil, citrate of magnesia, wine of ipecac [a South American plant], powdered alum, tincture of ginger, essence of peppermint, soda mint tablets. One of the first four laxatives will usually give relief

in any ordinary case. The wine of ipecac and alum are efficient emetics. The ginger, or peppermint will relieve pain in the stomach, and the soda mint checks nausea and relieves flatulence.

All of us who have had to give children unpleasant tasting medicine, or as children have had to take it, will appreciate her suggestions for making the procedure less traumatic.

Medicine that has a disagreeable odour should not be held under the nose. A little cologne on a handkerchief to sniff will divert the child's attention. A pill can be put into jam or pressed into a square of bread cut like dice.... Cod-liver oil can be made into an emulsion with the yolk of an egg, beating it like mayonnaise, adding a few drops of oil at a time; flavor with extract of bitter almond or lemon, and sweeten if desired. A little salt taken after the pure oil removes the traces of it, and baked apple is efficacious for the same purpose.

Bessie's ever present awareness of the psychology of good care is evident in the last two sentences of this chapter. "Do not destroy confidence in the truthfulness of grown persons by saying the medicine is not nasty. Say nothing about it, or make a virtue of the bravery of taking it when it is not nice."

The chapter on "Physical Deformities" includes everything from freckles to curvature of the spine, from bow legs and knock knees to cleft lip and extra fingers. Bessie's usual approach is to seek medical advice early if the problem appears serious, otherwise, she offers often simple treatments such as the mixing and applying two acids for warts.

Mothers must have been especially grateful for the forty-one page chapter on "Children's Diseases," which gives precise instruction for nursing scarlet fever, measles, diphtheria, croup, mumps, chicken pox, typhoid fever, pneumonia, bronchitis, asthma, rheumatism, chorea (St. Vitus' Dance), rickets, and tuberculosis.

The chapter also includes general information on ventilation, gavage (forced feeding), poultices, disinfectants, fumigation, formentations (application of hot packs), and nutritive enemata. Following Bessie's recommendations would mean early observation and appropriate care by the mother, which would be much appreciated by the visiting doctor when his assistance was required:

> The mother must remember that it is often difficult for him [the doctor] to make a diagnosis in an obscure case, or early in the disease, and she may be able to throw much light on the subject by telling him of symptoms that seem to her unimportant.

Again, Bessie's writing reminds us of the huge responsibility carried by a mother, possibly already weighed down by another pregnancy, in caring for her sick children. In the 1890s, well before modern drugs, vaccinations, and highly effective treatments, death from childhood disease was common and must have hovered in the mind of any parent whose child became ill. One only need to walk through an old graveyard to see repeated evidence of the brutal effect of disease upon the young. Bessie, herself, was one of eleven siblings only four of which survived early childhood.

Caring for a sick person was clearly more labour intensive than it is today. Under "articles useful in a sick room" Bessie lists "bent glass feeding tube," which underlines that drinking straws had yet to be invented. Imagine the cleaning and sterilizing time for such a utensil, instead of throwing it in the garbage and reaching for a fresh one as would be the practice today.

Sudden childhood injuries and health emergencies are times of high anxiety for parents. Bessie undertakes to dispel some of this anxiety by presenting fourteen pages of calm, sensible and medically informative instructions. She covers a wide range of accidents and emergency circumstances that may have to be dealt with—for example stings (baking soda or moist earth); bites (suck and spit); drowning (keep heat over the heart and apply artificial respiration—precise instructions given); a severed finger (wash in salt and water, put in place and fasten with strips of adhesive plaster and bandage — "there is good hope that the parts will unite, and at least the experiment ought always to be tried"); swallowing foreign bodies ("a masterly inactivity is the best course to pursue; an object that can pass down the throat can pass through the intestine and probably will do so safely if not interfered with, even pins; give potato, porridge or bread to form a soft coating"); foreign bodies stuck in the throat ("a quick blow between the shoulder blades"); broken bones ("place the limb in as natural a position as possible and make the as child comfortable as possible until the doctor comes").

Bessie's recommendation for an emergency box lists twenty articles including "a quarter pound of baking soda" and "a box of carbolic vaseline 1-30," both frequently used in emergencies. Carbolic acid was then the great anti-septic, preventing serious infection and an even more serious outcome to skin-breaking accidents.

She provides a short elaboration on bites from dogs and the possibility of hydrophobia [rabies]. Free ranging dogs were common at that time, so the chances of a child being bitten by a rabid dog was a real worry for a mother, especially where rabies was present in wild animals, which could well be the case but the frequency unknown. Bessie offers information on the treatment known to be effective to prevent the development of this fatal disease in persons who have been bitten or scratched by a rabid animal, though it is unlikely to have been acted upon except by New Yorkers or Parisians:

> Pasteur's method of the prevention of hydrophobia by injecting the virus, properly prepared, has warm advocates. There is an institute in New York where patients can be sent to undergo the treatment, as well as in Paris, where it originated.

Bessie would be delighted that widespread immunization for most childhood diseases is now given, thus preventing great misery and early child deaths for a large percentage of the young.

The chapter on "Physical Culture" opens with the statement that pre-school children do not need special exercises because of their "ceaseless activity."

> When a child is cut off from play and forced to sit still for several hours every day, often in a constricted, unnatural attitude, systematic exercise of the muscles becomes a necessity. We call the system of movements devised for this purpose gymnastics. The mind cannot be trained and expanded to its fullest capacity unless its companion [the body] is able to keep pace with its demands.

She looks forward to the day when "competent teachers will be provided to train the body, developing the weak points in the physical frame of each child and strengthening the whole by judicious exercises." Again, Bessie's thinking is very advanced. Even in our so-called modern education systems this common sense ideal is rarely attained, except perhaps in well-run private schools.

She observes that country children are not in such need of organized gymnastics as their town and city counterparts as they usually "lead an active outdoor life, running, jumping, often rowing, swimming and riding, sometimes engaging in work that calls many muscles into play." To be on the safe side, Bessie recommends two books to the mothers of children who lack sufficient exercise: *How to Get Strong* by Blakie and *Manual of Calisthenics* by Watson, the latter "although not as recent a work, has one point of advantage, music to which the different exercises can be executed." She goes so far in emphasizing the importance of physical exercise as to suggest that parents set up home gyms in order to support the childhood development of healthy bodies:

> With very inexpensive apparatus, light dumb bells, and a pair of parallel bars, and perhaps a pair of pulley-weights, feats can be accomplished which will

give keen pleasure to the children and be of lasting
benefit to their rapidly growing bodies.

In case readers do not acquire either of the books she
recommends, Bessie gives precise instructions on how to encourage
proper standing, breathing, sitting, and walking postures, and
on how to strengthen the muscles in general, including using a
skipping rope, which, however, "should not be overdone."

In keeping with her advanced ideas, Bessie includes
"stammering" in her chapter on physical culture. She advises the
practice of deliberate, correct breathing, speaking slowly, and
standing erect. Though she didn't have the precise knowledge about
airway muscle contraction that recent research has shown to be
cause of stammering and speech blockage, her recommendations
for dealing with the problem were intuitively correct. She notes
that "whispering and singing do not present the same difficulties
as speaking, the child rarely stammering then."

Twenty-one pages discussing "The Care of Girls" and eleven
for "The Care of Boys" conclude this ground breaking book.
Bessie warned against the temptation to deflect a child's curiosity
about where babies come from with joking or fanciful stories. She
advocated the importance of being honest when children want
honest answers to their questions.

> If fathers and mothers were frank with their boys and
> girls, telling them modestly and truthfully the things
> that they ought to know and warning them against
> the dangers into which they may fall from ignorance,
> much sin, anguish of mind and suffering of body
> would be saved. ...
>
> Nothing so rapidly and fatally destroys a child's
> confidence in his parents as to find that they have
> deceived him, and girls are fully as sensitive on this
> point as boys. The unthinking jest, or subterfuge, that
> stopped or satisfied the inquirer for the moment, is

looked back upon, when fuller knowledge comes, with a resentment that parents would find it hard to understand unless they can remember vividly the experiences of their own childhood.

Early in the chapter on "The Care of Girls" Bessie discusses the menstrual period and what is now call PMS (pre-menstrual syndrome). She is especially attentive to this concern in young girls, even before their periods begin. The mother is encouraged to show "infinite patience and tenderness" to the behaviour upsets that may occur. She cautions that "the child does not mean to be naughty and her feelings are as much a problem to her as they are to her mother."

Bessie observes that "…until a girl is ten years old her life may be much the same as her brothers"; after that, and especially after her periods begin, she should make a habit of resting quietly for a few hours "during these days" with "no violent exercise, tennis, riding on horse-back, rowing, or swimming." Even "long walks should not be taken, hard study prohibited [and] dancing injurious; although an occasional indulgence in this pastime might not do harm, it should not be an habitual amusement under these circumstances." No "plunge baths"; only sponge baths with warm water are allowed. No wonder the term "unwell" was applied to girls who were missing from some function they were expected to attend, as they were considered to be just that.

By 1894, "Sanitary towels can now be purchased to take the place of napkins. These are used once and then destroyed. They cost about sixty cents a dozen." That was expensive for a throw away item, and not available to women of small means, especially if she had a large family of girls. Bessie advises they "can be made more cheaply of cotton waste and cheese cloth."

Under the heading of "Hysteria," Bessie writes:

> Girls of a nervous temperament are apt to have a variety of symptoms at this time, which are included under this general term. There may be fits of excessive laughter, or crying, a general want of self-control,

shown in acts of wanton mischief, fits of unprovoked ill-temper and apparent attacks of fainting or convulsions. These can be distinguished from true faintness or fits by two symptoms. The girl never hurts herself, as by biting her tongue or striking her head in falling, and the eyes are sensitive, which is not the case when a person is really unconscious.

This attempted deceit is a part of her mental and physical condition, for which she is not fully responsible. Medical treatment is necessary, tonics, nourishing food, baths, gentle exercise, sleep, and all hygienic measures, to restore tone to the system. ... At the same time her moral nature should be appealed to and a desire to struggle against her weakness be awakened in her. ... She must be made to understand that self-control is a virtue, and that a girl who willfully gives way to foolish manifestations loses the respect of right-thinking persons.

Moving on to more general considerations, Bessie warns mothers to remember—

...that girls cannot go to school and meet the claims of society at the same time. Late hours are absolutely incompatible with keeping the young, growing body in good condition. A school girl should not be allowed to go to parties in the evening, except possibly occasionally on Friday night.

Again showing her advanced thinking, her final paragraph on the subject of "school work" slips in an amazing suggestion as though there were nothing unusual about it:

If a girl wishes to go to college she wants to take there unimpaired health, steady nerves, and the power of close application. This she cannot do unless her physical well-being has been carefully attended to during the formative period of earlier youth.

Helping a daughter become proficient at needle work is discussed in some detail and with an eye to independence, if necessary. A girl who "has a taste for millinery" should be given lessons in the art. "Any girl can earn her own living who can do well what everyone wants to have done." No doubt remembering her own mother's dependence on her bankrupt husband and eventually on her original family, Bessie adds two powerful sentences to this section:

> Every mother should choose one [useful art] for her daughter and see that she is perfected in it whatever it may be. If she never requires to use it to gain her daily bread, it will still be a desirable accomplishment and in the changes that life brings, it may be the sheet anchor that saves her from destruction.

A "moderate amount of housework" is desirable exercise for young girls as it "develops muscles, improves circulation, and so the complexion, and if it roughens the hands a little vaseline, or glycerine and rose water, with a pair of gloves worn at night, counteracts the ill effect." We forget what life was like before rubber gloves. Since "home-making is the primary business of a woman's life," every girl should learn to cook at the side of her mother as well as learning the other domestic arts. "She will find ample opportunity to practice them, if it is only to make a home for herself in one room." On the other hand, "Should her sphere be a wider one, she will have the satisfaction of filling it with ease and command efficient service. ...."

The common sense with which Bessie wrote in 1894 has not been diluted with the years. It will be forever applicable:

> Most people like to do what they can do well, and girls are no exception to the general rule. The mother

must be patient with failures and not give too scanty a measure of praise when it is deserved. The efforts to render service that is sometimes more hindrance than help must be accepted and encouraged. It is much easier to do things oneself than to teach others to do them, but training is the mother's mission and she must fulfill it faithfully in small things as well as great.

Saturday morning is a good time to devote to the special lessons in house-keeping. If some triumph of cookery can appear at the festival dinner on Sunday, the family approval will be a reward the young maker will remember all her life.

Bessie includes seven pages on "Preparing Girls for Boarding School." She is particularly insistent that students be able to communicate freely with their parents:

The mother should insist that the home letters are to be free from surveillance and the girl should be encouraged to write freely. While being free not to interfere between the pupil and the constituted authority, many misunderstandings may be smoothed out by a little advice from the calmer judgment of the elder, and many questions settled by helping the child to bring them to the touchstone of right or wrong.

The theory does not always accord with practice. According to my mother, all letters home from Edgehill School for Girls, which was later attended by the three nieces under Bessie's care at Meadowlands, were strictly monitored and censored if the Matron thought it necessary to protect the reputation of school and prevent parental interference. The situation was so intolerable for my mother that she was permitted to return home after just one term.

Bessie then details the wardrobe requirements for boarding school, including five dresses of different kinds for different occasions, with special attention given to garments and accessories needed for winter wear.

Bessie is careful to underline the need for the mother to remain "the chief authority in her household" and not allow her daughter to "usurp her privileges." In other words, no matter how clever, pretty, talented, well educated and headstrong a daughter might become, she should never be allowed to rule the roost. Deference belongs to the mother by right of her position and she must exact it from her children. They may have had greater advantages than she has had, but, while this may increase her pride in them, it must not alter the natural relation.

With a large helping of optimism, Bessie unfolds more of "a daughter's privileges," including "to be her mother's right hand, serving and sparing her in every way that love can devise. If this service is always exacted as a tribute of love it will never be felt a burden." The mother is the one who must receive and welcome "any friends her daughter may invite to her home and there must be no visitors who come and go unseen and unwelcome." The mother must "make it plain that she regards them as hers as well as her daughter's friends."

And then, comes this advice about the father/daughter relationship:

> It is a daughter's especial privilege to be the companion and caretaker of her father. The tie between them is very strong and she should strive in every way in her power to repay him for all he has done for her. She brings a brightness into his life, often clouded by business cares and worries, of which she has no conception. She should cultivate all the little ways of pleasing him that she has found to be successful. She should submit cheerfully even to restrictions for which she cannot understand the necessity because she does not know the reasons that lie behind them.

These suggestions for producing "Daddy's little girl" are uncomfortably to me, a clear rehearsal for being a submissive and unquestioning Victorian wife, which was the only career most daughters would or could aspire to at that time. Did Bessie play this role for her father during the years she remained at home before leaving for nurse's training, a professional career, and a life of independence? Perhaps; her father was in special need of care after his business and professional failure. But this advice, as a general rule for girls, seems odd coming from one who never conformed to the implications of its message. Perhaps, Bessie thought the advice in a book that addressed a wide audience should be conventional. Yet, we know that at the same time, she was writing articles that encouraged young women to seek careers in nursing as she had. The quest for independence was in tension with the old order of Victorian social roles.

The chapter on boys is much shorter than the one on girls. Bessie glides over puberty with this opening paragraph:

> The change from boyhood to youth is much slower in boys than the corresponding period in girls. The friends do not always remember that the awkwardness and bashfulness, the tendency to uncomfortable blushing, the irritability and moodiness that often accompany it, are nervous manifestations to be dealt with consideration. The father can do much to guide his boy at this time, and he should not neglect his duty toward him.

The advice to the father is a little scanty. However, the book is primarily directed at the mother who can, at least, point to the above advice and hope her husband is up to the challenge. "Good food, active outdoor games, a cheerful home atmosphere, and pleasant associates, help a boy through this transition period as he passes on to the responsibilities of manhood."

Having said that, Bessie ships the boys off to boarding school. While she admits that the preparation is "not as serious a matter as preparing girls for a similar goal," she none-the-less lists the recommended wardrobe and accoutrement items needed in some detail, concluding with the following parental advice "While extravagance should be discouraged, a boy's requests should be listened to with attention, carefully considered, and granted if there is no good reason against it."

The chapter on the care of boys is notable in that it devotes several pages to encouraging intellectual development as well as practical training. This contrasts with her suggestions for girls, which dwell chiefly on preventing exhaustion, illness and strain, encouraging helpfulness to mother and appreciation of father. Bessie is reflecting the prevailing attitudes. However, she does slip in her heartfelt insistence that all girls should acquire an accomplishment with income earning possibilities, in the unlikely event that she would have to support herself, and that college may be considered. Girls are also included in her directives for fostering a general love of books.

In the boy's chapter, Bessie recommends that mothers prepare themselves by acquiring a book by Mr. George E. Hardy of New York, entitled *Five Hundred Books for the Young*, to help guide their choice because it "gives much valuable information as to the best books for children. "No mother should permit her children to read books of which she knows nothing." Reading material has much influence on children's ideals and standards. "The heroes and heroines become the readers."

We can see from the following that Bessie was well read as a child and a true lover of books:

> Let the children learn to cultivate the dear book friends, who never grow old or change, and who, when they turn to them in after years, will still have the power to recall something of the sweetness of the childish days when they were first known and loved.

Under "home training" she offers a rather unorthodox suggestion for the early 1890s. "It does not hurt a boy to know how to make his own bed, darn his own stockings, or even cook his own dinner." "Collecting," as an educational activity is covered in the same section. "Collections are invaluable as a means of exciting a boy's interest." She includes stamps, stones, mosses, flowers, woods, observing birds, animals, butterflies and other "works of nature."

Bessie concludes this last chapter and *The Care of Children* with her usual neat, inspirational sentence: "If she [the mother] keeps her own standards high, her ideals will impress themselves upon her children and they will never be satisfied with lower ones."

*   *   *   *

Preparation For Motherhood, published in 1896, is the third jewel in the crown of this much read author. Like her first two books, this one aims at increasing the health and happiness of women and children. The publishers, Henry Altemus of Philadelphia, lost no opportunity to promote Elizabeth Robinson Scovil as a well informed and experienced nurse and popular author. The following personal information appeared on the title page under her name:

Late Superintendent of the Newport Hospital
Associate Editor of The Ladies' Home Journal
Author of *The Care of Children*

In case anyone missed that little plug for her previous book, the next page contains a full citation:

In Uniform Style. By the same Author.
The Care of Children.
New and Revised Edition.
With a practical and copious index. 360 pages.
Cloth. $1.00.

The publisher no doubt realized that diffidence at reading a book on so delicate a subject as pregnancy and childbirth could be somewhat lessened once the potential reader discovered the author was not only a nurse but an editor of a highly respected women's magazine and an expert on caring for children. The book is attractively designed, with a cover of cream linen, black capitals for the title, half way down, and smaller ones for the author's name; an eye catching scroll pattern on the spine and around the edge of the front cover gives it a distinguished appearance. The book is only 6½ by 4½ inches, with 316 pages, making it companionable and easy to hold.

The four-page Introduction explains the author's open discussion of pregnancy and related subjects. First, mothers are responsible for preparing their daughters for their probable role as future mothers. She then adds:

> It has been the fashion to educate girls in total ignorance of the subjects that in coming years many of them will most require to be fully informed upon. The structure of their own physical frames, the laws that govern the reproduction of the species, the proper care of children, before and after birth, demand and should have at least as much attention as the study of foreign languages, or the higher mathematics.

In case any excessively prudish readers are about to raise objections, Bessie very cleverly brings in the Almighty on her side and, with progressive daring for the time, embeds "the secrets of nature" in an appreciation of the Divine.

> There is nothing indelicate in the secrets of nature. We may look with pure and reverent eyes at her processes, as far as she permits their mysterious workings to be seen, and find only cause for awe and admiration. Unseen but ever present is the Lord and Giver of Life, in whom we live and move and have our being.

After a paragraph underlining the sacredness of life and the need for it to be "impressed upon the minds of some women" so that "it might lessen the tragedies of ruined health and burdened conscience that overshadow too many homes," the author counsels that too frequent childbearing becomes an "oppressive weight." Without actually using the word, Bessie emphasizes the criminal and moral aspects of abortion:

> The remedy does not lie in the desperate woman taking the law into her own hands and staining her soul with crime by crushing the germ of the new life just begun. This is fraught with terrible consequences to body and soul alike. After the birth of the child, the best and wisest physician within reach should be consulted and his advice implicitly followed in the future.

There is no more specific reference to birth control than this. Just how sophisticated a doctor's advice in the mid 1890s might be is a good question. Perhaps it stopped at separate rooms for husband and wife or visiting mother during the most likely week to become pregnant. The fact that she suggests seeking out "the best and wisest physician" indicates she realizes that not all doctors will be equally adept in giving good advice on this matter.

Bessie knows that "some of the great central facts of life" are not sufficiently known and understood by some mothers, so they are unable to "talk frankly yet modestly with their daughters" thus preventing "unhappiness, suffering and ill health" in later life:

> The little girl, as her curiosity awakens, comes to her mother with questions which should be truthfully answered, as far as it is possible to make the subject plain to her limited comprehension. Instead of this she is put off with some well-worn fiction which she soon discovers to be untrue. Her absolute trust in her mother is shaken, never to be wholly restored, and she seeks from others who have no right to give the information she should have had from the one whose duty it was to have imparted it.

This introduction is bursting with common sense for any time:

> ...Innocence is not ignorance, but reverent knowledge. It is the atmosphere which surrounds an object that gives it its coloring. The simple facts of physiology, properly taught, convey no hint of impropriety. Make this a principle in the elementary teaching, never tell a child anything that is not absolutely true.

Bessie's advice regarding the birds and the bees, begins almost literally:

> Draw illustrations at first from plant and animal life. Describe in simple language the wonderful structure of the pelvic organs. Tell how day by day the little frame grows until the child is perfected, and the tiny, helpless being comes into the world to be loved and cherished. Further details can be left until the inquirer is older, but there need never be silly mystery in the beginning.

In her continuing effort to educate her readers, Bessie decried the lack of "a good text book of physiology for mothers." There seems to have been nothing available for them other than school books which "do not deal with the pelvis further than to say that it contains some important organs, which is not sufficient information for women," and "the text books intended for students of medicine [are] too technical for the ordinary reader and presuppose a knowledge that she does not have." To fill the gap Bessie wrote:

> It was thought that a chapter devoted to this subject would not be out of place in this manual. It may be of use and interest to those who desire to know something of the anatomy of this region and yet have not time nor opportunity for more extended study.

What a revelation to young women, still in the Victorian era, contemplating parenthood or not, to be told that knowing about the anatomy of "this region" was not a disgrace but a desirable duty of womanhood.

Nurse Scovil then presses for a good state of general health as "the more vigorous, healthy and well-developed a woman is, the better chance she has of coming safely through the perils of child-bearing." Knowing that a delicate and sickly child is unlikely to develop into a robust bearer of children, the experienced nurse recommends "good food, pure air, cleanliness, exercise, proper clothing, sufficient sleep," as tending to "build up and develop the frame of the girl," preparing her "the better to fulfill the function of motherhood. …In so doing she will add greatly to her capability for usefulness and to her happiness in life, whether she ever becomes a mother or not." Bessie may have added that last phrase, thinking of her own childless but generally healthy state.

Preparation for Motherhood consists of twenty chapters: The Pelvic Organs; Menstruation; Indications of Pregnancy; The Progress of Pregnancy; Food; Baths; Exercise; Rest; Clothing; The Baby's Wardrobe; The Baby's Belongings; The Mother's Room; The Mother's Comfort; The Mental State; Ailments; Miscarriage; Premature Confinement; Labor; After-care of the Mother; After-care of the Child.

My Great Aunt Bessie certainly had an ability to write facts wrapped in poetic presentation, which prompts the reader to continue. Her first chapter entitled, "The Pelvic Organs," opens with an unexpected sentence: "The word pelvis is derived from a Greek term meaning a dish, or bowl." With that, I already know more than I did and want to continue reading.

Several paragraphs describing the appearance and function of the pelvis and nearby organs would not be very different in a modern book (though unlikely to be expressed with such literary flair), but caring for the uterus after delivery is a very different matter:

> It is very important that there should be rest in bed for nine, or ten days, and great care should be exercised

in walking, or standing, for some time, as the uterus does not return to its usual size for about six weeks. The motion of going up and down stairs is particularly injurious, and should be avoided as long as possible.

Up until the late 1920s this advice was still followed. By the 1950s, a week recovery with exercise beginning a few day after given birth was the norm. By the 1980s, rest in bed ended at two days in hospital. This routine was given Royal approval when, after an equally short hospital stay, Princess Diana held the heir to the British throne for the world's approval on the steps of St. Mary's Hospital in London. We can imagine that Bessie—always ready to accept progressive changes— would heartily approve.

The paragraphs titled "Conception" describes the process with correct terminology, but with the notable absence of any mention of how "the semen, or seed of the male, entering the uterus from the vagina…" manages to arrive there. The male member, it seems fair to say, should be worthy of some note but escapes any billing at all in this important life drama. It may be that Bessie did mention the role of the penis in her original manuscript and it was edited out by the publisher. Or, she may have omitted this detail because her aim was to be sufficiently inoffensive to Victorian sensibility so her knowledge would be circulated without censoring. She was already breaking ingrained taboos by writing about the subject for the general public in the first place.

In the section on "Growth" [fetal] the author describes "the impregnated egg," its journey, development, and nourishment in its "perfectly designed amniotic sac." She perceptively mentions that in carrying the baby the liquid in the sac not only "protects the child from a sudden jolt, or jar, to the mother," which is commonly recognized as its function, but "It also defends the uterus from contact with the hard surface of the child," which is, of course, equally desirable. In the first chapter, the birth process is covered with these deceptively brief words: "When the child has been expelled from the uterus…" However, later in the book, there are many references to the complications involved in "expelling" and how to avoid them, mostly by being in good physical condition.

The chapter on, "Exercise," is especially encouraging as a prevention against undue difficulties:

> It is all important to the expectant mother that every muscle should be in good order, able to perform its proper work with ease. If she were told that by spending fifteen minutes a day in some simple observance, she could greatly lessen the fatigue of her labor and minimize its pain would she not gladly do so? Judicious exercise will surely do this. It must be steadily persisted in, as it is the daily repetition of the same act that strengthens and develops any part of the body.

As in most modern get-fit and keep-fit manuals, walking is suggested first as the most accessible and simplest forms of exercise and "within the reach of all." However, according to Bessie, there are right ways and wrong ways to walk for strengthening exercise. "It may be so done as to render it perfectly useless for practical purposes and it may be so used as to make it an efficient aid in the development that is needed." She describes the former as "an aimless saunter" and the latter as "a brisk constitutional, taken with an object in view." Even that is not enough. She describes the "correct position" which involves the usual shoulders back and arms swinging easily at the sides, but also "the lower part of the body thrown a little forward and the weight allowed to fall on the ball of the foot as it touches the ground." Considering the fashion of the time — the popular bustles of the 1880s only recently discarded (and perhaps not entirely) — there would be a need to think about changing the position of "the lower part of the body" to improve carriage and therefore muscle fitness.

By 1894 bicycles had become popular for both men and women with clothing fashions adapting to the needs of this energetic pursuit. Since it was impossible to ride a bicycle in a trailing skirt, divided skirts were introduced as were baggy knickerbockers called "bloomers." They caused almost as much excitement as the original bloomer campaign of the 1850s. They were ridiculed in the press and denounced from the pulpit (domains of male opinion), but it was all to no avail. Strong spirited young women with independent minds enthusiastically continued to wear them. Indeed, the new enthusiasm for outdoor sports of all kinds made it necessary to wear more rational garments in general and there was a new vogue for the tailored suit, consisting of jacket, skirt and "shirtwaister."

With the publication of *Preparation for Motherhood* in 1896, nurse Scovil must have realized that some of her readers would likely have indulged in more vigorous exercise than "a brisk constitutional," so she sensibly deals with the possibility:

> A celebrated physician has said, "One might hesitate to prescribe gymnasium exercise for the pregnant; yet I recall one patient habituated from early childhood to gymnastic exercise, who continued her training during nearly the whole of her gestation, omitting only the heavier work, and she had a most rapid and easy labor and an uneventful convalescence."

Bessie's only mention of bicycle riding is that it should be "discontinued at this time" along with other "violent exercise, like riding on horseback, playing tennis, dancing…" However, she does recommend going up and down stairs to build muscles:

> The dress must be perfectly loose and easy, with no constraining bands, or pressure anywhere, particularly about the waist. The progress should not be too rapid, nor the journey [up and down stairs] repeated too often at first.

She states that a healthy man does not complain about climbing stairs, so why should a woman. But she must be properly dressed; if she is, there is no reason why

...[she] should not be able to mount stairs with as much ease as he can. I can testify from personal experience that the absence of corsets and correct habits of breathing deprive the ascent of all its terrors. In going up and down stairs keep the mouth closed to ensure breathing through the nose, hold the shoulders back to expand the chest and do not carry a heavy weight in the hands.

The author is doing her best to dispel the myth that "...going up and down stairs, is...peculiarly injurious to women" and that it's practice "may be made to serve the same purpose [as walking] developing these muscles [at the sides of the waist." I can see Great Aunt Bessie, divesting herself of corsets, breathing through her nose and triumphantly and repeatedly ascending and descending stairs, either as an experiment for the purposes of this book or in order to become as fit as possible and maintain her strength.

There would have been ample requirement when she was Superintendent of the Newport Hospital to climb stairs for other than therapeutic reasons, but I cannot imagine she would have lowered her standards sufficiently to remove her corsets, unless making a point to her student nurses that health came before fashion, a strange concept at the time for most of them, no doubt.

Along with walking, going up and down stairs and breathing properly, Bessie advocates a drive in a carriage for those unable to walk because of fatigue, not only for the fresh air but for a "change of scene." However, "nothing is more injurious than long sitting in one position bending over a writing table or a sewing machine." She does not leave the problem without a solution, presumably for pregnant seamstresses or those with already large families who must spend long periods sewing clothes. The alternative to using a foot-treadle machine, "which should be interdicted," is to remove the drive band from the treadle, "when the machine can be turned by hand, thus making sewing upon it possible without injury to the worker." This would have increased the time spent sewing many fold.

"Prolonged standing is also injurious." Again, the ever-practical Bessie offers an alternative. "Women who have to do their own ironing will find great relief in using a high chair and sitting while they are thus occupied. The feet must be comfortably supported on a foot stool." Anyone who has ironed for an hour or two knows the wisdom of this suggestion. (The need for any serious ironing in the 21st century has, of course, almost evaporated.) Standing for "domestic operations" such as washing dishes or bread kneading may be eliminated "by having a chair of the proper height. By the exercise of a little ingenuity much unnecessary weariness can be avoided."

Gardening is encouraged, though nothing more energetic than weeding. "Bending over as in weeding strengthens the muscles of the small of the back, and being in the open air is always beneficial." Bessie's advice extends to many possible situations. She is anxious, for example, that the need for long bed rest does not cause loss of "vigor." She recommended massage by a professional masseuse and if that is not possible "amateur rubbing, and if the doctor permits them, a regular course of exercise in bed." A full description of suitable exercise follows, along with a warning that the bed ridden woman "should spare no pains to cultivate them" in order to firm her muscles as they "will be of great advantage to her in her hour of need." Bessie, characteristically, is firm but gentle in her promotion of short term pain for long term gain:

> There is one precaution that must not be neglected. No violent exercise, nor indeed bodily exercise of any kind, should be taken at the time that would not have been in the menstrual periods under ordinary conditions. This rule must be implicitly observed. Its neglect may cause the loss of the child's life and serious injury to the mother.

Taking into consideration the restricted life for a woman in the 1890s and medical knowledge of the time, this chapter on exercise is full of good sense and practical application, with the exception of the "precaution" strongly recommended in the previous paragraph. The fact that attitudes toward the physical potential of the female body have changed so much in the last one hundred years makes Bessie's progressive views an interesting comparison. However, well exercised muscles are no less a benefit in the birth of a baby today than they ever were, in spite of so many advances in medical science.

Preparation for Motherhood also takes up the possibility of "premature confinement"—premature birth in modern terms. Bessie wants expectant mothers to be fully informed and ready to act appropriately should they have to deal with this situation. In her chapter titled "Indications of Pregnancy," she takes up the question of viable duration premature births "In this country [USA] the law recognizes as legitimate children born after a possible pregnancy of two hundred and seventeen days." She goes on to suggest ways of caring for pre-mature children including "roll in lambs' wool instead of being dressed" and uses this opportunity to highlight the human qualities of a foetus.

> As soon as the twenty-first day after conception, the ears, eyes and mouth have begun to develop, and at the end of the first month the tiny beginnings of the limbs are plainly evident. It is no formless mass that is crushed out of existence if the operations of nature are interfered with, thus early in her work.

Here is one of many references in this book and scattered throughout her writings against abortion. As a nurse she would have seen many examples of a woman taking an unwanted pregnancy into her own hands or having a less than skilled abortionist attempt the operation, with seriously negative results for the women and, of course, obliteration for the foetus. Beyond that, Bessie has a traditional religious belief in the morality of respecting all life. I have not seen any reference in her publications to the moral dilemma presented by a pregnancy or birth which calls for a decision about which life to preserve, if both are not possible, especially when the woman already has ten children needing her care. But this and much of her other writings are aimed at the lay person and not at the professional medical/nursing practitioner on whose shoulders the decision usually falls, with input from the family, if there is an opportunity.

At the end of this chapter is a sub-heading, "Sex" where readers may have hoped for some guidance on when to give up having it or when to resume, after the birth. Their expectations would have been dashed. The paragraph deals instead with forecasting the sex of the unborn child. After mentioning several theories, Bessie writes: "…none has been found to be infallible. It is such an interesting and important matter, one would think that some bold explorer would by this time have succeeded in filching the secret from nature." One possibility is worth looking at, even though it was already debunked in the 1890s. It was once thought that the eggs from one ovary produced females, and those from the other, males. This was disproved when women from whom one ovary had been removed by an operation, have afterwards borne children of each sex. She concludes the chapter with a couple of witty double entendre. "The whole subject is wrapped in mystery. It remains for some earnest student of the future to penetrate the darkness and discover the truth."

Chapter V, titled "Food," takes up thirty pages and is in keeping with the times and Aunt Bessie's general attitude to the subject. Relatively bland, carefully cooked food is best and you should make an effort to eat at least a little of everything, even if it is new to you or you do not care for it. However, in treating the problem of nausea, she also caters to the women who cannot keep anything down, suggesting that albuminized water [egg white shaken with very cold water] which, she advises: "Must be the chief reliance in extreme nausea when the stomach persistently rejects food."

Longing for certain foods when pregnant is a reality which most pregnant women experience. Bessie writes: "It was once thought that longings for a special article of food, if not gratified immediately, would surely be attended with evil consequences to the child." She dismisses this and correctly assures her readers that these cravings "…are only indications that the system is clamouring for some material that the coveted food is rich in." Her advice is to obtain the food if it is easily available, or something similar. If that is not possible, the mind should be "resolutely turned away from it [and] no harm will follow." When the longings are for "slate pencils, chalk, vinegar or pickles… the doctor should be consulted, as some form or iron, or dilute acid is probably required."

Aunt Bessie could never be described as a gourmet cook. This is evident from my mother's comments, her recipes that have survived in two Fredericton Cathedral cookbooks, and reinforced by the final paragraph in her chapter on food. "Eating is a means, not an end, and never more so than during this time of waiting, which is also a time of preparation and development." Though this is her approach in general, she presses the point here because just previously she mentions "unselfish women are too apt to think that their special likes and dislikes are matters of very little importance and put them aside as too trivial to be attended to." She urges them to think again and goes on to admonish these seemingly admirable women, reminding them "there is another life depending on them." so they should make an effort to eat for "it" even though they might not for themselves.

You might think the subject of "baths" could be covered in a line or two, but in the days when few homes had bathrooms or hot and cold running water, thirteen pages are probably not excessive. Filled with useful advice, the chapter on this subject covers both the routine for the expectant mother and the newborn's first bath in minute detail. Bessie's introduction is geared to emphasize the historical importance of body care, giving it the weight and importance of the centuries:

> The early Greeks, who had strong and beautiful bodies, were particularly careful and punctilious in their care of them. They were bathed, rubbed, and oiled, in fact groomed with a care that is now sometimes exercised with valuable horses, but very seldom with the human form divine.

She elaborates on the procedure, precautions and benefits of every type of bath imaginable: friction, plunge (both hot and cold), sponge (hot and cold), sitz, foot (hot and cold), foot bath in bed, sponge bath in bed (blanket bath), local, and baby, including special attention to the eyes of newborns. When imagining any of these, I think of a tin tub in front of the stove or open fire with endless jugs of hot water carried by servants (or mother, sisters, aunts) from the kitchen range to the bedroom, or in the kitchen itself, from where all men and boys would be banished. A bath was an event that had to be carefully orchestrated.

Though Bessie is no modern feminist, she is dedicated to the possibility of women developing their potential and is careful not to use words which might limit their estimation of themselves. Her opening paragraph of the chapter titled, "Clothing," is a perfect example:

> Dress is generally an important subject in the estimation of women. Our garments are so much more complex than those of the sterner sex that naturally they require more consideration than men accord to theirs.

No trite cliché here. After spending a fair amount of ink encouraging women to build up their strength in quite vigorous activities, she is not about to undo her good words and use the term "stronger sex." "Sterner sex" serves well to indicate a difference without implying inferiority. The reason for dress being considered "an important subject" for women is left to the reader to decide as Bessie continues with her introduction:

> Whether this is at the root of the vanity with which we are credited, or not, we all have the feminine desire to please and wish to look our best under all circumstances. Dress must be fitting and appropriate, or this natural and laudable wish cannot be fulfilled.

Bessie lays down the law with three principles: no pressure on the waist or breasts in particular; hang clothes from shoulders and not the waist; no garters around the legs. "These are not mere arbitrary rules; there is a reason for every prohibition. The thoughtful woman will recognize their necessity."

Bessie pushes home the absolute need to abandon constricting corsets during pregnancy, if the woman has been "in bondage" to them previously. After some discussion about the "vital organs which are arranged in the abdomen with wonderful nicety," she quotes an illustration to show the "great mischief" brought about by corsets, even to the woman who is not expecting. "One variety of malformation of the liver is known as the 'corset liver' because it is deeply indented by the pressure which is maintained by even moderate tight lacing."

Though generally optimistic, Bessie despairs of offering anything that will help an expectant woman recover from years of tight corseting and to heavy skirts pulling downward from the waist:

> Pressure continued for many years may have distorted the bones of the pelvis, altering its shape and diminishing its capacity. The weight of heavy skirts dragging on the lower part of the flexible spine may have bent it inwards. For this there is no help now.

She again emphasizes that "preparation for motherhood should begin in early girlhood," guided by mothers who should instill in their daughters the need to look after their bodies. Bessie does provide a chink in the prophesy of despair over the possibility of a corset spine, by trusting that nature will do the best she can, once restraining garments are discarded. (Fashion still ruins women's bodies, most often now days by way of their feet.)

Bessie recommends the most suitable type of clothing required by a pregnant woman in the 1890's. Although she had never been pregnant, she is able to put herself inside the needs of an expecting woman to a surprising extent. Her nursing knowledge would have provided her with requirements in dress for physical health, though

I suspect sharp eyes and female relatives probably provided much information.

Bessie is keen that a woman's pregnant condition be concealed for as long as possible, reflecting the custom of the time and long afterward. Maternity dresses are described in detail:

> It is impossible under the circumstances to preserve the graceful lines of the figure. Any attempt to do so is labour thrown away. Tight fitting garments only bring into prominence what it is desired to hide.

She recommends what designers of maternity clothes have been promoting for decades: "loose, softly flowing draperies… which give the impression of ease and fitness." She again emphasizes their tendency to be "effectual in concealing the form."

"A maternity dress should be made with long jacket fronts and a full vest falling well below the waist line. This vest can fasten down the middle, the lining being concealed by the fullness." Hiding pieces of elastic, various petticoats of suitable warmth for summer and winter, linings, lacing, hooks and eyes, hems for lengthening the front, choice of colour (dark, as it is "slimming") and many other fine points for the well turned-out prospective mother are considered. Several pages ensure that she will know exactly what indoor and outdoor garments are appropriate and comfortable, including shoes, stockings (and supporters), bed socks, underwear, wrappers, cloaks, night dresses and bed jackets (flannel). She completes her chapter on clothing with a warning:

> Delicate persons of a nervous temperament should husband the heat of the body, preventing its escape by sufficient clothing. Its production is a tax on the nervous energy which should be made as light as possible.

The chapters, "The Baby's Wardrobe" and "The Baby's Belongings" cover forty-five pages. They include precise directions for homemade versions of a new baby's needs. By 1896, when this book was published, Elizabeth Scovil had been an associate editor of *The Ladies' Home Journal* for six years, answering a multitude of questions from unsure and nervous mothers in her columns.

She must have amassed many notes and sources to answer all imaginable inquiries. Anticipating that women from a variety of economic backgrounds would read her book, Bessie quotes the cost of store bought articles comparing them with the lesser amount of homemade necessities and even includes that of "very elaborate" designs.

Thinking of the other end of the economic scale she is careful to encourage re-cycling, which most people did as a matter of course. Wastefulness carried a weight of immorality and poor management, not to be tolerated:

> Tiny shoes, to be used instead of socks, may be fashioned of stockinet. The best part of old, fine underwear answers very well for the purpose — flannel, jersey flannel, or eiderdown flannel... The Butterwick pattern number 4257 shows how to cut them in two ways."

But what if the reader is a hopeless seamstress; should she employ someone to make garments for her baby? Bessie knows the mother will not be satisfied with badly made "dainty little garments." If she is competent at sewing and "knows how to purchase the materials judiciously, it is cheaper to make than to buy them. When a seamstress has to be employed the ready-made clothing is less expensive."

The discussion of baby's clothing includes recommendations for the layette, which "is based upon the supposition that the clothes can be returned from the laundry punctually once a week." Again, Bessie is looking at the possible need for frugality. The items in the layette "should not be much curtailed, unless the facilities for washing and ironing are exceptionally good, or the need of economy is very urgent." A fully equipped layette includes:

...three bands, four shirts, six petticoat, forty-eight napkins [diapers], six night slips, eight dresses, two wrappers, twelve pairs of socks, three blankets, two cloaks, two hoods, and eighteen bibs.

The first necessity on the list—"three bands"—requires some explanation. "Three strips of soft flannel about five inches wide, by twenty-four long, torn off and not finished in any way are all that is needed." They are wrapped around the baby's tummy, to keep the navel flat, and fastened with small safety pins. Excessively tight bands worn too long are an anathema to the nurse/author. She writes with authority on the subject:

When linen shirts were worn, bands were an important part of the wardrobe, affording warmth and protection to the abdomen. They were usually pinned too tight and did harm in that way. It is no more necessary to bandage a young baby than a young colt. It is true there are weak points in the abdominal walls, but the unyielding bandage, as it is usually applied, forces the intestines down against these when the child cries and actually increases the danger of rupture, which it was meant to guard against.

Now that the use of the soft, warm Jersey shirt is almost universal, the band is only required for a few days to keep the dressing in place and care should be taken not to put it on too tightly.

Much of the information on baby's basket and its contents as well as on baby's bath and bed in *Preparation for Motherhood* is the same as noted earlier in this chapter in the section on the book, *The Baby's Requirements*, with, however, a notable addition—the hammock.

When space is a consideration, as it is to the dwellers in flats, a hammock makes a convenient bed for the baby. A small one occupies little space when slung on two stout hooks and is easily put out of the way when it is not occupied. A long pillow and blanket is all the bedding required. …If there is a fear that the baby will fall out, it can be fastened in with two broad bands tied around the hammock.

When my eyes fell on this suggestion, my mind went back several decades to a book titled *Christ Stopped At Eboli* by Carlo Levi about life in an impoverished hill town in southern Italy, which I visited in 1960 during travels in that stark and wildly beautiful part of the country, long after I had read the book. A description I have remembered for more than half a century is of the sleeping arrangements of humans and animals. The father and mother and children, except the most recent, all slept in the matrimonial bed; the hens clucked underneath, providing warmth for the family and security against theft. This year's baby slept in a hammock over the bed, from which the nursing mother need never stir in order to quiet her fretful infant, if she found a gentle push of the hammock was not enough.

Bessie, ever practical, was not about to overlook such an economical and space saving solution in the search for a bed to suit impecunious or crowded circumstances, especially one proven to be satisfactory in many cultures, for centuries.

The chapter on "The Mother's Room" warns of dangers lurking literally in every corner. With neither vacuum cleaners nor modern bathrooms, anti-septic conditions were almost impossible to achieve, but easier than in the days before carbolic acid, before Lister and Pasteur. After a cheery introduction on choosing "a large airy room…with a sunny aspect in winter and a cool, shady one in summer…when there is an opportunity," Bessie immediately sets out to inform the mother of a new danger at the time — sewer gas. "If there is plumbing in the house [mother's room] should not open into the bath room nor should there be a set basin in the room." If there is no alternative room, the connecting door should be closed "and the cracks carefully stuffed with paper."

The overflow holes in the basin "should be stopped with moist plaster of Paris and the basin kept filled with water, to form a water seal. The water must be changed every day by the nurse."

Though sewer gas may be a major danger in Bessie's mind, carpets, old mattresses and pillows are close behind as sources of contamination. The cleaning is to beat vigorously, leave in the sun, and re-cover when practical. A polished wood floor with a few shakeable mats is much preferred to a fastened carpet. Bessie is entirely modern in her anti-carpet stance, now known to reduce dust mites and related allergy causing conditions.

She was much concerned with the transference of infection from old carpets or mats to the mother in a vulnerable state or from mother to baby via unwashable floor coverings and a less than careful nurse. Once serious infection took hold there was not much that could be done other than trust a strong constitution and the power of prayer. At the time nurse Scovil was urging strict hygiene in all matters relating to baby's and mother's care, women and newborns were still dying from preventable infections, as I noted earlier about my paternal grandmother and four of her friends who all died within a few weeks of one another.

In her effort to put the prospective mother at ease, Bessie lists a dozen ailments in a chapter on illness that may be encountered during pregnancy starting, of course, with "morning sickness" and including piles, sleeplessness, and faintness. She offers simple remedies available to most readers. She is careful that her book not be seen as a substitute for medical assistance; if an ailment persists and worries the woman, she should consult a doctor.

> A few cheery words from the doctor may dispel a phantom which has haunted her for weeks to the great detriment of nerves and spirits, and which might as well have been laid to rest earlier. If there is a real evil to be faced, the sooner it is met and dealt with the better...ease of mind should be as jealously guarded as strength of body."

A short chapter on "Miscarriage" is unusual for its advanced content:

> There are various causes which contribute to a miscarriage. It is not to be overlooked that disease in the father, or other circumstances connected with him, may affect it. Alcoholism, exhausting chronic disease, lead poisoning, working in sulphur and extreme old age, or youth, are some of these.

The working environment of the father has, indeed, been proven to produce negative effects on the foetus. This is at least the second time Bessie mentions alcoholism in the father being reflected in the child. This is given some consideration by modern experts who cite the possibility of chemical imbalance contributing to the tendency, which could be genetic. "Women who work in tobacco are said to be peculiarly liable to miscarry and excessive indulgence in it by the father may have the same effect."

Several pipes during a day and a cigar or two after dinner were common for a middle class man in the 1890s. A few miscarriages were common for many women, so who knows the result of "excessive indulgence" or the effect of second-hand smoke which is now known to affect the health of non-smokers. It is easier, of course, to identify causes of miscarriage directly related to the woman:

> If the mother takes too violent exercise, or very hot baths, wears tight corsets, has a fall, or a severe blow on the abdomen, suffers from an infectious disease, as scarlet fever, or some forms of chronic disease, is subjected to extreme emotion, or any prolonged strain, it is very apt to bring it [miscarriage] on.

The first two, at least, were well known methods of encouraging the abortion of an unwanted pregnancy, whispered as general knowledge among all but the most sheltered young women.

After alerting her readers to the possibilities of a miscarriage, Bessie adds a chapter on the disquieting subject of "Premature Confinement" (birth). She goes into such detail for precise care that the reader cannot help but be hopeful of a successful outcome. The baby should not be bathed, but rubbed with warm oil daily, and wrapped only in lamb's wool. Exact instructions for converting two tin tubs into a "hot cradle" as described by a Dr. Worcester in his book on maternity nursing, would have been easy to arrange, but would require constant supervision. "The inner tub is lined with cotton wool or thick folds of flannel, and the baby, well wrapped and covered, placed in it." Warm water is placed in the outer tub and kept at a constant temperature. "An incubator cannot always be procured when it is needed. One for chickens might be modified so that it could be used." When the infant is too feeble to breast feed or suck from a bottle, gavage, or forced feeding, "is said to have saved many lives." The method is a softer, gentler one than is used in institutions, with "not more than a tablespoonful...given at once."

The chapter, "Labour," is composed in a way that would be helpful to any perspective mother in any era—what to expect and how to cope even if a nurse or doctor has not arrived or no one at all is present. Whenever Bessie writes something that is presumed to be commonly held knowledge, but for which she quotes no authority and is unwilling to be one, she begins by writing, "It is said." This allows the reader to be informed and yet decide for herself whether to accept it or not. For example, Bessie writes. "It is said that labor usually commences between nine and twelve o'clock at night and the birth takes place between nine the next evening and the same hour the following morning." This seems excessively long, but if the time is counted from the very early signs of labour, and the baby is the first one, perhaps not.

In the chapter, "After Care of the Mother," we find circumstances and advice that remind us of the times, over a century past, in which Bessie lived:

> The state of the nipples should be reported to the doctor. When the skin is actually cracked and painful

an application of cocaine is usually ordered. This has to be washed off with special care before the baby nurses.

Bessie was writing well before the introduction of "bobbed" (short cut) hair. She recounts the extreme difficulty and consumption of time in untangling long hair, which has not been parted down the middle at the back and arranged in two braids at the sides of the woman's head, early on in her labour.

> Hair forty inches long that had been untouched by comb or brush for three weeks, has been disentangled, but it is a task that equals one of the labours of Hercules.

Bessie then devotes three paragraphs in such detail on just how to go about this Herculean task that I suspect she worked out the method herself, when confronted with having to solve the problem. Of course, cutting the hair would have been unthinkable.

One more surprise — the eyes:

> For a few days, the mother's eyes should be shielded from a bright light. The room can be partially darkened during the day and the gas, or lamp, shaded at night. Even if she feels well she should not read until after the third day. Rest of the mind and body is all important.

Bessie is probably right about giving the whole system a rest. She has, as I have mentioned elsewhere several times, good reason from personal experience to pay special attention to the needs of eyes.

Producing a baby in the 1890s up until the 1930s meant being an invalid for about a month. No matter how well the mother feels, "it is only a reasonable precaution to stay quietly in bed until the ninth, or tenth day. She may then move quietly to the easy chair…but still sit with her feet up." However, "If she wishes to go downstairs after the third week the progress should be made slowly and carefully. In summer a drive in an easy carriage will do no harm." I am sure many young mothers today would be astounded to read that a century ago an expert on mothers and babies would write: "The fifth week is quite time enough for her to leave her room to begin to take up her ordinary duties again."

In addition, the fear of infection was such that Bessie recommends the letters to a new mother should be opened by "some near relative" as "many of the eruptive diseases, as scarlet fever, can be conveyed by letters."

This seasoned nurse is always careful to give doctors their proper place in the hierarchy of caregivers. Not only is the doctor supreme but the new mother should have complete confidence in him and "should not permit any feeling of false modesty to induce her to conceal from her physician any unusual sensation, or circumstance, during this period of convalescence." Though the nurse is there night and day (presumably for four or five weeks) all may not go smoothly in their relationship.

> The mother should make a point of seeing the doctor alone for a few minutes during each visit, even if she has to request the nurse to leave the room that she may do so. Then should anything occur to make his private counsel necessary she will feel no embarrassment and find no difficulty in securing it.

Throughout her writing, Bessie never suggests that the nurse, no matter how experienced or knowledgeable about a case, should queen it over the doctor. But she also knows that a good doctor relies heavily on a competent nurse to steer him in the direction of problems needing his attention, and thus possesses a subtle power.

In her final chapter, "After Care of the Child," Bessie includes every imaginable situation "from colic to the lack of and great need for mother love."

"A child that is looked upon as a burden and an encumbrance is defrauded of its just due. The mother who does not give to her baby the love and devotion that ought to be inseparable from her relation to it, loses the sweetest reward of motherhood."

What better ending to a book on effective mothering.

* * * *

The same year *Preparation for Motherhood* was published (1896), Elizabeth Robinson Scovil added three more publications in the *Eternal Life Series* published by Henry Altemus of Philadelphia. Her devotional books were titled *Morning Strength, Hymns of Praise and Gladness,* and *Evening Comfort.* They were priced at twenty-five cents and joined a list of thirty-two other books, mostly by clergymen. The publisher advertised the series as "Selections from the writings of well-known religious authors, beautifully printed and daintily bound in leatherette with original designs in silver and ink." The authors included Thomas Arnold (Headmaster of Rugby boys school in England), the Honourable William Gladstone (Prime Minister of Great Britain — several times), and Professor Henry Drummond (an old friend and allegedly one time romantic interest of Lady Aberdeen, wife of the Governor General of Canada and founder, along with Bessie, of the Victorian Order of Nurses).

Of the three titles in this series I have a copy of only *Morning Strength,* an attractive 7 by 5 inch volume in pale green leatherette with silver lettering and decoration of tiny stylized silver butterflies on the front cover, as promised by the publisher. The format is simple and effective. Thirty-one pages, one for each day of the month, all begin with a short quotation from the Bible followed by a poem or part of a poem by a well known author, Bessie's interpretation of the poem followed by a two or three word "Keynote of the day."

Morning Strength, and the other books in the series, would have been read mostly by women, though not produced exclusively for them. By the late 19th Century women were beginning to assert themselves as individuals rather than being solely male possessions. ERS is a perfect example, entering the careers of a trained nurse and of journalist and author, eschewing marriage and dependence on a man.

Of special interest to me in the copy I have is the surprisingly formal inscription on the flyleaf in Aunt Bessie's distinctively slanted Victorian hand; "S. John Scovil, from his sister, E.R.S., May 2nd 1898."This was a present to her eldest surviving brother, "Jack" on his forty-second birthday, who was living in New York with his wife, Adeline, two sons and a daughter.

Many of the thirty-one selections are from the works of prolific and well-known Victorian and earlier writers and public figures whose names are still familiar, such as Lord Alfred Tennyson. Others have not travelled the decades well and their names are generally not remembered, though their works may be, as, for example, Isaac Watts and his many favourite hymns including "Jesus Shall Reign Where'er the Sun." Bessie also chose poems by John Greenleaf Whittier (1807-92), an American Quaker, prolific poet and journalist, who became passionately involved in the slavery abolition movement.

Here is an example of the format and content:

Twenty-Seventh Day
For even Christ pleased not Himself. – Romans xv.3

We lose what on ourselves we spend!
We have as treasure without end
Whatever, Lord, to Thee we lend,
Who givest all.

Christopher Wordsworth.

It is not only through material gifts that we may know the blessings of giving. It is often a harder sacrifice to give time, or service, or even to yield our own will, or give up our own pleasure for another's comfort or good. Be sure these offerings are not passed by unnoticed and uncared for. The generous soul that gives freely of such things as it has, that seeks first not to please itself, but to please others, is truly a follower of Christ.

Keynote for the day: Self forgetfulness.

This theme of putting others before self is a favourite of Bessie's. It recurs in her magazine columns, her speeches to audiences of nurses, her other books and on many pages of *Morning Strength*.

The second page I have chosen has a quotation from probably the best remembered of Bessie's selection of authors, with the exception of Tennyson. Oliver Wendell Holmes's inclusion is not a surprise as he was immensely popular, not only for his witty after dinner conversation, but for his essays and poems. He was also a practicing medical doctor, which might also have influenced her decision, as well as his death two years before the publication date.

Nineteenth Day
I can do all things through Christ, who strengtheneth me. Philippians iv 13.

O Love divine, that stooped to share
Our sharpest pang, our bitterest tear!
On Thee we cast each earth-born care;
We smile at pain while Thou art near.
On Thee we rest our burdening love,
O Love divine, forever dear!
Content to suffer, while we know,
Living and dying, Thou art near.

– Oliver Wendell Holmes.

We shall never be content with our lot in life until we accept it as God's appointment for us. Then we know that He who gave the duties will give strength to perform them. His mighty power is behind our feeble efforts, and we need not fear.

Keynote for the day: Dependence on God

The good Dr. Holmes had reason to call on the Almighty to help those in pain as he had relatively few tricks up his sleeve for relieving it compared with his modern colleagues. There is no doubt that accepting "one's lot" as having some purpose gives discomfort meaning and makes it more bearable, especially when there is no possibility of improvement. The religious philosophy of the Victorian era of acceptance may also have allowed the discovery of desirable qualities otherwise hidden.

It would be interesting to know which Bessie chose first, the biblical quotation or the poem, though I imagine the latter. Her knowledge of the Bible must have been even greater than was normal for Victorians brought up in a heavily Anglican atmosphere. Her great-grandfather, grandfather and uncle were all professional churchmen and we know she spent considerable time at their Rectory on the Kingston Peninsula when a young woman. I suspect she memorized many texts from the Bible and would have had little difficulty pulling an appropriate quotation out of her mental filing cabinet to suit her selections of poetry.

* * * *

There is no record of Bessie publishing any new books between 1896 and 1920, though reprints were probably made of her books that continued to sell. Perhaps she found that being an Associate Editor of *The Ladies Home Journal,* including writing a monthly column and occasional feature pages, along with her nursing, was enough. In addition, she would shortly take on a twenty-year associate editorship of *The American Journal of Nursing* and in seven years would be living at Meadowlands on a permanent basis, running the household for her widower brother and his five young children until they were adults.

Some time prior to 1920 she turned her attention to producing books of Bible stories suitable for young children just beginning to read. Perhaps the experience of "mothering" her brother's children made her aware of the lack of this kind of book. Possibly her old friends at Henry Altmus in Philadelphia asked whether she would fill this gap. Her previous books had been highly successful for this publisher and Elizabeth Robinson Scovil had name recognition as an author.

Bessie's second period of book writing began with *Wee Folks Stories from the Old Testament in Words of One Syllable*, published in 1920. It is an innovative collection of short stories in simple words enhanced by fifteen colour illustrations. The tales are a mixture of Bessie's setting the scene, paraphrasing from the Bible, and direct quotation. If a word used contained more than one syllable — there are surprisingly few — it was broken up with hyphens and an accent on the appropriate syllable. The first paragraph of the second story, "Man Sins," is an example of the author's ingenuity:

> In the place where God had put Ad'-am and Eve there was one tree whose fruit God told them not to touch, for if they ate it they would die. Eve did not know what death meant, no one had died yet, so she did not fear it as much as she would have done if she had seen death. The fruit was ripe and full of juice, and she longed to taste it.

Enough parents and grandparents must have snapped up the book to convince Altemus to ask Bessie to create an obvious sequel for publication in 1921, *Wee Folks Stories From the New Testament in Words of One Syllable*. It was in the same format as the previous year's success, 5 ½ by 4 inches, in mauve with a red spine, and sixteen colour illustrations, including one on the cover. The opening paragraph of the first story, "Christ is Born," follows, which is a little more complicated than those in the first of what eventually became a series of three.

> We are all glad when Christ'-mas comes. It is the birth-day of our Lord Je'-sus Christ. We give gifts to those we love, for on that day God gave us His son to live in this world and teach all men how to live while they are here and how to die. His moth-er Ma'-ry's home was in a small place called Naz'-a-reth. She went with Jo'seph, her hus-band, to pay a tax, to Beth'-le-hem, which was once Da'vid's town.

Wee Folks Bible ABC Book, the third in the series, was also published in 1921. Elizabeth Robinson Scovil, the book author, was on a roll with three new, highly successful books for children. *Wee Folks Bible ABC Book* was republished in 1996 by Applewood Books with the same colourful illustrations.

Starting in 1924, Henry Altemus published another series of Bessie's books on religious themes. They were small, embossed hardcover volumes with a raised design in the front, reminiscent of a woodcarving, and with the titles printed in gold. The first book in the series was *Prayers for Girls.* The copy I have has an inscription on the fly leaf in Aunt Bessie's slanted and flourished hand: "Helen DuVernet, with the author's love and Christmas good wishes." Betty DuVernet Hamilton of Gagetown, Helen's eighty-year-old daughter, now deceased lent it to me. Helen was related by marriage to Bessie's sister-in-law, Harriet Lavinia DuVernet Scovil, Morris's wife.

The Reverend Charles B. Scovil, Executive Secretary, Department of Religious Education, Diocese of North Carolina, Bessie's nephew, son of her eldest brother Jack, wrote a two-page "Introduction" to *Prayers for Girls.* My Mother remembered her cousin Charlie as a self-centered fourteen-year-old boy during the year she stayed with her Aunt Addie and Uncle Jack in New York. Not being at all pleased at having to escort his five-year-old country cousin to kindergarten on his way to his own school, Charlie offered her only his little finger as he whizzed along the streets, praying he would meet no one he knew, while Mary's tiny feet flew to keep up with him. Between then and his writing the introduction for his Aunt Bessie's book, Charles had clearly become more empathetic toward the "youthful life" of girls. He praises *Prayers for Girls* as being "a human little book" and goes on to encourage wide readership:

> It enters into the inner sanctuary of the girl's heart, and enables her to give utterances to longings and hopes, which before she has been unable or unwilling to speak in the presence of God. A prayer for Courage, for Cheerfulness, for Fortitude under Failure, in Perplexity, in Sorrow, in Disappointment. These few titles show the wideness of this little book's range, and the depth of its understanding and sympathy. We have long needed such a book as this. Here it is. May our girls make use of it.

With sixty-four pages and usually two prayers per page, Bessie covers most likely needs of a teenage girl. Many are praying for some quality, such as "For Unselfishness," "For Tact," "For Success." Others are "Against Gossip," "Against Evil Speaking," and "Against Prejudice." Some are for particular days in the church year: Christmas, Easter, and Sunday. Bessie is careful to include prayers close to her nursing life, aware of the need for more than the medical and nursing worlds offer—"In Pain," "In Illness," "Before an Operation," "In Convalescence," and, being a realist, "In the Loss of Friends." In 1959 Thomas Nelson and Sons of New York republished *Prayers for Girls* exactly as the original, including the same type of lettering. The price increased to sixty-five cents.

Bible Prayers was published in 1925. The copy I have has "Buckland" written in pencil in a childish hand on the flyleaf. The Reverend Basil Buckland was an Anglican clergyman in Gagetown, followed by his son, Basil. The signature is probably the son's. Though the format of *Bible Prayers* is similar to that of

Prayers for Girls, the prayers are longer and all have lengthy Biblical quotations, introduced by a little background and concluding with Bessie's comments in her own words or those of the Bible. Again, this is obviously from the pen of someone who knows her Bible. The subjects are more adult than in her previous book, such as "The Prayer of Confession" and "The Prayer of Intersession."

She presents the "The Prayer of Pride and of Humility" in the following way:

> The two characters in our Lord's parable of the Pharisee and the publican have come down to our day as the symbols of pride and humility. The two men went up into the temple to pray. The Pharisee stood and prayed thus with himself:

> God, I thank Thee, that I am not as other men are, extortioners, unjust, adulterers, or even as this publican. I fast twice in the week, I give tithes of all that I possess.
> St. Luke XVIII: 11.

> The publican standing afar off, feeling himself unworthy to draw near the mercy-seat, would not lift up so much as his eyes unto heaven, but smote upon his breast, saying:

> God be merciful to me a sinner.
> St. Luke XVIII: 13.

> Few words, but embracing much. Jesus said, "I tell you this man went down to his house justified rather than the other; for everyone that exalteth himself shall be abased; and he that humbleth himself shall be exalted."

* * * *

Meadowlands was sold in 1923. Morris's three older children were now well established in their careers. Bessie and Morris and his two youngest adult children — my mother, Mary, and Roger moved to a modern house on King Street in Fredericton. As soon as Roger and Mary were out on their own, Bessie and Morris sold the Fredericton house and began spending spring and summer in England with Morris's oldest son, Morrie and his family, and fall and winter in South Carolina where Roger and his family now lived.

In 1927, the next little mauve book, *Joy in Sorrow,* was published in the same sixty-four-page format. Bessie and the publisher obviously had a good thing going with this series. But, considering what was to come, it is almost as though Bessie anticipated the stock market crash of 1929, which brought so much misery and caused once prosperous men to jump out of windows. The Crash reduced the living standard of millions and produced a general economic and psychological depression that lasted until World War II, which started for Canada in 1939 and for the U.S. in 1941. The chapter titles include: In Disappointment; In Financial Cares; In Restricted Means; In The Loss of Riches; In Poverty; In Want; In Worry — all apt subjects for the soon to be afflicted.

In 1927 Bessie was seventy-eight and Morris sixty-sevencan appropriate time for a new book titled *Light at Eventide — For the Homeward Traveller,* again with sixty-four pages in the same embossed, mauve cover. The copy I have has Bessie's inscription: "Priscilla A. DuVernet, with Christmas greetings from the author. Christmas, 1928." Priscilla was the second wife of the much older Harry "The Squire" DuVernet and lived directly across the river from Meadowlands on the Gagetown side. By 1928 she was living in Boston with her two unmarried, adult daughters, Florrie [Florence] and Muriel.

Light at Eventide consists of cheerful one-page reflections and optimistic philosophical pronouncements, including occasional Biblical references, on the acceptance of old age when death is on the horizon. Typical, is a reflection on the story of Moses, which seems especially appropriate since Aunt Bessie was not far from Moses' age at the time:

> Moses was fourscore years old, and Aaron fourscore
> and three years old, when they spake unto Pharoah.
> – Exodus 7:7.

Eighty and eighty-three is not an age at which, as a
rule, men begin new enterprises. Yet it was at this age
that the Lord said to Moses and Aaron, "Bring out
the children of Israel from the land of Egypt." It was
an arduous undertaking, fit to tax the youngest and
strongest. There must have been younger men among
the tribes who, under the guidance of the Almighty
could have assumed the leadership, but God did not
choose them.

Is not this a reminder to us that age is no excuse for
shirking responsibility? If a task is set before us, and
it is our plain duty to perform it, we shall have the
strength that is necessary to carry it through. We have
reserves of power of which we are utterly unaware
until the need arises and we call on them. We can still
say, "The Lord is my Helper."

I wonder whether the author thought of that quotation from
Exodus when she was asked to give a fifteen-minute lecture on the
radio in her 85th year. She did not exactly have to part the waters,
but it still must have been quite a challenge, along with being the
guest speaker at a large nurses' convention in South Carolina on
the same day.

Henry Altemus published three additional books by Elizabeth
Robinson Scovil in this series: *Prayers for Boys*, *Prayers to be Used
at Sea*, and *Little Prayers for Little Lips*, but I have not been able
to locate copies. Bessie's last book, and one in my collection, goes
back to the subject of child health, *Common Ailments of Children*,
released in 1930 by her loyal publisher, now in the hands of Howard
Altemus, the son of Henry. The readers in 1930 would be a new
generation from her followers in the 1890s, so Altemus thought it

prudent to place under the author's name, "Late Superintendent of the Newport Hospital."

The book is a 6½ by 4 inch, 137-page hardback with a dark green cover. The signature inside the front cover is in the firm backhanded style of Elizabeth A. Karsten, Bessie's niece (Jack and Addie's daughter). By the time she received this book, Bess, as Bessie's namesake was known, would have mothered three of her four surviving children. Charles, the eldest, remembers his mother as a scholarly, well organized and delightful woman.

Common Ailments of Children is written simply and easily understood. Basic symptoms and appropriate treatments are clearly described. Specific advice is given on when the doctor should be called. In those days when the doctor still made house calls, but charged a fee, the author encouraged the mother to be realistically confident in her own abilities, up to a point. In the section on "Convulsions," for example, she writes: "One convulsion is not alarming but if they recur a doctor should be consulted."

The sections about "Bites" is a good example of a mother working with what she has at hand and making unusual use of household implements.

BITES

Children are sometimes bitten by cats, dogs, or other pets. The wound should be immediately sucked. If the skin of the mouth is unbroken and the saliva is not swallowed there is practically no danger to the person doing it.

The wound can be cauterized by applying a white-hot button hook, or piece of wire heated white-hot. The hotter the iron, the less the pain. Treat the wound like a burn.

The animal inflicting the wound should be confined, given food and water, and carefully watched. If it does not develop hydrophobia [rabies] much needless anxiety is spared.

This graphic advice makes us realize how reliant we have become on the professional medical world with the introduction of Medicare in Canada, the National Health Service in England, and similar public programmes in many parts of the world after World War II. Home knowledge for dealing with injury or illness is no longer looked on as the first line of treatment. The appearance of antibiotics as the cure-all triggered this loss of knowledge and lack of confidence. We may not think of a buttonhook as a household tool that could be used in emergency medical treatment, but it was in the early 1930s. I have a firm memory as a toddler in 1933 sitting on the floor in front of my Great Aunt Bessie, absorbing the unusual presence of this august person, and looking at the little black buttons on her black kid-leather shoes as she stretched her feet toward the fireplace in my home. *Common Ailments of Children* is a volume of common sense knowledge and effective home treatments with the materials, techniques, and tools at hand.

Elizabeth Scovil continued to prepare material for book publication throughout her last years. I have seen several references to a book of poems authored by Bessie and published by Altemus in 1932, but have not been successful in finding a copy or any individual poems. That this author, so deft at writing prose, would compose poetry comes as no surprise. In a letter to her future sister-in-law, Adeline Barker, in the 1880s, she makes a reference to some "trifling verse" she had composed for her "own amusement." It seems likely this practice continued and the 1932 volume collected this additional creative writing. What a happy surprise and fitting conclusion to my quest if a copy of this book would yet emerge from someone's collection of old books and be found on the shelf of a used and rare bookshop. I can imagine Bessie during her many Atlantic crossings, well installed on a cushioned deck chair with a tartan rug over her knees, in a sheltered corner of the ship, glancing occasionally at the rolling waves of the open ocean, and, with fountain pen in hand, putting down her thoughts in poetic form.

During the time of these trips to England, she also wrote a dozen one-page stories for her young nieces and nephews she was on her way to visit. I have photocopies of the originals, which, unfortunately, were lost in my cousin's house fire in Amherst, Nova Scotia in 2004. They were never published and perhaps not intended to be; however they may have been the nucleus for a future book as they are precisely the same length and for the same age group—3 to 5 year olds, as her previous series.

I continue to look for Great Aunt Bessie's missing books, but until found, if ever, I must be content with those I possess or at least have seen. They place her solidly as a talented and innovative author, with a wide knowledge of nursing and religious subjects, a natural teacher and a compassionate woman who dared to be independently ahead of her time.

Addendum
Books Written and Published by
Elizabeth Robinson Scovil

I have seen and read all of my Great Aunt Bessie's books except *In the Sick Room, The Littlest Loyalist, History of the Kingston Peninsula, Names for Children, Stories of Angels Prayers for Boys, Prayers to be Used at Sea,* and *Little Prayers for Little Lips.* These missing books have been referred to by credible sources.

In the Sick Room: What to Do, How to Do and When to Do for the Sick; the Art of Nursing. Springfield, Mass; C. W. Bryan Co, 1888.

A Baby's Requirements. Philadelphia; Henry Altemus, 1892.

The Care of Children. Philadelphia; Henry Altemus, 1894.

Preparation for Motherhood. Philadelphia; Henry Altemus, 1896.

Morning Strength. Philadelphia; Henry Altemus, 1896.

Hymns of Praise and Gladness. Philadelphia; Henry Altemus, 1896.

Names for Children: A Dictionary of Baptismal Names for Children Containing Upwards of 1200 Names with Their Meanings and Language from which They were Derived. Philadelphia; Henry Altemus, 1896.

Evening Comfort. Philadelphia; Henry Altemus, 1897.

Wee Folks Stories from the Old Testament in Words of One Syllable. Philadelphia; Henry Altemus, 1921.

Wee Folks Stories from the New Testament in Words of One Syllable. Philadelphia; Henry Altemus, 1921.

Wee Folks Bible ABC. Philadelphia; Henry Altemus, 1921. Republished by Applewood Books, Carlisle, MA, 1995.

Little Prayers for Little Lips. Philadelphia; Henry Altemus, 1921. Republished by Platt & Munk, New York, 1934.

The Wee Folks Life of Christ. Philadelphia; Henry Altemus, (date ?). Republished by Platt & Munk, New York, 1935.

Prayers For Girls. Philadelphia; Henry Altemus, 1924. Republished by Thomas Nelson & Sons, New York, 1959.

Bible Prayers. Philadelphia; Henry Altemus, 1925. Republished by Kessinger, Whitefish, Montana, 2010.

Light at Eventide for the Homeward Traveller. Philadelphia; Henry Altemus, 1927.

Stories of Angles. Philadelphia; Henry Altemus, n.d.

Joy in Sorrow. Philadelphia; Howard Altemus, 1927.

The Open Window. Philadelphia; Howard Altemus, n.d

Prayers for Boys. Philadelphia; Howard Altemus, n.d.

Prayers to Be Used at Sea. Philadelphia; Howard Altemus, n.d..

Daily Help for Daily Need. Philadelphia; Howard Altemus, n.d.

Little Tales for Little Ears in Words of One Syllable. Philadelphia; Howard Altemus, n.d.

The Littlest Loyalist. (No publishing information)

History of the Kingston Peninsula. (No publishing information)

Common Ailments in Children. Philadelphia; Howard Altemus, 1930.

Chapter Five

Journalist

There is a fine line between the definitions of "journalist" and "author,"—some might say none. However, for the purpose of delving into Elizabeth Robinson Scovil's many published works, I have decided to consider her articles and speeches published in magazines, journals and newspapers separately from her books.

In 1932, Margaret E. Lawrence, a member of the Canadian Women's Press Club, documented the beginning of Bessie's career as journalist based on correspondence with her.

> It was while in [nurses] training that Miss Scovil began to write for publication. In 1879 she sent to the then *Scribner's Magazine*, the predecessor of *The Century*, a paper on domestic nursing which to her 'joy and delight' was published and for which she received what seemed to the young author the magnificent sum of $25. Shortly afterward the *Christian Union*, which later became *The Outlook*, accepted a series of seven papers on "Home Nursing," and "Thus' says Miss Scovil, 'my modest literary career was launched."

Margaret Lawrence continues, quoting from her correspondence with Bessie:

> "I wrote innumerable papers on different subjects for my periodicals. ....After I had graduated, I wrote an article [on nursing] for *The Youth's Companion* which brought, it was said, 1,200 applications for admission

to the Training School of the Massachusetts General Hospital, and which brought me the thanks of the [hospital] committee."

It was a remarkable journalistic achievement for Bessie to write about her two years of training in a way that encouraged a large number of young women to follow her example. We don't have the text of this article, but it is fair to assume that while she wrote truthfully, the article did not dwell on the difficulties of nurses training—lack of sleep, overwork, tired feet, poor food, little money or appreciation, and lack of equipment. Instead, she must have concentrated on the satisfaction of helping patients recover from illness or injury and on the opportunity to follow in the footsteps of the great Florence Nightingale, still active in advancing the nursing profession. Bessie must have strongly hinted that professional nursing was one of the few roads open to gentlewomen leading to independence. In 1880 there was scant acceptance of young ladies being anything but dependent on their fathers and then on their husbands. The role of *The Youth's Companion* was not to inflame young women's ambitions with any thought of independence and a radical change in the status quo but the implication would have been implicit in her encouragement and example.

Bessie's early writings began with a mission to promote the profession of nursing. Later, when she became an associate editor of *The Ladies' Home Journal*, she concentrated on writing about the care of children and child development. Still, later, in other publications, she broadened the focus of her journalism to include new information from medical research and practice and, eventually, from the fields of science and technological innovation and progressive social development in general. In this latter phase she regularly shared her wide-ranging interests, well considered ideas, and astute observations with her readers.

The Ladies' Home Journal, established in 1890, was the innovative publishing product of Philadelphia's Curtis Publishing Company. By February 1891, Elizabeth Robinson Scovil had become an associate editor of the new magazine with responsibility for a page titled, "Mother's Corner." Bessie's career in journalism blossomed from this position. The response from readers to her writing and to the helpful information and advice she imparted to new mothers made her a valuable writer. In an era of booming magazine production, *The Ladies' Home Journal* was an outstanding success. It grew to have the largest circulation of any periodical in the world. Bessie's contribution undoubtedly helped boost the magazine to this level of popular appeal and its spectacular commercial success.

Payments for her contributions provided a steady and growing source of income, which must have been a sweet addition to her nursing income considering the recent impecunious condition of her family. In addition to her income from writing, she was a wise investor. We know that Bessie came to hold a significant investment in Curtis stocks. According to my mother, Aunt Bessie was an original stockholder in the Curtis Publishing Company. Her income from employment as a nurse was probably adequate for living expense but hardly enough for stock market investments. It is likely she was paid for her work as an associate editor of *The Ladies' Home Journal* and as a contributing writer, in part, with Curtis stocks. As the company's publishing efforts met with increasing financial success, their stock would have become increasingly valuable and her dividend income would have increased.

In addition, it is clear that her "Mother's Corner" page and her feature writing led directly to the writing of her books, which were received by a large audience with great enthusiasm and sold well. Her royalty income from books sales added to her financial resources over a number of decades.

Amazingly, Bessie became a wealthy woman. In 1929, she confided to her niece, Courtney Scovil, that she was a "millionaire on paper." Though part of this "paper" wealth was diminished by the stock market crash at the beginning of the Great Depression, Bessie never lacked financial resources for the rest of her life. In fact, her continuing wealth became a regular source of financial support for family members at various times when assistance was needed or could be employed to make good things happen for them that otherwise would not have occurred.

Bessie took advantage of opportunities to become a regularly published journalist. Whether a desire to impart knowledge and guidance, or the pleasure of seeing her work in print, or the need to make sure she would never be in the impecunious position her father endured following his bankruptcy in 1868, we have much evidence that she wrote with conviction, insight, authority, literary knowledge, sensitivity, and, on some occasions, with humour.

* * * *

The Ladies' Home Journal began as a large format, eleven by sixteen inch, magazine. It was filled with articles chiefly of interest to women: gardening, child rearing, food preparation, fashion, household management, appropriate furniture and furnishings, and all aspects of interior decoration. It included short biographies of well-known people, adventurous stories of faraway places, well illustrated stories of socialites, and occasional articles of international or national political interest that a self-respecting husband would not feel embarrassed to be found reading.

Every few months, *The Ladies' Home Journal* would dedicate a full page to promoting books it also made available for purchase. The books were not potboilers or the equivalent of Harlequin Romances. The authors included Alfred Lord Tennyson, Charles Dickens, Sir Walter Scott, George Eliot, and Agnes Strickland (a writer of popular biographies of royal women). The advertising must have been effective as the offers were repeated every few months.

For many curious and intellectually able women with no formal education beyond secondary schooling, without books at home, and little or no access to libraries, the opportunity must have been enticing. The opportunity to purchase books that exposed them to all sorts of ideas never before encountered, especially if they lived on a remote farmstead, made them feel part of the sisterhood of informed women across the country.

In writing her "Mother's Corner" page, Elizabeth Scovil used terminology her readers could easily understand. The information she gave them was not only useful but comforting, helping women on the way from being uninformed and fearful to being competent mothers. Judging from some of the basic questions asked in her question and answer columns, many new mothers felt very uncertain about caring for their infants and lacked the skills to do so.

In the early 1940s, when I was staying with family friends who had rented a house for the summer near Grand Lake, not far from Gagetown, New Brunswick, I made a heart-pounding discovery. In the back of an old barn I found several issues of *The Ladies' Home Journal*. Each issue featured a "Fifty Years Ago Today" section. One of these sections displayed the headline, "Elizabeth Robinson Scovil Said," which was followed with a quotation from one of her advice-to-mothers' columns. Even at age eleven, I knew my great aunt must have been a famous person to be quoted in such a magazine, especially for her advice given fifty years previously. Thus began my interest in learning more about her life and legacy.

In order to research the full scope of Bessie's journalism, I obtained photocopies of *The Ladies' Home Journal* from 1891 through 1906 from Cambridge University Library in England where the magazine is preserved on microfilm. Her regular "Mother's Corner" page ran through August 1902 with an article titled "The Truth About Baby Foods" (she did not think much of them—better to make your own). However, she continued writing for the magazine and published the following articles: "The Children on Christmas Day" (December 1902), "Good Books for the Young" (February 1903), "Old Games" (November 1905), and her last, "Children's Merry Frolics" (1906). This final contribution included instructions for the following group activity games along with the accompanying verses to sing or chant: "A Menagerie," "Birds in the Nest," "Peter in the Bramble Bush," and "The Dukes of Marlborough,"

By 1906, Bessie had been caring for the day-to-day needs of young children for three years. In 1903 she had stepped in to manage the home and family of her younger brother, Morris, whose wife, Hattie, had died leaving five young children motherless. The articles she wrote for *The Ladies' Home Journal* during the next three years reflected her experience in this new role. However, she did not teach the game in the "Merry Frolics" article to her nephews and nieces, perhaps lacking enough participants on their isolated farm. My mother did not remember them and was seven in 1903 when Aunt Bessie took over the care and management of the Meadowlands household. Bessie may have eventually abandoned these games with respect to changing cultural mores at the time. She was a founding member, along with Lady Aberdeen, of the National Council of Women of Canada and was increasingly sensitive to gender bias which some of the old games displayed. In addition, the chant for "The Dukes of Marlborough" game included unmistakable racial slurs.

As an associate editor of *The Ladies' Home Journal* over all those years, Bessie's articles covered a great variety of topics relating to the care of babies and children, the mother's care of herself, and the cultivating of healthy and nurturing relationship with children. Articles written by other authors and published under her editorial guidance added to the helpful information and advice offered to readers of the magazine. The question-and-answer features allowed young mothers to know that any query they had, no matter how basic, would be given thoughtful and serious reply. No subject, within the bounds of propriety of the time, was too much of a challenge.

Bessie published sixteen articles on the health of the baby and the small child, which included close attention to infectious diseases, injuries, sleep difficulties, baby's healthcare in relation to the seasons, the invalid child, as well as many other sickness and health issues.

In addition, Bessie wrote thirteen articles on the broad subject of education, including advice on suitable books, schooling at home, simple playthings, the importance of exercise, the habit of saving, appropriate Sabbath activities, and various games. She wrote twelve articles that can be categorized as advice on "up-bringing," such as punishing, table manners, rewarding, encouraging kindness, dealing with temper outbreaks, and even the problem of "untrained daughters." Eight articles focused in detail on feeding babies and children, with a special concern for "delicate children." She provided helpful advice on breakfast and lunch preparation, food changes in summer, and on how and when to allow the drinking of tea.

She wrote eight articles about seasonal holiday activities: Christmas Day, Christmas gifts, Thanksgiving, summer luncheons, and summer amusements. Three articles dealt with clothes and dressing for babies and children, two on nursery furnishing, and one on birthday parties. She also wrote the following articles concentrating on the welfare of the mother: "A Wise Selfishness," "Worries of Our Daily Life," "Order in The Home," and "A Wife's House-hold Allowance."

These articles were either one column of a thousand words on the page she edited, or occasionally three columns of approximately three thousand words. The size of the print varied, depending on the space required. Sometimes more than one article appeared in the same month.

In May 1898 she published a full column under "Suggestions for Mothers" that answered fourteen question submitted by readers. The same issue carried a full page article titled "The Life of a Trained Nurse" that was presented in the following sections: "About the Choice of a Hospital," "Qualifying for Institution Work," "Making Application to the Superintendent," "The Time of Probation," "The Routine of the School," "The Nurse's More Important Duties," "Part of the Hospital Routine," "The Uniform of the Nurse," "The Compensation Which is Received," and "After She Has Graduated." What else might a girl thinking of becoming a nurse — or the mother of that girl — wish to know?

This article was a major revisiting of the topic with which Bessie began her career in journalism — the promotion of the nursing profession. It begins with this striking paragraph:

> To most people who have never been inside of a hospital it seems as though the life there must, of necessity, be sad, and the constant sight of illness so depressing as to render cheerfulness impossible.

To such, the aspect of a sunny, well-kept ward, clean and fresh, with its white beds and neat appointments, would be an agreeable surprise. The nurses in their dainty caps, white aprons and light uniform dresses are not overshadowed with gloom. If their responsibilities have banished careless gayety from their faces there is a serenity and calm brightness in its place which is far removed from sadness. Outside the ward their own quarters are, as a rule, pleasant and attractive. They lead busy lives, but there are stated times for rest and recreation, which is not always the case with busy workers in the outside world. Most of them love their work and would not exchange it for any other.

A young woman, or her mother, would be inclined to read on, especially if this were their first glimpse into the world of nursing. In the next section, "About the Choice of Hospital," Bessie offers the enticing prospect of promotion to positions of power and influence, along with some practical advice:

The woman who wishes to make nursing her profession should decide whether, after her graduation, she would prefer to nurse individuals in their own homes, or to undertake Institutional work, as head nurse of a ward in a large hospital with a view to becoming a superintendent of a small school for nurses.

Looking ahead so soon to quick promotion must be read in the context of 1898 when few nurses had a two-years of training like Bessie. She knew that nurses with professional training could choose their employment as they wished, as they were still rare and sought after.

She advises the aspiring nurse to "... choose a training school attached to a hospital of moderate size. In these is more leisure to be devoted to what may be called the niceties of nursing."

Bessie encourages the potential candidate to think about her post-training future even before she begins, and for good reasons. Where she goes for training has a bearing on the type of preparation she will receive and therefore her readiness for her particular choice of practice.

As the article proceeds, she presents an increasingly realistic picture of life in nurses' training. Under "The Time of Probation," she writes,: "Untidiness is considered a crime of the first magnitude. Carelessness is a fatal fault; too much depends on a nurse's exactness for the want of it to be easily forgiven in a probationer."

A sheltered young lady (and her mother) may wonder just how much she would be expected to do when caring for men, surely nothing too intimate. Bessie writes:

> In the men's wards an orderly or ward-tender give the male patients their general baths, but the nurse is still responsible for the cleanliness of hands, finger-nails, ears and feet. These duties are not always pleasant, and it is best for the aspirant for hospital work to understand that there are disagreeable things to be encountered, that she may decide whether she is sufficiently eager for it to overlook them.

Later she stresses the inevitable complaint of every nurse:

> Most pupils suffer very much with their feet when beginning duty. The hard floors are very trying; those in the wards are of hardwood, while the corridors are sometimes paved with brick, or tiled. Standing and walking continuously during the long hours of duty are very fatiguing to those who are unaccustomed to being constantly on their feet. Well-fitted stockings, free from darns are indispensable.

On the subject of payment Bessie is equally informative:

After graduation head nurses in hospital wards receive from twenty to thirty dollars per month; superintendents from five hundred to twelve hundred dollars a year. District nurses, who are employed by various churches, societies and sometimes by private benevolence, to work among the sick poor, receive about the same salary as a head nurse in a hospital, exclusive of board. Private nurses receive from fifteen to twenty-five dollars a week. They have to pay the rent of a room to use as a headquarters, and their earnings are more or less precarious. It is rare for a [private care] nurse to be employed all the time, and her work is so arduous that it would be impossible for her to stand the strain of continuous work.

Bessie concludes her article with a section discussing life after graduation. The last sentence is surely a most accurate and unadorned summary of a career in nursing: "In any case she holds in her hands the means of obtaining an honest living in a useful way as long as she has health and strength to exercise it."

Fifteen years later, during the Great War, Bessie's speech to the Canadian National Association of Trained Nurses used an extremely dramatic backdrop to highlight the devotion and out-of-the-ordinary service of nurses to the wounded, saying, "Our profession has its saints and martyrs." However, in the relative peace of 1898 nursing was prosaically an exhausting but a worthy profession. Promoting good health, preventing illness, nursing the ill, and nursing to assist recovery are all topics close to Bessie's heart. She would have felt relaxed and competent writing articles about them with very little if any need for checking reference books or even her own notes.

Bessie's first sentences and first paragraphs are often impressively crafted no matter the subject. She had the knack of inclusion and assumes her readers have inquiring minds and a desire for accurate information. Consequently, her first words are enticing and spur the readers to continue. This must be one of the basics taught in schools of journalism, but Bessie knew this instinctively. Here is a good example. Since many of her readers would experience extreme weather conditions in the summer months, it is not surprising that early in her associate editorship, July 1891, she prepared an article on the health of "Children In Summer":

> Every mother knows that summer is a trying time for children who have not finished cutting their teeth. If they are fed artificial food, any change in the diet or want of care in its preparation, is sure to disorder the digestion, and perhaps cause serious illness. Intelligent mothers are alive to the dangers which surround their children and are on their guard against them.

> It is not always remembered that older children also require care at this season. The chilly winds of spring and autumn and the frosts of winter rouse a mother's anxiety and make her watchful; but summer seems to her time when vigilance may be relaxed without doing any harm. There are some points in relation to dress, bathing, food and sleep which should be carefully attended to, and then an ordinarily healthy child may be permitted to go on its own way.

> To talk of guarding against cold in summer seems absurd, and yet it as necessary as in winter. Where the climate is changeable, a hot day is often followed by a cool evening, or a sudden rain storm chills the air, or a cold wind springs up, grateful after the heat, but dangerous to those who are thinly clad unless they are protected from it by proper covering. Cotton is a good conductor of heat and allows it to escape rapidly from the surface of the body. As soon as the surrounding air becomes cooler than the skin it steals the heat which the body requires for its own needs. A fresh supply of heat must be produced, and thus

the system is overtaxed to supply the demands of the robber. Flannel is a bad conductor and guards the tender body more faithfully, retaining the heat.

What caring mother could resist the logic of this scientific explanation of the need for flannel in the summer especially with an overtone of drama in the form of lurking danger, a "robber"? But there is more — merino wool flannel:

> Children should wear light merino undershirts in summer, as thin as can be procured, but always with an admixture of wool. They can have cotton dresses and as few under-garments as possible, not to overheat them, but flannel next the skin is indispensable. Long stockings should be worn, and these may be of cotton. The shoes must be light, with broad toes and low heels, perfectly fitting, not to cramp the foot. An extra jacket should be provided to wear in damp weather and in returning from expeditions in the evening when the dew is falling.

> Young children should wear night-dresses of thin flannel; older ones may have undershirts like those worn in the day, or light jackets of Shaker flannel.

It is easy to take a cynical 21st century view of what seems like unnecessary precautions. But in the pre-sulfa-drug, and pre-antibiotic era, before free medical care and hospitalization, and before routine immunizations, a simple chill could lead to complications and be a forerunner of serious illnesses.

Bessie continues with advice on summer bathing, food, and bedtime:

> Vigorous children should have a cold or tepid sponge bath every morning. Delicate ones require more care in this matter, as frequent bathing exhausts them. Salt

should be added to the water and the bath given every other day, alternate with rubbing the whole body with a towel, followed by friction with the hand.

When children live near the water they should not be allowed to bathe more than once a day, and then not immediately after eating. Wading is such a dear delight that it cannot be prohibited, but it is dangerous if the water is cold.

Though Bessie writes extensively about food elsewhere, she neatly summarizes her views on diet here:

…meat not more than once a day.…The cereals should be used abundantly: oatmeal, rice, hominy and farina are usually liked. Even when there is a distaste for them it can be overcome with patience. In this case a very little should be offered at once with sugar and milk, or with syrup poured over it.…plenty of fresh ripe fruit should be eaten.

She urges the drinking of milk. "Every effort should be made to induce them to take it. The addition of a little salt, or sugar will disguise the milky taste that is disliked." She adds that if this diet is "too loosening, scald the milk, remove oatmeal, introduce rice instead, and no fruit with little seeds." And finally, "If there is any suspicion that the drinking water is not perfectly pure, it should be boiled and filtered."

Bessie continues her advice for summer by writing that children should be encouraged to take an afternoon nap as long as they will put up with it so they will have the stamina to play into the "cool of the twilight instead of fussing in a too warm bedroom." Houses at this time lacked good insulation and upstairs bedrooms were frequently hot in the summer. To induce sleep at bedtime she recommends a soothing nursery rhyme or a little song. Reading a bedtime story or, if no children's books are available, a story told from the imagination can help bring on sleep. If the family has a music box or a windup gramophone, these can be played at bedtime as well.

An inexperienced mother, with her first child, must have felt well informed and more confident after reading just this article. No wonder Bessie remained an associate editor of *The Ladies' Journal* for so many years and was urged to write the book, *A Baby's Requirements*, after streams of young mothers asked her for advice, often the same advice, over and over again.

In 1892, Bessie wrote an article for *The Ladies' Home Journal* that is of particular significance for illustrating her progressive views on the care and development of children within the life of the family. "Children at Christmas Time" is an extensive treatise that literally overturns the rigid and harsh strictures of Victorian culture in favour of a new, joyous, and nurturing ethic of family life and parent/children relationships. While this social revolution in family dynamics was emerging in many contexts of everyday living, Bessie chose to focus on its significance for the Christmas holidays. Her opening lines set the stage for what is to come:

> Christmas is the Children's Day. The household that is so unhappy as to contain no children loses half the beauty of the festival. It seems specially fitting that the birthday of the Holy Child should be dedicated to the pleasure and delight of the little ones.

It happened I was in the middle of reading Joan Perkin's absorbing and shocking book, *Victorian Women* at the time I was researching Bessie's articles in the 1892 issues of *The Ladies' Home Journal*. The contrast between the miserable lives of women and children of all classes during the first half of this era, especially in England, and the culture of family celebration depicted in "Children at Christmas Time" could not have been greater. Bessie was clearly on the other side, and an unequivocal promoter, of a social revolution in parent/child relationships, so much of which stemmed from, and depended on, the family leadership taken up by mothers who aspired to a better life for their children and for themselves.

The Victorian era carried forward the dominant class structures of the very wealthy and the very poor, neither of which experienced December 25th as a day dedicated to pleasure and delight of children. It was not until the emergence of a middle class with a growing measure of financial security and, at the same time, a woman's movement for social equality, that the change in family dynamics so evident in Bessie's holiday recommendations could be fully realized. The rise of the middle class occurred earlier and with greater fluidity in Canada and the United States than in England. The appeal of *The Ladies' Home Journal* to an expanding audience of middle class women who were eager to provide a better way of life for their children, for themselves, and for their whole family was the key to its commercial success.

By the 1890s, many families whose grandparents were distinctly working class aspired to middle class values and behaviour as their economic position improved. Bessie was ideally suited to address this audience, starting with the health and physical wellbeing of children and moving on to their emotional and intellectual development. She seized the opportunity with skill and conviction. It is sobering to think of the thousands of mothers she influenced in this regard and the benefit that was then spread to many more children who would grow into adults and also become parents.

"Children at Christmas Time" is a prime example of the change in family life that was taking place at the end of Victorian era. It presents a picture of the ideal, progressive, middle-class North American family in the early 1890s on Christmas Day. It is an inclusive guide for a memorable holiday. Brief quotations on each topic will provide the scope and thrust of Bessie's advice:

> Children never forget their early Christmas days. It is worth any sacrifice to make them so full of joy that in after life this memory shall be a precious possession guiding all their childhood. The festival should be made different from every other holiday,

with its own peculiar observances, sacred to it alone. Music appropriate to the festal season, hymn and song and story that tell its glad tidings, games played at no other time, dainty dishes which only Christmas brings to the larder, decorations that charm the eye, and, if they are of fragrant evergreen with its spicy odour, press the sense of smell into service; all lend their aid to weave the subtle web of association which in years to come will revive for many men and women the happy past.

Later comes "the pleasant fiction of Santa Claus" and the best way to give children Christmas presents:

So much poetry clusters about the legend of Santa Claus that the ideal celebration of Christmas must include the filling of the stockings. First there is the delicious ceremony of hanging them by an open fireplace, if possible on Christmas eve; the procession of father, mother and happy children, each child with a stocking, all eager to find a good place to deposit them, the important business of fastening them securely so that they will not fall with their precious burdens; the lingering glances of the children as they go to bed picturing those limp, dangling receptacles filled to overflowing from that wonderful sleigh the tiny reindeer are bringing nearer and nearer. Who would relinquish all this? If the older members of the family are wakened at an unreasonably early hour the next morning, by whispers and footsteps and irrepressible gurgles of delight, is it not Christmas, the children's day?

Bessie continues to paint an increasingly detailed picture of the ideal Christmas morning:

Warm dressing gowns and slippers will prevent the truants from taking cold from exposure, and as the stockings should be emptied nowhere but in mother's bed, she will be able to see that they are worn. When there is to be a tree later in the day only the smaller presents need be put in the stockings. Each article should be wrapped up separately and tied. The exquisite uncertainty as to what may be in the parcel when it is drawn from the stocking is half the fun. A rosy apple or an orange should fill the toe, and candy be rather sparingly distributed among the other treasures, as it is too early in the day for a refection[7] of sweets. It requires tact on the mother's part to prevent too many from being eaten under the most favorable circumstances.

"A Christmas tree is only a shadow of itself if it be not lighted, so it is best to have it after dark," Bessie writes. She describes in detail the "proper precautions," which if taken… "there is very little danger of fire." In the near future when electricity becomes a little cheaper, incandescent lights will make the tree a blaze of glory and there will be no fear of a catastrophe.

The proper precautions in decorating the Christmas tree with tapers[8] were complicated:

> …care must be exercised in placing them and one person should be deputed to watch that nothing flammable swings within reach of the light. There should be a wet sponge at hand, tied to a long stick, a pail of water and an old blanket, or rug, to smother the flames should anything catch and the fire spread. The damp sponge will extinguish sparks without trouble.

---

7   According to the Oxford English Reference Dictionary, a "refection" is a small meal. It is an example of a number of words in Bessie's vocabulary that are no longer in common use.

8   "Tapers" are tall, slim, slow burning candles.

> If there is a carpet it is best to have a large, old rag
> spread under the tree for fear of accident.

Christmas presents are given close consideration:

> Presents, of course, occupy the place of honor at
> Christmas-tide, but they should be kept in place,
> and not allowed to monopolize time and strength
> and money to the exclusion of the other forms
> of good cheer. …If a girl longs for a silver pin and
> gets a dozen pocket-handkerchiefs, the fact that her
> initials are embroidered in the corner, making them
> more expensive than the pin, will not sweeten the
> disappointment.

Bessie goes on to say that children are "reasonable beings" and if,
as a parent, you cannot afford their "inordinate desires" you should
say they cost too much. "[You] will be surprised to find how fully
they acquiesce when they are treated with confidence."

> There is nothing so sweet to a child as to be placed
> on an equal footing with grown-up people. To be told
> to "run away because you cannot understand what we
> are talking about," is an injury that rankles long in the
> sensitive, imaginative heart.

This change in attitude toward children at a time when they
were generally meant to be "seen and not heard" and encouraged
to "speak only when spoken to" must have seemed quite a
revolutionary approach to child rearing for the readers of *The Ladies'
Home Journal* in 1892. The "run my way because…" approach suited
parents who were unwilling to allow children into their world. But
adequate explanations that take children into parental confidence
create a sense of family understanding and promote the emotional
and intellectual growth of young people. Bessie was confident
that when parents moved from a stance of authoritarian power to

nurturing guidance the quality of family life would improve for everyone. On the matter gift giving, Bessie continues:

> It is foolish to waste money on expensive toys for children. The mechanical ones are easily broken, and simpler ones give an almost equal amount of pleasure. Painted toys are to be avoided...[for infants] as sooner or later all their belongings find a way to their mouths.[9]

> Books are a never-failing source of delight to the child who cares for reading, and is accumulating a library. Each book is a personal friend, loved and cherished as they seldom are in later life. Who does not recall with tender affection the beloved aspect of some dear old favourite?... It seems almost defrauding children of their natural rights not to give them an opportunity to know and love the classical treasures that have charmed the generations before.

It is not surprising that such a well-read and literate woman put books high on the list of desirable presents. We can well imagine that hundreds, perhaps thousands, of mothers took her advice and encouraged their children on the reading road with a copy of *The Adventures of Robinson Crusoe* or a *Gulliver's Travels* under the Christmas table napkin:

> The dear doll families that lie close to the hearts of so many little mothers should be increased at Christmas time. Fine Paris dolls, beautiful to look at but useless to cuddle, are best passed by in favor of the humbler

---

9   Though it was not well known in those days that lead was a brain toxin with permanently damaging effects, especially on the brains of children, and that virtually all paint contained lead, Bessie either knew something about this from her medical training, or she had an intuitive precaution about the hazard of painted toys for small children.

members of the guild, who can be rocked to sleep in comfort, and put to bed without arranging their hair.

Tools for boys, and sewing implements for girls, some of the kindergarten gifts, anything that can be used and not merely played with, will help in the development of the active little minds and bodies we are trying to train aright. A world of wonder and beauty lies around us, with avenues into it on every side. If we can turn into the right channels the desire for knowledge inherent in children, and excite their interest in the wonderful things happening about us, we have done much for them. A microscope will open realms of which they have never dreamed. If they have shown an interest, however slight, in any branch of natural science, encourage it by some gift of book, or specimen or implement that will help them to pursue it.

Bessie's balanced recommendations are impressive—cuddly dolls to microscopes. Other than "tools for boys" and "sewing…for girls," Bessie does not differentiate on the basis of gender. Her own scientific training would have prevented her from seeing presents that feed an interest in "any branch of the natural sciences" as being only for boys.

Bessie turns her attention to food served on the holiday:

Christmas fare is a tax on the children's digestion, and as there is a good deal of it to come during the day, so the breakfast should not be too elaborate, but include one favorite dish as a special treat. …Someone has said that the turkey and not the eagle should be the national bird [in the USA], so it must not be excluded. It is not the substantials that endanger the digestion, it is the dessert that needs most careful guarding. Ice cream or sherbet is always acceptable to children, and does not hurt them. It seems a pity to lose the traditional plum pudding, which should be served in a blaze with a sprig of holly stuck on top. A little brandy poured over it and lighted at the last moment produces the desired effect.

Whether children were to have their appetites satisfied with a small portion of holly crested and brandy blazing plum pudding, Bessie wisely leaves ambiguous. The reference to the eagle reminds us that the readers of *The Ladies' Home Journal* were primarily American.

Speaking to the religious context of the holiday, Bessie's writing turns poetic:

The Christmas services are bright and joyous, and children should go to church with their elders. Even the little ones can understand something of the sacred story. The music will linger in their memories and in the after years the dear old hymns will seem like an echo of their mother's voice.

After Bessie describes the main activity of the evening—presents distributed from around the Christmas tree, "dressed with plenty of tinsel and many glittering ornaments"—she recommends the following as the grand finale:

A game of "Snap Dragon" may finish the evening. A shallow dish is spread with raisins and a little alcohol poured on them; this is lighted, and daring fingers snatch the raisins from the fiery dragon. Whoever gets the most wins the game. "Hunt the Thimble" and Blind-man's Bluff" are time honored amusements. Before they are ended, the children's cheeks will be crimson with excitement, and they will be too sleepy to do more than murmur: "Good-night and thank you for a merry Christmas."

This depiction of an ideal Christmas in 1892 is clearly the result of Bessie's own middle class experience of family and friends, with the mother of the house at the helm conducting the core of the festivities. What went on in the house was mother's business, and it was for the mothers who formed the core of *The Ladies' Home Journal* readers that Bessie compiled her Christmas day advice.

* * * *

Another article of note, "The Best Reading for Children," appeared in the February 1893 issue of *The Ladies' Home Journal*. As usual, the opening sentence and the lengthy first paragraph invite the mother to identify with the child. In requiring the precise repetition of stories night after night, Bessie compares the child's insistence with "the eagerness with which we listen to a familiar strain of music, experiencing fresh delight every time it falls upon our ears. If one note is altered or one chord omitted, it spoils the melody for us." She then asks for understanding of this "apparent unreasonableness" in children and for the "patient mother, a little worn with the monotony of the often told tale" to continue to fill the child's need.

Bessie draws her readers into a thoughtfully devised article that suggests substituting "true stories of the wonders that lie all about us" for traditional tales like "Little Red Riding Hood" or "The Three Bears." She writes that the "land of science has domains as fascinating as anything in the realms of fiction. ... Tell them of the habits of birds and plants and animals, of the wonderful snow crystals and the black diamonds of coal." In case the mother feels inadequate as the weaver of true tales, Bessie assures her there are many books available where the authors "have recorded their observations for our benefit, so that we have only to profit by their labours."

Bessie anticipates busy, tired mothers, exhausted by children "constantly asking questions and inquiring into the reason of everything that strikes them as being unusual. They should receive intelligent answers; explanations that will satisfy them as far as possible, when the subject is beyond their grasp." Writing in an era when there was still general acceptance of the advice that children should be "seen and not heard," Bessie dared to confront the norm:

> Nothing is more exasperating to the inquiring mind than to be told, "You cannot understand that now; you must wait until you are older," or given one of the other excuses that serve to conceal the ignorance of elders....An attempt should be made to solve the problem, or explain the phenomenon that is puzzling them in a way that is suited to their childish capacity....The effort must be made, for what the children learn in these early days is seldom forgotten, and it is the duty of both parents to see that it is something worth remembering.

This article would have influenced thousands of mothers, with many more thousands of children benefiting. In addition, Bessie insists both parents share this duty. Father is definitely required to come out from behind his newspaper and his cloud of pipe smoke to support mother in this activity of childhood learning. Bessie recommends that if no other time can be found by a busy mother or father, that at least ten or fifteen minutes in the evening or at bedtime be devoted "to talking with the children or reading to them."

> Establishing this habit will accomplish a good deal in the course of a year....Choosing always the best books, a love of good literature will be established. Boys then, will not crave the unhealthy stimulus of the Five-Cent Library...and girls will not be attracted by sensational romances.

Bessie knew that her page in *The Ladies' Home Journal* appealed to a broad spectrum of readers who wanted a better life for their children. The Editorial Board of *The Journal*, on which Bessie sat, knew that offering quality books through their pages helped to encourage subscriptions and individual sales of the magazine. It was likely that many of the girls who had developed good reading habits from having access to the books available from the magazine would become readers of *The Journal* when adults. Bessie extends the offer:

> Because the books chosen in "The Best Reading for Children," may not be accessible to the average mother, I have been privileged to say that the Book Department of *The Ladies' Home Journal* will undertake to secure any book here mentioned at the prices given; there will be no charge for forwarding or postage.

The following paragraph lists fifteen titles with prices and comments, starting with *The Young Folks Cyclopedia of Common Things* in three volumes at $2.50 per volume, and ending with *The Wonders of Pompeii,* one of a series at $1.00 each.

Bessie's own love of reading prompts a desire that children pick up a similar enthusiasm. She regularly returns to writing about suitable books for the young. The last of these articles for *The Ladies' Home Journal* was published in December 1903. By this time she had been living for three months at Meadowlands, the Scovil farm across the St. John River from Gagetown, New Brunswick as previously noted.

Her judgment and choice of books to recommend was no doubt conditioned, at least in part, by her experience with her nieces and nephews. Bessie's final book list was a substantial compilation presented under the title "Good Books for the Young," published just in time to assist mothers in selecting Christmas gifts for her children. Bessie divides the article into five categories: "For Children from Six to Ten Years," "Books that Will Please Boys," "Books that Will Please Girls," "Fact with Fiction," and "For Boys and Girls Alike."

While many of the recommended books were written by American authors and published in the United States, Bessie clearly made an effort to include books by Canadian authors writing about Canadian settings and subjects. This included *Cruising on the St. Lawrence* and *Indian Boyhood* by Charles Eastman/Ohíye S'a in the section on books for boys. Adventure stories from around the world and from ancient times to the present day were included in her list.

Bessie was adept in choosing age appropriate books. In the recommendations for "girls of twelve and over," the books appear to be dealing with the lives and emotions of girls in social settings. For example, her list includes Louisa May Alcott's *Little Women*. I remember reading that book at age twelve, easily identifying with the characters, and unexpectedly crying at the sad parts. It was the first book that affected me in this way.

"Fact with Fiction" included a variety of stories based on historical events, often wars, including *Between Boer and Briton*, and *Under Colonial Colors*, about Arnold's expedition against Quebec in 1775, and, *In the Camp of Cornwallis*, which tells of the experiences of a boy in the New Jersey campaign under Washington in 1777.

Books on natural history depicting the interesting lives of birds and animals are featured among her recommendations. *The Story of Joan of Arc* and *In the Days of Queen Elizabeth* are suggested under "For Boys and Girls Alike." It is notable that these books feature women who accomplished feats previously thought possible only by men. Bessie's bibliographic mission was more than to just encourage reading as a pastime. She knew books could influence values, attitudes, and even lifelong behaviour.

* * * *

The year 1895 brought a new name for Bessie's page in *The Ladies' Home Journal*— "Suggestions for Mothers" with the byline, "By Elizabeth Robinson Scovil." An ornate decoration showing the heads of a mother and child, surrounds the title under which is printed, "Questions of interest to mothers will be cheerfully answered on this page whenever possible," along with the statement, "Any books mentioned in this department may be ordered through the Journal's Literary Bureau at advantageous prices." These would have included Bessie's two books, *A Baby's Requirements* and *The Care of Children*, which, by this time, she had been inspired by the response to her column to write and publish.

In addition to the new name for her column, the format gradually changed to one in which readers' questions and Bessie's answers came to dominate the page. Over the previous four years, Bessie had undoubtedly covered the full range of advice she had to offer on the care of infants and children. Responding to mother's specific questions and circumstances, though often restating advice previously given, gave her column a lively new format. As the circulation of *The Ladies' Home Journal* continued to expand, new readers would not have seen Bessie's early articles so the question-and-answer format gave her the opportunity to continue sharing her information and advice in personalized ways. Question-and-answer journalism has been a popular and enduring feature of magazine and newspaper publication. Bessie's practice of engaging with readers of *The Ladies' Home Journal* in this way on issues of child care and family life made her a valuable asset for the magazine.

The questions from readers were given headings such as "Obstruction in the Nose" or "A Boy's Financial Education." They were usually signed with a first name and last initial or sometimes with a phrase like, "Anxious Mother." In answering questions, Bessie offered straightforward advice and sometimes recommended books by other writers as well as her own:

> It depends upon circumstances whether it is cheaper to purchase the baby's wardrobe ready made or make it at home. If you can sew neatly and have plenty of time, make the underclothing, at least, yourself. *A Baby's Requirements* gives the needful preparations for the comfort of the mother as well as the directions for meeting baby's requirements. *The Wife and Mother*, by Dr. Albert Westland, would be a useful book for you. *The Care of Children* fully covers all the points of which you speak.

Another example of her practical advice comes up in answering a letter from a distressed mother about the choice of a family name for a new baby:

> It is unfortunate that you are obliged to give your child a name that you dislike. If for family reasons this is imperative, can you not choose a nickname for everyday wear that pleases you? Few names offer as wide a choice in this matter as Elizabeth. The following are in common use: Eliza, Ellie, Bessie, Betsey, Bettina, Betta, Libbie, Lila and Lizzie. There is a baker's dozen to select from. Besides these Elsie, Lily and Elspeth are sometimes pressed into service.

Bessie must have been reasonably happy with her parents' choice of name for her as she was not reluctant to suggest its versatile qualities to her reader.

This has been a selective look at a small fraction of Elisabeth Robinson Scovil's contributions to *The Ladies' Home Journal* from 1891 to 1906—writing of consistent quality, full of inspiration and practical help for the thousands of loyal readers, and of great influence on many North American mothers and their children.

* * * *

In addition to her work as a journalist for *The Ladies' Home Journal*, Bessie was a key figure in the founding of *The American Journal of Nursing* in 1900 and *Canadian Nurse* in 1905. "Miss Elizabeth Robinson Scovil" was listed on the masthead of *The American Journal of Nursing* from its inception as one of five editors. Her great friend, Sophia I. Palmer, was the Editor-in-Chief from the beginning and for the following twenty years. The other three were Miss L.L. Dock, who wrote many books on nursing and the history of nursing, Miss Mary E. Thornton and Miss S.M. Durand. Bessie remained as an editor of *The American Journal of Nursing* for two full decades and retired from her post when Miss Palmer died in 1920.

For each monthly issue during that time, Bessie wrote an article entitled, "Notes From The Medical Press." She also contributed special articles from time to time. In a 1911 issue, entirely dedicated to Florence Nightingale, Bessie wrote of her unique experience with the revered icon. The publication marked fifty years since the founding of the first training school for nurses by Miss Nightingale at St. Thomas' Hospital in London, England. Bessie was in a position to enrich the issue with her personal comments and dramatic writing. I will look at this article in detail later in his chapter.

The date of Bessie's graduation from nurse's training and the course of her nursing and journalistic careers following graduation has always been a bit uncertain; fortunately for my research, an event in Fredericton, New Brunswick that I attended a few years ago, dispelled this uncertainty.

At a show-and-tell session of Fredericton women interested in antiquities, Hughena McNeil brought a box of family papers she inherited from an attic in Cape Breton, Nova Scotia when her last aunt died. Various members of her family had journeyed to the "Boston States" for work and education, which was common in the last half of the 19th century and well into the 20th. Among the papers in her box was a booklet, published in 1903, listing the graduates of The Nursing School at Massachusetts General Hospital in Boston. This little booklet answered two questions. In all the biographical sketches, obituaries and oral histories of my Great Aunt Bessie, no mention is made of the exact date of her graduation from The Nursing School, but here it was; "The Massachusetts General Hospital, 4th graduating class, 1880, Scovil, Elizabeth R.; occupation: In charge Infirmary, St. Paul's School; residence: Concord, N.H."

This information, printed in 1903, explains why Bessie was free to help look after her dying sister-in-law at Meadowlands, during the summer of 1903; St. Paul's School would not have been in session during the summer. My mother told me Aunt Bessie originally came for the summer only, but after the death of Harriet Lavinia in early September, she took a leave of absence from St. Paul's School and stayed on.

There is a reference in a newspaper article to her having been in charge of the Infirmary at St. Paul's at two different times, which this booklet confirms. We know that her first employment following graduation was at St. Paul's School. We also know this was followed by a well documented six year stint as the Superintendent of Nursing at the Newport Hospital in Rhode Island from 1890-1896. We now know she returned to her position at St. Paul's and was working there in 1903.

In addition to clarifying the sequence of Bessie's nursing employment, attending that show-and-tell meeting shed light on how she probably came to know Sophia Palmer, the founding Editor-in-Chief of *The American Journal of Nursing*. In that 1903 list of all the graduates of the Massachusetts General Hospital School for Nurses, Sophia I. Palmer is shown in the class of 1878, the year Bessie began her training. Sophia's occupation is given as "Editor-in-Chief, *The American Journal of Nursing* and her residence as Rochester, N.Y. Bessie and Sophia were not classmates in their training, but it is likely they met and became close friends through their mutual association with the Massachusetts General Hospital School for Nurses.

Before launching into Bessie's twenty year contribution as a journalist for *The American Journal of Nursing*, it is interesting to note what the editor wrote about her after only three years of work. In the October issue of 1903, the following appears under "Editorial Comment":

CHANGES IN THE JOURNAL STAFF

We regret exceedingly to announce to our readers the resignation of Miss Elizabeth R. Scovil as editor of the department of "Notes from the Medical Press." Miss Scovil is leaving her old home in New Brunswick to accompany her brother and his motherless family to a new home in the Far West, and she feels that the regular work and time which the department requires will be more than she can continue to give under the changed conditions of her life.

The editor of Medical Notes has not only to put her material into form for the press, but must examine a dozen or more medical journals each month and cull out such ideas or items as will be of special interest to nurses.

Miss Scovil's gratuitous work has been splendidly done, her copy always on time, and the *JOURNAL* makes full and grateful acknowledgement for the liberal service of such a high order of excellence that she as given to it for so long a time. We extend to Miss Scovil for the *JOURNAL* and its hosts of readers earnest wishes for great happiness in her new environment. Miss Scovil will make up the department for the November number and in that number we hope to announce her successor.

Luckily for everyone these plans to settle in the "Far West" were apparently abandoned and in an issue, a few months later, the following notice appeared under "Changes In the *Journal* Staff":

We announced some time ago the resignation of Miss Elizabeth R. Scovil as editor of the Department of Medical Notes. Fortunately for the *JOURNAL* Miss Scovil's plans were changed to some extent and she has been able to continue her work on the staff, her residence being now in St. John, N.B.

Taking up residence in Saint John may have been a brief consideration or it may have been a mistake on the part of the *Journal*. Bessie may have written to Sophie Palmer while visiting Robinson relatives and used a Saint John return address.

My mother never spoke of a move to the "Far West" as a possibility or intention. However, she was only seven in 1903 and her mother had just died, so plans like this may not have been mentioned to the younger children. Government advertising free land for farming settlers may have been temporarily attractive to Morris and Bessie. With the sadness of his young wife's death ever present at Meadowlands, Morris, may have thought about making a new start elsewhere. Their parents had both died and their youngest brother, Barclay, had settled in western Canada, employed as a government agent for distributing treaty money to Indigenous communities.

If at all, Bessie and Morris must have entertained the thought of a move for only a short time, which is just as well. Twenty years later Morris' son, Morris A. and family returned to Meadowlands after three years of crop failures on a farm near Selkirk, Manitoba. Although he had his World War I gratuity and a diploma from the Nova Scotia Agriculture College in Truro, the drought conditions at that time made it impossible to establish a new farm.

It is surprising to read that Bessie was praised for her "gratuitous work" for *The American Journal of Nursing*. Based on the evidence of her sharp eye in financial matters, it seems odd that she did not hold out for some remuneration. There may be several reasons why she did not press this point: 1) the Editor-in-Chief was a close friend, and for a new publication operated by women in 1900 funds would have been scarce; 2) her monthly contributions to *The Ladies' Home Journal,* which continued, must have brought in a comfortable sum and also enable her to acquire valuable stocks in the Curtis Publishing Company; 3) she had already sold several books to publishers on favourable terms and had the prospect of writing and selling still more; 4) the thought may have appealed to her that this gratuitous work would keep her name circulating in the nursing profession; 5) she may have thoroughly enjoyed researching a dozen medical journals each month and bringing new information and fresh ideas to the nurses that would assist in the upgrading of their knowledge and practice.

Following the announcement of "Changes in the Journal Staff" in 1903, another editorial contribution, titled "The Collaborators," announced a further development for the periodical. "Collaborators" were nurses who "represent the JOURNAL" wherever they live. Two new ones are welcomed and their responsible positions in the nursing world mentioned. One is in charge of the operating rooms at the Seattle General Hospital and the other is the corresponding secretary of the Nurses' Association in Detroit and responsible for nurses' registration in the State of Michigan.

Although Bessie was more than a "collaborator," this editorial gives a better understanding of her motives for being on the editorial staff for so long without financial compensation:

> We take this time to remind our collaborators that the JOURNAL looks to them for information on all nursing matters from their districts, and expects them to induce nurses especially to contribute to its literary pages. The office is not in any sense complimentary. It carries with it an obligation for the advancement of the profession. The collaborators are the JOURNAL'S special agents to stimulate nurses to literary effort, a department of progress in which it is often said nurses are very lacking. Such development is essential for professional growth, and this JOURNAL is the product thus far of the literary standards that nurses have attained, but it has been too much the work of a few rather than representative of the profession as a whole. One of the very important educational motives for the JOURNAL'S existence was to stimulate nurses to literary effort, and in promoting such effort the collaborators have been and must continue to be great factors.

These sentiments are entirely in accord with Bessie's beliefs and motivation. In many of her speeches and articles she took advantage of all opportunities to encourage, publicize, and ennoble the work of her beloved profession.

* * * *

During the twenty years Bessie was an editor of *The American Journal of Nursing*, her primary responsibility was to produce a several page section titled "Notes From the Medical Press" for each monthly issue.[10] During those years she also wrote twenty major articles, ranging over topics as varied as "Moral Influences of Superintendents and Head Nurses" to "Instructing Children in the Origin of Life," to "Use of Gelatin in Food for the Sick." When I read the index of the sixty subjects covered in "Notes," I was amazed at the spectrum of topics covered and can only imagine the vast number of items Bessie must have read in making her selections. There are too many to comment on but I want to glance at some of the topics Bessie thought nurses ought to be familiar with at the beginning of the 20th century.

Except for the years 1900-1903, when she was still working at St. Paul's School in New Hampshire, this research, selecting, culling, quoting, and paraphrasing for her "Notes" took place at her small, elegant, oak, desk with spiralled front legs, pigeon holes for letters and one long, thin drawer, the width of the whole desk, that opened with two handles, looking as though they were tassells dipped in brass.

I grew up with this desk and occasionally did my homework on it, always knowing it was "Aunt Bessie's desk" but having no idea how much work was completed on it. According to my mother, the desk sat on the second floor in a hallway nook under the peaked eves above the front door of the Meadowlands house. This location provided good daylight from side and front dormer windows. In many of New Brunswick's older houses this feature of construction is still a special nook, not shut off from the rest of the upper hallway but because of the sloping ceilings on either side capable of suggesting a private space.

One of Bessie's early "Notes" in *The American Journal of Nursing*, pinpoints how life threatening disease was treated in her time, before antibiotics:

---

10   All available on microfilm at the Harriet Irving Library at the University of New Brunswick.

TENT LIFE FOR CONSUMPTIVES – Dr. J. Edward Stubbert in an article of this subject in the "Medical Record" strongly advocates sleeping in the open air for the relief and cure of consumption. Patients who are obliged to remain in cities, he says, should sleep on the roofs of their houses when this is practicable, or at least in the open air. Some slight protection is necessary only in the case of rain. Heavy dew is not objectionable. He advises tent life whenever possible. Rugs may be admitted if they are exposed to sun and air everyday, but draperies should be avoided. The tent should be pitched on the edge of a wood for protection from wind and shade from heat, but not in the wood, to permit free circulation of air. A substantial tent may be occupied with benefit in winter even in a cold climate. A warm place to dress is desirable. Two tent colonies are to be established at Liberty, N. Y. In one the cost will not exceed ten dollars a week.

Liberty is a little distance north west of New York City, just south of the Catskill Mountains and in the early 1900s must have been a relatively small town. The uncontaminated air, benefiting from the nearby mountains, would make it an ideal setting for tent colonies. Sleeping outdoors or in tents was a common treatment for tuberculosis well into the 20th Century.

About the time Bessie chose this article, my mother, age five was sent to New York for a year to stay with her Aunt Addie and Uncle Jack, Bessie's brother. Someone was living at Meadowlands in a tent, in order to overcome T.B. I have not been able to discover the name of the patient, although I assume it was a relative. Little Mary was so inquisitive, I am sure no one was confident she could be kept out of that tent. The patient either died or recovered as Mary returned to her beloved Meadowlands, full of big city ideas, within a year.

Bessie's gleanings very often concentrated on the discovery of simple methods that were surprisingly effective. In the same issue as the previous article, "Inunction with Cod-Liver Oil" is a good example. "Inunction," a word no longer in use, means rubbing or massage:

> E.J. Kemp reports in the "Medical Standard" a case of a girl suffering from spontaneous dislocation of both knees who was pale, emaciated, weak and loose jointed, with a slight hacking cough and exaggerated respiratory murmur over both lungs. The family history was tuberculosis. After six-months' treatment with general massage and inunction with cod-liver oil the patient recovered perfectly. Another case of acute tuberculosis recovered under the same treatment, as did a third, a girl suffering from hystero-epileptic attacks following several bites by a dog.

Here, again, TB is lurking in a family history. Bessie selected many "Notes" on tuberculosis over the years, suggesting the prevalence of this killer in the early part of the 20th century. Though the first tuberculin tests were made on dairy cattle in Canada in 1892, mandatory testing was not in place until 1923. Though the use of "inunction" must have seemed an improbable method of healing for such diverse range of illness and health concerns, Bessie found it worthy of communicating to the nursing profession. The present day use of Reflexology, Reiki, and Therapeutic Touch as healthcare practices confirm her judgment in this regard.

The possibility of patients suing healthcare practitioners or institutions when they believe they have been injured by treatment or malpractice is an ever present hazard. Bessie chose the following "Note" to impress upon her readers that extreme care must be taken in all matters related to their profession:

> BURNING WITH A HOT-WATER BAG – A suit which is of interest to nurses has just been tried for the fourth time. The Boston "Medical and Surgical Journal" says Miss Helen Ward brought suit against

St. Vincent's Hospital to recover thirty thousand dollars damages for injuries alleged to have been received by improper treatment at a hospital. This resulted on March 21 in a verdict in her favor for nineteen thousand four hundred and twenty dollars, which includes an allowance for counsel's fees. Miss Ward, who is sister-in-law of ex-Judge Howland, had an operation performed on one of her legs while she was a private patient at the hospital, and after the operation a nurse carelessly allowed a hot water bag to remain in contact with the limb, in consequence of which, it was claimed, permanent injury had resulted. At the first trial of the suit the case was dismissed; the second resulted in a disagreement of the jury; on the third she secured a verdict of ten thousand dollars. The case was then appealed, and the Appellate Division reversed the judgment on the ground that the hospital was not bound to provide a patient, even though a private patient, with its best nurse, and ordered a new trial, which resulted as above.

Though most selections made by Bessie discuss technical discoveries or innovative approaches to the treating or curing disease, many are of general interest, aimed at the general education of the nurse readers. Here are two that fall into the latter category, the first from 1901 and the second from 1903:

THE WORLD'S DEATH RATE – The death-rate of the globe is estimated at 68 a second, 97,920 a day, or 35,740,800 a year. The birth-rate is 70 a second, 100,800 a day, or 36,792,000 a year, reckoning the year to be three hundred and sixty-five days in length. [no source mentioned].

NON-ALCOHOLISM IN GREECE – The "Greece Medicale" of Syria calls attention to the fact that although the use of light wines is almost universal in Greece, alcoholism is practically unknown there. The purity of the wine drunk is supposed to account for this. It is made exclusively from grapes, and so contains the most harmless form of alcohol. There was no word for alcoholism in the ancient Greek language, showing that the condition was unknown.

Bessie paid special attention to information on eye problems with which she had considerable personal and family experience. She knew that if left untreated, various forms of optical disorder can seriously affect a person's whole life. The following is one of Bessie's emphatic "Notes" on the subject:

THE VITAL IMPORTANCE OF DETECTION AND RELIEF OF EYE STRAIN – Ambrose L. Ranney, says the "New England Medical Monthly" presents a comprehensive series of conclusions and deductions, some of which are as follows: Eye-strain can be a potent factor in disturbing the normal development of both mind and body and in causing and perpetuating physical ills. Near-sightedness, when uncomplicated, causes little or no eye-strain. An imperfect centering of a strong myopic glass to the pupils may create great nervous disturbance, however, because of prismatic effects. Far-sightedness and astigmatism should be recognized early in life and corrected by glasses. Both cause an unnatural expenditure of nervous force in proportion to the extent of the defect. Maladjustment of the eye muscles may exist as an independent deformity. It is a most prolific cause of physical and mental ills. Imperfect mental or physical development is very apt to be associated with some type of eye-strain. No child should ever be allowed to begin its education without preliminary testing of the eyes and also of the eye muscles. The full amount of maladjustment of the eye muscles is not usually disclosed because sufferers of this class unconsciously acquire "tricks of adjustment." A very large proportion of eye defects are congenital. Eye-strain predisposes to the development of cataract and other eye diseases. The writer believes that many inmates of institutions for the feeble-minded, insane hospitals, and epileptic colonies owe to eye-strain their confinement or social ostracism. This statement is based upon careful clinical data. Legislative enactm*ent should compel an eye examination of every child before it enters the public schools.*

In addition, her own experience with headaches prompted Bessie to give this disorder and its treatment repeated attention:

HEADACHE AS A SYMPTOM – "The New York and Philadelphia Medical Journal" has an editorial on Dr. Ellis's paper on this subject. Dr. Ellis believes that sixty per cent of all headaches are due in a greater or less degree to some fault in the eyes. Those arising from this cause are oftener dull and heavy than very sharp. When they are not due to a diseased condition they are most commonly found in persons who make considerable use of the muscles of accommodation and convergence. When a person complains of headache after riding in a car, going to church or the theatre, or after shopping, it is reasonable to suspect the eyes. When headache occurs as the result of an ocular defect it almost always comes on within a few hours after the eyes have been taxed, but sometimes it holds off until the next day, especially when the eyes have been used to a considerable extent at night. In patients subject to attacks of sick headache, it is always wise to look for eye defects. They occur in about sixty percent of such cases, and their correction leads to amelioration and frequently to cure. Headache is common as a result of nervous exhaustion from almost any cause, and particularly from prolonged mental effort or worry. When it is caused by anemia it is general frontal. In congestive headache the pain is of a throbbing character. Toxic headaches are frontal and deep seated. Syphilitic headache is neuralgic and limited to the temples. Stomachic and hepatic headaches are usually occipital or vertical, but they may be frontal or general. Ocular headache must not be confounded with neurasthenic headache (in neurotic patients), which is probably toxic and continues after every source of peripheral irritation has been removed.

Occasionally, items from the medical press Bessie deemed worthy of being called to the attention of the nursing profession were truly offbeat and, in the case of the following "Note," we can say "sensational." While it is true, nurses need to be reminded that infection, no matter how spread, can lead to serious illness and even death, adding kissing to the list of high risk health concern is a cultural shock.

Was there a reason why Bessie chose to highlight the hazards of this practice? Was she subjected to expectations of embracing and kissing ancient relatives as a little girl? Did their beards and moustaches smell of tobacco mixed with the odours of insufficiently washed bodies? Did the much-plucked chins of invalid dames in stuffy rooms repulsively scratch the delicate face of childhood? My mother said Aunt Bessie was not physically affectionate with her. Was there some special reason for her aversion of this practice and for her now warning her readers of its grim possibilities? The following "Note" was published in 1903, shortly before Bessie returned to Meadowlands.

THE HYGIENE OF KISSING – "The New York and Philadelphia Medical Journal" has a synopsis of an article in "Revue de Medicine" on this subject:

Féré observes that kissing is not only an expression of sentiment; it is, in addition, the means for exciting and exalting it. The act of kissing produces a psychological excitation apart from all association of ideas by the simple fact of irritation of integument. Those portions of the face which are nearest the natural openings are the most sensitive, especially those portions which are contiguous to the lips and the extremity of the tongue. The teeth often enter the act of kissing, and especially is kissing unattractive if the lips are unsupported by teeth. If the nasal passages are impermeable or adenoids are present, the act of kissing is subjected to unfavorable conditions. The odor of tobacco and certain odors peculiar to certain individuals may render kissing repulsive. Among many savage tribes kissing is not practiced. It is a mark of treachery, of disapproval, or veneration, or of religious fervor. It is often the medium by which very infectious diseases are propagated, notably syphilis, hydrophobia, leprosy, pestilence, purpura [eruption of purple patches on the skin] itch, etc. The kissing of books or of religious relics is objectionable because unsafe.

Kissing may cause traumatism by the action of suction; thus the skin may be injured, the drum membrane of the ear may be ruptured, the eyelids may be wounded. Children who are compelled to kiss others may acquire such a repugnance to it as to result in painful impressions when they are forced to practice it. The effects of sexual perversions by this means are well known. In a word, kissing is accompanied not only with dangers of traumatism and infection but with those which are neuropathic, psychopathic, and moral. Promiscuous kissing should be suppressed, and it is especially desirable that such possibilities for evil should not be forced upon children.

Though no selection from the medical press for Bessie's "Notes" is without interest, space forbids a year by year survey. Moving to February 1910, she selects the following "Note," which also addresses an issue of public health:

> THE PUBLIC DRINKING CUP – The new periodical, "The Cup Campaigner" has made its début with the December number. The journal introduces itself as "A militant little paper published at intervals by persons striving to banish that most prolific medium for spreading disease — the public drinking cup; containing authentic reports of the rulings of health officials, the growth of public sentiment through the press, and other developments of the crusade." The editorial offices are at 115 Broadway, and the editor is Mr. Hugh Moore.

I am reminded of the little aluminum cup that sat beside a bucket of drinking water in my one-roomed school house in East Amherst, Nova Scotia in 1937. Twenty-seven years after Bessie and her fellow campaigners on this health hazard sounded the alarm, the message had not yet penetrated rural Nova Scotia. On a visit in 1986, I saw it had not reached Moscow.

Ten months later, in the December 1910 edition of *The American Journal of Nursing*, Bessie is able to quote from an unmentioned source that things were moving in the right direction in Boston.

> PUBLIC DRINKING CUPS BARRED – On October 1, the regulation of the Massachusetts State Board of Health forbidding the use of public drinking cups went into effect in Boston. Under the new rules no such cup can be used in any public park, street, or way; in any building or premises used as a public hotel, theatre, public hall or school; in any railroad car or station, steam or ferry boat. In many places the sanitary bubbling fountains have been installed.

I wonder what happened to all those public drinking cups? Some are probably gazed at in museums of bygone days in little country towns.

In the June 1910 of her "Notes," Bessie passes on this little gem:

> THE TRAINED NURSE – *The New York Medical Journal* says in the April [issue of] Red Book [Magazine], Dr. Regan plays a conspicuous part in "The Jewel Consistency" by Elliott Flower, who gives us this bit of philosophy: "Revolt against a good, trained nurse is quite impossible. You may defy a doctor, you may tell a male attendant to go to the devil, but the trained nurse with gentle firmness rules you absolutely."

In many editions, of her "Notes" Bessie appended a long list of "Current Literature of Interest to Nurses," which must have taken her no small amount of time to peruse and compile. This bibliographic flourish is yet another indication of her devotion to the ongoing education of nurses and the continuous upgrading of the nursing profession.

In the July 1911 issue of *The American Journal of Nursing*, Bessie included the following "Note" for the benefit of nurses, their clients, and their patients. We must bear in mind that 1911 was still within an era determined to mold the female form:

> GOOD AND BAD CORSETS – G. B. Somers describes in the *Journal of the American Medical Association* the requisites of a good corset as follows: "It is laced about the hips and holds in place independently of garters or straps. It supports the lower abdomen and reduces the hips. It has a straight front. It is only form-fitting or loose about the waist and bust. It does not diminish the waist measure. It laces from below upward by means of two or more lace strings. A bad corset exercises its greatest

compression about the waist and diminishes its measure from two to four inches. It is loose above the hips and held down by garters or by the tight lacing above."

If this advice needed to be given in a medical journal, think of what the fashion magazines must have been advocating! James Laver, in his book, *A Concise History of Costume* (1969, Thames & Hudson), writes the following about the period around 1911:

Fashion favoured the mature woman, cool and commanding with a rather heavy bust, the effect of which was further emphasized by the so-called "health" corsets, which is a laudable effort to prevent a downward pressure on the abdomen, made the body rigidly straight in front by throwing forward the bust and throwing back the hips. This produced the peculiar S-shaped stance so characteristic of the period.

It must have produced a lot of backache as well. No wonder the 1920s responded with straight, short dresses, lacking in waist definition with the boyish look of a flat bust. This was comfortable and easy to achieve if you were naturally slim, but women who were fashionably well endowed in 1911 had to be bound and their curves minimized to fit in with the expected silhouette. According to James Laver, the look was achieved with the help of the "flattener" intended to abolish the bust. This was a tubular under-garment, a type of loose-fitting corset.

*　*　*　*

The February 1911 issue of *The American Journal of Nursing* was devoted to a celebration of the life and work of Florence Nightingale. Producing this tribute issue of the *Journal* was a highlight of Bessie's twenty-year career as a contributing editor. She was in a unique position; she had several times met with and interviewed this tireless pioneer and promoter of the nursing profession and contributed a major article titled, "Personal Recollections of Florence Nightingale."

The recollections are fascinating for a number of reasons, but particularly because they settle speculation about what actually happened at these meetings. On the first visit, Tuesday, March 30, 1897, Bessie was shown into Miss Nightingale's bedroom, two flights of stairs up from the ground floor. She found Miss Nightingale's room to be quite unlike a typical room of the period. Victorian rooms in the 1890s were usually packed with brick-a-brac, the walls covered with pictures, tables with fringed cloths, stuffed birds under glass domes, patterned cushions, and wall paper and carpets adding to the confusion; curtains were, mercifully, often of plain, heavy velvet.

Expecting a room characteristic of the age, Bessie was surprised with what she found. Apparently, Miss Nightingale's progressive ideas on cleanliness had swept away all dust collecting clutter:

> The first impression was of freshness and brightness and bareness. No superfluous furniture, a screen between the bed and the door. Miss Nightingale was even at this time confined to bed with rheumatism and seldom left it.[11] Her face lighted with a welcoming smile as she held out the firm, strong, beautifully shaped white hand, whose tapered fingers had revolutionized the world of nursing, and took mine in it, bidding me welcome as a friend because I was a nurse. Across the head of her bed within easy reach was a shelf of books, and on her bed lay the little books which I had sent her. She took one of them up and began to talk about it, saying with a laugh, "I am so glad your book has not a skeleton in front."

---

11   It was not generally known at the time that she probably suffered from brucellosis, a bacteria born illness developed from eating insufficiently cooked beef from sick cows when she was in Crimea.

It was not clear what Miss Nightingale meant by that comment until I looked again at the letter she sent to Bessie two months later on May 28th to thank her for another of her books which had just arrived:

> We have tons of Nursing books: full of Technical and not Common Sense words; full of analyses of food ta da, (by which even Doctors themselves never guide themselves) copied from one another—full of Physiology (with a skeleton of course at the beginning. We want not a skeleton but a wholesome baby) also all the Physiological mistakes copied from one to the other—full of bacilli and all the fads of the present day—and not of cleanliness.

Such verve and wit and common sense permeate the expression of her views, so far advanced beyond most of those of the Victorian period. It is hard to imagine that these and other equally spirited comments in this letter were written by an elderly woman—seventy-seven was considered an advanced age in 1897—who had been an invalid for the past thirty years and confined to her bed for much of that time.

Bessie admits to "trembling with emotion and excitement" before a maid opened the door. Even after some conversation, her euphoria did not diminish. She writes:

> After a time the maid brought in the afternoon tea, an indispensable adjunct to an afternoon call in England. I drank the cup of tea poured out for me, but could not manage anything more solid, much to Miss Nightingale's concern. "Won't you have an egg," she said, "or something more substantial?" When I said, "Oh Miss Nightingale, I am too excited to eat!" she smiled, as if she could not understand what there was to be excited about.

The day before this visit, Bessie bought a photograph of Miss Nightingale at the London Sterescopic Company. She brought it to this first meeting and asked whether she would autograph it. "I always disliked having my photograph taken," she replied. "This one was done by the command of the Queen when I returned from the Crimea." Bessie responded by saying she had seen an excellent and more recent photograph of her. "I don't know when they got it, the villains," came the retort:

> After a few minutes she took the card up again, and twirling it in her fingers, said, "If I write my name on this, people will think I gave it to you." Seeing that she really did not want to do it, I bethought me of my birthday book, which I carried with me, and said, "Well, Miss Nightingale, if you won't write your name on the photograph, will you in my Birthday Book?" She gave a whimsical glance, a flash of the eyes which I have never forgotten. "Oh, you monkey," and wrote the coveted words.

At age eighty-five, in the last year of her life (1934), Bessie's memory of this incident was as sharp as ever as she recounted it to a reporter for a Greenville, South Carolina newspaper. (The reporter was preparing a story on Bessie's long nursing career in connection with her forthcoming address to the graduating class of a local nursing school.)

In August 2002, I had the great fortune to hold Aunt Bessie's precious Birthday Book in my hands and read through its memorable autographs while visiting my cousin, Anne Purdy, in Amherst, Nova Scotia. Like all Birthday Books of the time, it was a chunky, well-bound volume. It had been well cared for and was in remarkably good condition. Bessie died at the home of Anne's grandparents in England, my Aunt Madeline and Uncle Morris A. Scovil. Not only did Anne inherit this Birthday Book, with the historic signature, but a substantial photograph album, as well, with a collection of well labeled, sober Victorian faces, both of which affected me in a way that made it difficult to leave off my viewing of them.

Two years later, Anne brought both books to Fredericton, New Brunswick for a two-day visit, at which time the New Brunswick Provincial Archives photographed their contents. That was a fortuitous move. The Birthday Book later perished in a house fire and the photograph album was badly damaged. The *Amherst News* had been previously interested in the story of Florence Nightingale's signature and a photograph of Anne looking at the original and an enlarged reproduction of it over an article about the Purdy/Scovil family's possession of it has been preserved.

A Birthday Book was a clever way of collecting autographs under the date of the person's birthday that gave the owner a special record of friends and relatives' birthdays along with their signatures. Each page in Bessie's Birthday Book was headed with a short, appropriate, sentimental verse. In reading through the book, I recognized many names of family friends. Seeing the well-rounded script of my mother's young hand under January 10th gave me special pleasure.

As her first meeting with Florence Nightingale was drawing to a close, Bessie recounts an incident that underlines social distinctions still ingrained at that time but completely removed by World War I, if not before:

> "Do you mind carrying parcels?" she asked. I intimated that I did not consider carrying parcels derogatory to a nurse's dignity. She rang the bell and the maid appeared with an exquisite bunch of flowers — roses, heliotrope, and many others. Miss Nightingale put them in my hands and in a few minutes the interview was over.

Before reading these "Recollections," I assumed Bessie had visited England in the late 19th or early 20th centuries for a meeting of the Victoria Order of Nurses (VON), accompanying Lady Aberdeen, its founder, and wife of the Governor General of

Canada. However, this was not the case, though the confusion is understandable. The VON grew out of recommendations made by the Women's National Council, of which Bessie was an active member and Lady Aberdeen the first president. The Women's National Council was later renamed, National Council of Women of Canada. I wondered why the Victoria Order of Nurses, an entirely Canadian organization, would traipse off to England for a meeting; Bessie's "Recollections" cleared up my confusion on this matter. She writes:

> Two years afterwards [July 1899] I was in London during the international meeting of the Woman's National Council. Miss Nightingale, whose health had not improved in this interval, consented to see two of the many nurses who were present in London on this occasion. By the great kindness of Lady Aberdeen I was asked to be one of the two, but I felt that this, the highest honor that could be bestowed on a nurse, should fall to the lot of some one else, as the great privilege had already been mine. I was permitted to name the person who should take my place and requested to go to Miss Nightingale's house and make the arrangement for the change. I submitted the name of Mrs. Grace Neill, deputy inspector of asylums, hospitals and charitable institutions, Wellington, New Zealand, who had come twelve thousand miles to be present at this congress, as a recipient of the honour.

The meeting in England in 1899 that Bessie, Lady Aberdeen, and many Canadian nurses attended was a conference of the International Council of Women, of which the Women's National Council of Canada was a federated member. (The International Council of Women was founded 1893. The Canadian counter part established in 1896.) The confusion arose and persisted over the decades because Lady Aberdeen and Elizabeth Robinson

Scovil, co-founders of the Victorian Order of Nurses, and a large number of VON nurses attended the meeting. But, in fact, they were attending as members of the Women's National Council of Canada. This becomes clear as Bessie continues her "Recollections":

> I went again to No. 7 South Street, with a little less awe, but no less pleasure than on the first occasion. The maid went up and down with messages two or three times between the dining-room, where I was waiting, and the third story, and finally said, "Miss Nightingale will see Mrs. Neill on Tuesday at three and would like you to come on Thursday at the same hour." To say that I felt as if I walked on air but feebly expresses my exultation.

> I found her visibly aged since my last visit but still bright and interested in all the doings of the nursing world. The blue eyes still shone under the quaint white cap, and the bands of white hair framed a calm and tranquil face, but there were slight lapses of memory, questions repeated, which showed that the infirmities of age were beginning to creep on.

Florence Nightingale had been dealing with the infirmities of age for some time and had become adept at adaptations enabling her to remain active and functioning. As far back at 1867 she experienced pain in her eyes from time to time, especially after working at night. In 1885 she wrote to Dr. Sutherland, an influential member of the Army Sanitary Committee with whom she had worked for barracks improvement for many years. "Please remember I have no eyes, or rather I have eyes but they are neuralgic. You must not tell me to look in the book but mark the passages for me."[12] In 1901, only two years after Bessie's second

---

12   Woodham-Smith, Cecil, 1950. *Florence Nightingale.* London, Constable. (Many subsequent editions.)

visit, Miss Nightingale's sight failed to the extent that she was no longer able to read or write, except with the greatest difficulty.[13]

As late as 1903, Miss Nightingale engaged assistance to hide her reduced mental faculties from an important visitor.

> ...before Lord Kitchener called on her, Miss Nightingale sent her companion to look up all the facts about Lord Kitchener's latest policy and memorized them just before the interview. Lord Kitchener remarked, on leaving, that it was astonishing how Miss Nightingale in her old aged followed what was going on.[14]

Though mostly confined to her bed for years, she enjoyed occasional respites when visited by family or able to enjoy walks in a park. As Bessie observed, Miss Nightingale even devised a way of bringing the outside into her line of vision, and so into her life:

> When tea was brought she had a dish of crumbs put on the balcony before her window for the sparrows, and told me what pleasure and amusement she found in watching them as they came daily for the food.

Bessie was charmed by this small focus of thoughtfulness and delight. Here was a world famous expert on the training of nurses, on the improvement in sanitation in army barracks in India, on the management of poor houses and asylums, the "heroine of the Crimea," the confidant of Ministers of the Crown and Prime Ministers, revered by thousands second only to Queen Victoria having a plate of bread crumbs placed on her balcony for the sparrows. The capacity to think of the needs of others, even the small birds, remained with her, though other faculties dimmed. The rapport deepened between the two women who had made the advancement of nursing their life mission. Bessie writes:

---

13 Woodham-Smith, *ibid.*
14 Woodham-Smith, *ibid.*

> We talked long of many things and when I rose to take leave she said, "I suppose you won't be coming to London again before you sail." Something in her tone made me say, in a flutter of hope, "You don't mean that you would let me come and see you again, Miss Nightingale?" "I should like it very much if you would," was the reply. I altered my plans so as to return to London and bid her good-by.

Though Bessie was elated to have the unexpected opportunity to visit her idol for a second time, and even more unexpectedly for a third time, it is clear from this report the pleasure was not one sided. These two pioneer nurses had much to talk about of mutual interest. For example, parental resistance to their embarking on careers in nursing was remarkably similar, as the next paragraph of "Recollections" illustrates:

> On this occasion [the 3rd] we were talking of the change in the status of women in recent years. I said, "When I wanted to take up nursing, my mother said, "I would far rather see you a housemaid than a nurse." "Yes," said Miss Nightingale. "It was the same in my case. When I first talked of it my mother said, "Why don't you want to be a cook?"

This parallel of parental reaction to their chosen profession must have brought the two women even closer, each knowing the other understood much of their shared struggle.

Two years before this conversation, the Victoria Order of Nurses was founded in Canada under the leadership of Lady Aberdeen with help from Elizabeth Scovil. Miss Nightingale responded with great interest to the work of the VON. It was similar to what in England was called "district nursing." Bessie must have been pleased to find a project that she had worked to establish was of great interest to her heroine:

She was deeply interested in the nursing of the poor, and discussed district nursing with eagerness. She was then nearly eighty years old and still full of enthusiasm and vivid interest in the work. If the years had slightly impaired her memory, they had not dulled her feelings. The warm heart that was touched by the sufferings of soldiers in the trenches of the Crimea still responded to the cry of miserable humanity wherever it was heard.

Bessie's last two short paragraphs are a fitting close for her memories of those historic meetings and her signal contribution to this special edition of *The American Journal of Nursing:*

As I turned to leave her, she was leaning back against the pillow she so seldom left, her blue eyes shining, her sweet smile radiating her calm face, her last words a cheer and blessing.

The great heart is still, the beautiful hands are folded in last sleep, but surely of her it may be said more fully than of any woman known to history, "She doth rest from her labours and her works do follow her."

After these "Personal Recollections of Florence Nightingale" there is a piece of information the readers of *The Journal* would certainly have found appropriate, though a most unlikely coincidence. The writing style is so similar to Bessie's it is likely from her hand.

The gist of the paragraph is that one of the first persons in Canada to hear the message that Florence Nightingale had died was "one of our own pioneer nurses, Miss M.E.P. Davis." Miss Davis was visiting her niece, also a nursing graduate, a Miss E. Katherine White, whose husband, Mr. F. F. Ramsay, was the telegraph operator at Hazel Hill, Nova Scotia. He received the message at 9 P.M. on August 15, 1910 and immediately crossed over to his home and put it into Miss Davis's hands. "Before the news was made public over the continent, these two nurses were paying homage to her memory."

Bessie continued submitting her "Notes" on a monthly basis from 1911 every year through World War I and on into 1920. In the May 1920 issue she also contributed a nearly four page article entitled, "The Later Activities of Florence Nightingale." There are also additional manuscripts among Bessie's papers on the subject of Miss Nightingale: 1) "Florence Nightingale in Relation to Public Health Work," which was her speech to the Fifth District State Nurses Association of South Carolina on March 16, 1931; 2) "Reminiscences of the Early Days of Trained Nursing," her speech to the State Nurses' Association of South Carolina on April 10th and 12th, 1934, a few months before she died in England; 3) a forty-four page history titled simply, "Florence Nightingale," and 4) a twenty-one page manuscript also titled "Florence Nightingale," likely intended for a speech that at this late stage in her life was never given.

* * * *

On April 27th, 1920 Miss Sophia Palmer died of a cerebral haemorrhage, just five months short of twenty years as the original Editor-in-chief of *The American Journal of Nursing*, with her friend, Elizabeth Robinson Scovil assisting her all the way. The June 1920 issue contained much comment about Miss Palmer's life and work, ranging over many aspects of the nursing world. A money raising campaign could not be organized for a memorial as their beloved Miss Palmer had expressly forbidden it. She believed nurses were called upon to make financial contributions too often and too much. The Editorial Comment in the June issue suggested that "entirely voluntary" contributions to the Nurses' Relief Fund in her name "would please Miss Palmer better than any other [memorial]."

From her antique oak desk under the Meadowland's eves, Bessie continued to February, 1921 when her last "Notes from the Medical Press"—restricted to one page—was published. "Editorial Comment" in the July issue reported that "Notes from the Medical Press and Book Reviews will be discontinued in their present form. ..." Then, after praise for the editors of the each department the following was added:

> Miss Scovil is the hardest to give up, for she has been longest with us, having been a contributor to the first issue of the JOURNAL and a member of our staff ever since. For many years she did her work with no compensation, as did all the earlier department editors, and she was as dependable as the sun.
>
> She will continue always a close friend of the JOURNAL and will occasionally contribute to its pages. Many who love to read her contributions may still follow her in the pages of *Canadian Nurse*, where she conducts two departments.

* * * *

Canadian Nurse was established in 1905. Elizabeth Robinson Scovil became a contributing editor in 1912. She served in this capacity for twelve years, writing two columns for each monthly issue. In addition, she composed three major articles during this time that were published in *Canadian Nurse*.

"The Care of Nurses" was a major presentation Bessie made to a meeting of The Canadian Society of Superintendents of Training Schools for Nurses and was published in 1915. "The Ethics of Nursing" was an address she delivered to the 1917 convention of the Canadian National Association of Trained Nurses in Montreal and was published the same year. "The Responsibility of the Nurse to Her Nursing Journal" was published in 1918 and appears to have been written in an effort to increase the written contributions of Canadian nurses to their national periodical.

Bessie did her best to stimulate interest in *Canadian Nurse* through contributing two columns in each issue: "News from the Medical World" and "The World's Pulse." Here is an example of the former taken from the February 1921 issue:

Heat as a Preventive of Shock

In a letter to a medical journal from a surgeon practicing in Korea, he states that cases of shock following operation are very few in his practice. Chloroform is the anaesthetic used. He attributes absence of shock to the practice of placing patients on the hot floor common in Korean houses. The floor is of stone, covered with mats and over this a thick layer of paper like linoleum. The floor is heated by smoke from the fire for cooking passing beneath it. Could not a system be devised by which hot air could be conducted to the under part of beds used by patients immediately after an operation?

"The World's Pulse" is filled with paragraphs of surprising news and dramatically reflects Bessie's wide ranging interests in the progress of science, technology, politics, economics, and the activities of societies around the world. Here are two examples:

Rocket Airplanes

Among the secret machines which the French Government is preparing to test is a man-carrying aircraft which has neither engine nor propeller. In the hull is an apparatus which produces gas under pressure in a combustion chamber and sends it backward into the air through specially designed nozzles. The reaction will drive the rocket airplane forward at great speed.

Bolshevists and Books

It is stated that the Soviet Government has resolved to abolish the right of private ownerships of books in Russia. All existing literature will be appropriated by the State, and in future it will be illegal for private individuals to acquire or continue to own a book.

These are typical of Bessie's informative snippets, quickly read, easily digested and perhaps made use of at a future date, if only to increase general knowledge. The latter report about the abolition of private book ownership in Russia sounds a bit odd and for which there is no subsequent evidence. She may have picked this up from alarmist, anti-Russian propaganda.

Bessie continued with her two columns until 1924. Helen Randal, the Editor since 1916, also retired at this time. In announcing this change, she announced Bessie's retirement as well.

> With the change of Editor and place of publishing the magazine [from Vancouver to the National Office in Toronto] comes the close of a series of contributions from Miss Elizabeth Robinson Scovil, who for so many years in *The American Journal of Nursing* and in our own *Canadian Nurse* magazine, has so willingly and…done what she could for us, and without any remuneration. To the Editor she has been most helpful, her contributions always to the point and what we as nurses needed to know, and as well she has been unique in her promptness in sending in her material. All her work had to be sent in in long-hand; but even with this handicap she always had it in the office in plenty of time for publication, and one never had to worry for fear it would be too late or come in at the eleventh hour.
>
> To the Editor, personally, she has always been most sympathetic and is among those whose friendship has been formed during the difficult pioneer days of the magazine.

The reasons for Bessie's retiring are unclear. It may be she did not want to start again with a new editor, or it may have more to do with the changes in her personal life. By September 1924, Bessie and her brother, Morris had moved from the farm at Meadowlands to Fredericton.

Roger Scovil, Morris's youngest son and Bessie's nephew, had moved to Greenville, South Carolina where he was working with his maternal uncle in his nursery business. Mary, Morris's youngest daughter, Bessie's niece, and my mother, had eloped. Within less than two years Bessie and Morris had sold their Fredericton house and would begin their semi-annual trips across the Atlantic. In the summer they resided with his son, Morris A. Scovil, and family in England and in the winter with Roger and family in South Carolina.

Though Bessie could have continued for another year or so with her columns in *Canadian Nurse,* the nomadic life which was in the planning would have made prompt filing difficult. She may have thought that the end of the editor's reign was a good time for her to retire from the schedules of regular journalism. However, at seventy-five she was by no means finished writing or giving speeches to rooms full of nurses, and continued to do so up to 1934, the year she died.

In addition, she began a new, creative, venture for the entertainment of her great nephew, Richard, and two great nieces, Courtenay and Ann, children of Morris A. and Madeline Scovil, with whom she was staying when she died. This new literary endeavour was the composition of ten, one-page, children's stories. Each story is exactly one page. She might have had some idea of adding to the collection and publishing them in a little book, similar to one she had previously launched. However, her final stories were very much geared to the resident children, for instance one being called "Ann's Cat." These stories were among the papers of Bessie's I photocopied before they were destroyed in the house fire suffered by Ann Purdy, Courtenay's daughter.

This overview and sampling of Elizabeth Robinson Scovil's journalistic production partially chronicles this aspect of her multi-faceted career. Fortunately, the Harriet Irving Library at the University of New Brunswick and the New Brunswick Provincial Archives, both in Fredericton, have holdings that make possible the studying of her writings in greater depth by anyone who might want to do so.

Chapter Six

Letter Writer

Although other chapters look mainly at segments of my Great Aunt Bessie's life based on various published sources, there is also much to be discovered in her letters and from those by others in my possession.

For example, less than three years after Bessie's family moved to the farm at Scovil Point, the tradition of hospitality was well established. According to a letter Bessie wrote to her brother, "Dearest Jack" at 10 & 12 Thomas St., New York, NY on January 14, 1883, a dozen or more Gagetowners attended "our tea party" before she returned to her position at St. Paul's school after her Christmas holidays:

> I could not prevent Mother from breaking [?] out into our tea party. We had Mrs. DeVeber, Emily, Gabe, Mrs. Neales, Helen and Ferris, Bate, the Peters and Lucy. It went off quite festively for a Gagetown party. We were at tea at Mrs. DeVeber's when Jack and Sue [Robinson cousins] were here and are going there again on Tuesday night when I believe there is to be a dance. [The DeVebers lived in a very large house, still standing and inhabited, at the far end of Gagetown and were also descended from Loyalists.]

She continues about travel plans:

> I wish very much I could see you and Addie for a day or two. Mr. & Mrs. Coit [Headmaster of St.

Paul's School and his wife] spend Sunday next in New York and wanted me to join them there but I could not spare the time besides the extra expense. Mrs. Kingsbury [very wealthy Scovil-born relative] has sent me a pass from Boston to Waterbury and return so my visit to them adds nothing to the cost of travelling. I expect to arrive there on Sunday and leave on Tuesday reaching St. Paul's the same night.

Bessie lists some of the presents she received, presumably while she was still at the school, but not before she expressed pleasure to her brother, Jack, that the paper knife he had sent her arrived safely. The Head Master and Mrs. Coit were obviously appreciative of Bessie as she regularly mentions them in a positive light. "Mr. and Mrs. Coit gave me a handsome lamp for my drawing room. The gas is high and hurts my eyes if I attempt to work or read by it." Perhaps she could not work from the light, but she could use it for background lighting. "I also got a nice leather case with three pairs of scissors. Lucy Pickett gave me a pretty thermometer on a stand of white and which she painted with fuchsias." Lucy P. is an old friend from the Kingston Peninsula, N.B. who began training at the Massachusetts General Hospital the year Bessie graduated, 1880, so would have also graduated by this time. They collaborated on the Pickett-Scovil Memorial Fund to provide retired Anglican clergy and their families with medical care in later years and remained friends until Lucy's death in 1910.

Bessie's mother was obviously not well and may have been spending some time in bed but determined not to miss the gaiety of visitors. "Mother is much better since I came. I make her take a tonic which has improved her appetite and brought her some sherry that has also had a good effect." Her father also remained less than well. "Father seems much the same as in October. He has a tolerably good appetite and I do not think is weaker than in the autumn."

On March 24th of the same year, Bessie writes again to Jack from St. Paul's. Other than thanking her brother "many, many times for the lovely Easter card you sent me…the design and the birds are so beautiful," the letter is full of illness of one sort and another. "I hope Addie is all right again now and that she will take great care of herself in future. Write me a line soon to tell me how she is." Two days later she writes directly to "Dearest Addie" who may have had a miscarriage, though no explicit reference is made. The nearest she comes to the word "pregnant" is, "I am very glad to hear of your prospects. You must take great care of yourself. Mother once had a similar experience and came out all right after all." Then she adds,

> I have made up my mind that I MUST see you this summer and I will spend a week with you either at the beginning of the holidays, in June, or at the end of them, the first of September, whichever you would like best. Mother must have had quite a sharp attack. I had a note from Mod [brother, Morris] which I enclose as giving the most trustworthy account of her condition. She always makes light of an illness for fear of alarming me.

She does not give her mother's "sharp attack" a name, but perhaps a heart attack. Her father's poor health was never given much of a description, though he was dead before 1883 came to an end.

This same letter includes two more tales of illness, first, her own—"I have one of my old headaches today and can scarcely hold my head up,"—and then one of the school boys:

> The son of the Hon. Stanley Matthews, Judge of the Supreme Court (US) is here, ill with pneumonia. His mother and sister have come to take care of him and a pair of more ill bred, unreasonable lunatics it has never been my bad fortune to meet. Luckily Dr. Coit is as much disgusted with them as I am. They abuse the Infirmary and everything connected with it in

most unmeasured terms. Well, it is all in a life time, but I wish the experience was over.

A follow up to that vivid little picture appears in another letter two days later:

> The Matthews lunatics have calmed down a little and I hope will be able to get off tomorrow. I am now the most delightful person in the world and the dear little boys whose lot is cast in the Infirmary the most fortunate of mortals!!

Though Bessie was only thirty-four and in her first position, she did not let unsuitable behaviour on the part of an influential parent depress her. She writes nothing about not being cut out for this type of work, but looks at the situation philosophically and with humour. More humour is lightly sprinkled throughout another letter, shortly afterward:

> Dearest Addie,
> I meant to have sent you a card [Easter] but could not get into town to find one and if one of my friends had not taken time by the forelock and sent me one in the middle of Lent which I transferred to Mother, I should have had none to send her.

Recycling greeting cards was a common practice at this time. Rural shops were poorly stocked and often distant. Women normally did not have their own incomes. Frugality was a prized virtue and recycling was a natural outcome. In Bessie's case, St. Paul's School was on the outskirts of Concord, New Hampshire and would have required an expedition into town. My mother's Aunt Lizzy DuVernet was known for her recycling of cards, without much vetting of original content. The story goes that one recipient was astonished to read some derogatory remarks about her, which the previous sender had written and Aunt Lizzy had neglected to remove. Aunt Lizzy's hand writing on an envelope was a cause for apprehension.

Card sending at Easter was especially popular as well as gift giving. In this same letter, March 26, 1883, Bessie writes the following to Addie:

> Mrs. Henry Coit gave me beautiful flowers, one of the masters brought me violets and another Florida oranges from a box that had been sent to him. I fared very well. Jack's mention of my poem was my first intimation of its having appeared in print. I am glad he liked it. Tell Jack that I have all the verses I have written pasted in a book but do not know in what numbers of the Churchman they appeared. They are well enough for a newspaper but not worth preserving.

Not only did the Head Master's wife give Bessie flowers but two of the masters *brought* her violets and oranges, rather than asking a school servant to deliver them with a note, which suggests they wanted to cultivate a closer association with the nurse in charge of the school's infirmary. Eligible women were in short supply in this almost all male school. She must have weighed the pros and cons of whether she was attracted to or could consider becoming attached to one of these well-educated men as opposed to excelling in her career. She knew she could not have both. Her nursing profession and her talent for writing, which was responsible for her eventually becoming a millionaire, might have been all but smothered if the gifts and attention of either of these two men were encouraged.

The poems she mentions in a self effacing manner are her early efforts at publishing her poetry in *The Churchman* magazine. I scoured appropriate copies of the magazine at the British Museum, in London, with no success. I then learned there was a New York publication of the same name and period, which I also thoroughly investigated, but without success in locating Bessie's first published poetry.

Being in charge of the school infirmary was not just dealing with expected illnesses and the occasional case of something more serious, like the Matthews boy with pneumonia. Again from her March 26th letter:

> There is a crowd of visitors here as there always is at Easter. One of the others staying at the Infirmary has gone to the exhibition of gymnastics tonight and the other is quiet so I am enjoying a few moment of leisure. I had cards from most of my recent patients who have gone home and a lovely one from the friends of the little boy who died.

So Bessie also had to act as a hostess to sometimes demanding parents as well as cope with the rare death of a boy, either under her care or after he returned home. In this short sentence there is no indication of which, but most likely in the infirmary.

Bessie finishes this letter with more proof of her appreciation for small gifts:

> When you feel able do write me a few lines and make Jack keep me posted by at least a note every week. I forgot to thank him for the stamps. With best love to him and yourself. Ever dearest Addie, Your loving sister, Bessie."

In the next letter I have, dated December 18, 1883, she addresses "Dearest Jack":

> I drove into town today and feel better for the air. There are no other boys in the house so I am not over worked.…Thank you and Addie, you dear, extravagant, wildly generous people for your lovely present of the cap. I always longed for one so much and I shall be provided with winter headgear for a

lifetime. It was very, very good of you both to think of it. I wish I could kiss you on the spot. ... If I do not hear until Thursday 27 perhaps you can still send my cap to Boston to wait me there. You see I am loath to go home without it.

Though this letter was written at St. Paul's just a week before Christmas, it appears that she plans to go home to Meadowlands for part of the holiday.

Apparently, they had not yet sent Bessie's Christmas present, but they did mail something for Jack and Bessie's mother for her to take to Meadowlands. Perhaps this was because all mail had to be collected from Gagetown and if the river ice was not yet safe for travel, the present's arrival would be delayed. Bessie is enthusiastic about their choice for their mother, too.

> The mantel cloth is beautiful. I am sure Mother will be charmed with it. The mantel piece is so hideous it will be a blessing to have it covered. Mod will have no difficulty arranging it, you have provided everything so nicely.

The mantle cloth would have had scalloped edges and embroidery and possibly a fringe much loved by Victorians who enjoyed living among clutter and multi-patterned decorations. The mantle had escaped this ornamentation for more than three years, but all appeared to rejoice that the "hideous" aspect was now to be covered.

Bessie's letter to Jack continues:

> Thank you a thousand times for the lovely card and box of candy. You know pink is my favourite color. ... Mother will like Mr. Crawford's new book... I think it is much the best of his works. Did you know he was an old St. Paul's boy?

Mother asked me to get a book for you and Addie and has sent the wherewithal. Has Addie read *A Little Pilgrim?* I thought of Macaulay's *Lays of Ancient Rome* for you, you used to be so fond of them, or *The Lady of the Lake* or *Marmion.* Write me which you would rather have, or if there is any other you prefer. Mrs. Kingsbury sent me a lovely little edition of George Herbert's poems, an English one in pale greenish grey binding. She is always so kind to me.

Mrs. Kingsbury [1828-1899] was Alathea Ruth Scovil whose father founded the Scovil Manufacturing Co. in Waterbury, Conn. In 1851 she married Frederick John Kingsbury who became president of the company in 1868. She was always well off and generous to Bessie, which is mentioned in various letters.

Books were very important to Bessie. She was clearly surrounded by them. When Meadowlands was sold many of Bessie's books were transported to my family's home five miles outside Amherst, Nova Scotia. As a small child, I remember many dark book cases, some with glass doors, lining the walls of our living room filled with these books, some of them almost too heavy for me to lift.

There is a gap of one year and two months until the next letter in my possession. It was written on January 18, 1885 from Meadowlands to "Dearest Jack." Bessie's opening paragraph is full of indignant steam:

I should like very much to know what become of all my letters to you. I wrote a joint letter to you and Addie, enclosing my photograph a few days before Christmas, a long letter to you, describing how we spent the day immediately after Christmas and another to Addie after our return to Fredericton, none of which seem to have reached you. I am sure they were all posted so they must have miscarried on the way.

Clearly she thought there was no excuse for leaving correspondence unacknowledged and unanswered. It was that important to her. Perhaps Bessie should not be so incredulous at their lack of replies. The young couple must have been completely taken up with the birth of their first child at this time. In spite of this indignant opening, Bessie continues with a letter more than twice as long as usual, full of details of family news:

Although, on January 18th of 1885, the St. John River was still open half way across, isolating Meadowlands from Gagetown, Bessie and her family were by no means cut off from the world's news and opinions. She recounts news from a recent trip to Saint John.

> Aunt Sophie read us Will's last letter [a nephew]. He seemed very jolly and expected to be sent to a town in the north of England where Armstrong guns are made, to study mechanical engineering. He hopes eventually to go to India. If he had not been out here [probably on leave] he would have been sent to the Sudan.

Bessie then reviews the newspapers and magazines that were sent on regular rounds to family members.

> If you care to see *The Standard* we will send it to you every week. I cannot but thank you for all the papers, dearest Jack. The *Bazar* [*Harper's Bazar*] goes to Mary after we have read it and *The Century* to Uncle Mod who then sends it to Pine Grove. ...Uncle Mod sends us *Harper's Magazine*.

Each copy of *The Century* would have been read by at least four households. She then adds:

> I want you to send me *A Beleaguered City*. It is by Mrs. Oliphant and is priced at 10 cents. There is no hurry, get it sometime when you are in a book store.

Dr. Coit says it is one of the most beautiful specimen of English he has ever seen and I should like to read it.

Bessie includes a little local church news as she is winding down her unusually long letter:

Mr. Hatheway [Rev. C.H. Hatheway, first rector of Saint James' Church in Jemseg] is still delicate and has obtained three months leave of absence from the Bishop to recover. A Mr. Raymond is to take his place. They are coming to tea tomorrow evening—roast turkey, scalloped tomato. I wish you were to be here! [Clearly "high tea" since meat is being served.]

She continues:

Dearest Jack how nice it would be if we lived nearer one another so Addie and I could be of some use to one another as sisters and we could all enjoy the dear, darling baby. Some year you must take your holiday in winter and Christmas here. [at Meadowlands, where Bessie regularly spent her long winter break from St. Paul's.]

The penultimate paragraph of this letter, for the first time, contains explicit reference to a health problem of Bessie and Jack's mother. "Mother is looking very well, really quite fat, she still feels the pain in her knee at times. She has generally an excellent appetite." The last paragraph adds farm news: "We have a new calf. Very early is it not?" She ends with effusive affection, "Worlds of love from mother to you all. Many kisses to the darling. Ever dearest Jack, your loving sister, Bessie."

The next letter to Jack is dated March 10, 1885 and includes farm news from Meadowlands. Bessie must have been on an extended break from her nursing duties at St. Paul's.

We are all well here and going on as usual. Mod killed a beef last week and sold two quarters. The other two we keep for our own use. He thinks of putting off his visit to Fredericton until next week. They will finish hauling out the barn frames in two days. As soon as the travelling breaks up and they cannot work elsewhere the men will come to hew it. ...

We like the girl we have very much and would keep her if she were strong enough for the washing. She will do very well for Addie. She is careful and has nice, quiet manners. Agnes, who is to come the first of April has written to say she must have eight dollars a month. There is no help for it, she is indispensable.

The "girl" going to work for Addie and Jack in New York will be joining the increasing flow of single girls from the Maritime provinces migrating to Boston and New York during this time for domestic, retail, and later, office employment. In 1885 there was no barrier for a Canadian who wished to work in the US, so Bessie could decide "she will do very well for Addie."

Bessie was thirty-six when she wrote this letter to her brother, an age when she undoubtedly knew she would not marry and become a mother. References to her first born nephew are always filled with longing to see him and unconditional delight in his existence:

We shall all think of the dear, darling boy on his birthday. I wish to send him something lovely for it, trust me! Oh if we were only near enough to see him often what a great pleasure it would be. I do wish, dearest Jack, you were coming to spend the summer, too, that would make it perfect and I am afraid poor Addie will be very homesick without you.

Apparently, plans had been made for Addie and baby DeLancey to spend the summer at Meadowlands although Jack would remain working in New York. Bessie frequently expresses her wish that they all lived closer to one another. Admittedly, it was a compliment to them both and to their offspring, but had Bessie been intent on seeing them more often she could have sought a position in New York when she became free to do so. Instead, by the fall of 1888 she was settled at the Newport General Hospital in Rhode Island as Superintendent of Nursing and in charge of the nurses' training school, which was still a considerable distance from her New York family. It is not hard to see why she made this choice; a senior position at the Newport Hospital and its nurses' training school was a highly desirable step in advancing her professional nursing career.

* * * *

Brother Mod (Morris) and Harriet DuVernet married on September 12, 1888, and settled in to living at Meadowlands. This allowed Bessie to return to her beloved profession, with twice yearly visits to the farm to see her mother, who lived until November 1894, and, soon, her brother's growing family. There is no impatience in her letters at needing to remain in New Brunswick for a few years when her mother was declining, and until Hattie took over the job of being the head of the household at Meadowlands.

But in 1885 this was all well in the future. I have five more letters from Bessie while she was continuing to live at Meadowlands: two are to her youngest brother, Barclay (November 21, 1885 and February 26, 1888); two are to Addie (January 1, 1888 and March 4, 1888); two are to Jack (March 2, 1887 and January 8, 1888). All these letters are filled with local news, weather, freezing and thawing of the St. John River, details of tea parties, illnesses, and farm activities. The letters to Barclay, who was only eighteen in 1885 and working in New York, were concerned with his general health and having sufficiently warm clothing and suitable boots for winter.

Bessie scarcely mentions Barclay, in the thirty-four letters I have, except in the two addressed to him. He continued to live at

Meadowlands from 1880 until he moved to New York, probably not much before her November 1885 letter. Barclay worked for an importing and exporting firm on Broadway for nearly two decades. Considering the frequency of family letters flying back and forth in those days and the details of activities of relatives, I am sure there would have been many references to little brother Barc in the many dozens of Bessie's letters not preserved.

In the November 21, 1885 letter to Barclay, Bessie writes:

> It would be as well for you to be vaccinated only you ought to have it done soon so as to be entirely well before Xmas, but I never told you there was any connection between vaccination and scarlet fever, you must have dreamed it.

> How do you like the new Society you have joined? I made some crullers today and only wish you were here to enjoy them. I am so glad you can go to Jamaica [to the home of Dr. Barker, Addie's father, in Jamaica, New York] for Christmas instead of having to spend it alone. You will not mind Thanksgiving so much as we never celebrated it.

> Mrs. Gabe [DuVebber] asked to be particularly remembered to you and says she misses you very much. She is not at all well and has no companion yet.

> I am glad your finances are so flourishing. How kind good, dear Jack is to you in sending stamps and in every possible way. What have you done about winter boots? With best love, Ever dearest Barc. Your loving sister, Bessie.

Seven years after the move from Pine Grove to Meadowlands, Morris, Bessie's second eldest brother, is definitely having success with horse breeding. In her letter to Jack on March 2, 1887, Bessie reports on this development and the prospect of additional funds for investment:

> The severe storms last week have made the travelling heavy and we have decided not to go to Fredericton. There is some uncertainty when the meeting of the Govt. takes place and Mod could not be present at it even if we were on the spot so we will wait until they are pleased to communicate their decision to us. I do hope they will give us the full amount claimed. I know if Mod had the capital to begin with he would soon make a good living from horses. He has nine now and has a new brown colt, and Nora, the black colt which he raised himself this winter. They will be fine, powerful mares when they are full grown. He is going to take Nancy to S. John next week and sell her if possible. She is rather a light horse for our work and is now in good condition to sell if he can get a fair offer for her. I may drive down with him if the roads and weather are good.

It is likely the full amount claimed was paid—whatever the nature of the claim was. Morris expanded his horse breeding and horse sales, which prospered to the point that he hired a groom from Scotland to live on the farm and take over the care and management of the stable.

The letter to Jack continues with domestic news:

> We have just changed servants and got back a girl who lived with us before and whom we liked then. I am sorry Addie is having so much trouble with cooks. Mary was a great loss. I hope Annie is tranquil.

Although I have not seen the letter to brother Jack and Addie that contained the announcement of Mod and Hattie's engagement, clearly there had been one. Jack responded with a need for more details about the DuVernet girl. Although Hattie grew up just across the river from Meadowlands, Jack moved to New York directly from Pine Grove, so did not have an opportunity to become acquainted with the Gagetown families. "You ask about Hattie," writes Bessie and then gives a physical description:

> She is a very pretty girl with nice eyes and complexion, hair lighter than Addie's, a straight nose, good mouth and teeth. She is just as tall as Mod, well built but not fat. She looks strong and in good health. She seems very fond of him and I think it bids fair to be a happy match. She has no photo in the least like her and must wait until she can go to S. John to have some taken.

If I had been the recipient of this letter, I would have appreciated reading something about Hattie's personality, as well as this somewhat clinical description; was she vivacious or shy, dreamy or practical? She was twenty-two. Her middle name, Lavinia, was in honour of her father's sister who was born in Ceylon (now Sri Lanka).

Harriet Lavinia was the fourth of six siblings born to her mother, the former Miss Susan Starr of Saint John, and her father, Henry James DuVernet. Harry, as he was known locally, was also referred to as The Squire. After his first wife, Harriet's mother died, The Squire and his second wife, Miss Pricilla Buzza, were well on their way to producing six more offspring by 1888, so Hattie was probably adept at fitting in to whatever circumstances were presented.

Hattie, my grandmother, was indeed pretty, though I have seen no photos of her smiling. A studio photograph required subjects to remain motionless for some time, so a sober expression was usually the result and certainly is on all faces in the family portraits I have, probably taken in the spring of 1903. The outdoor snapshot taken of the family a little later in the same year, when Hattie was pregnant and ill with pregnancy-onset diabetes, also produced serious expressions on everyone.

By the time of this 1887 letter to Jack, he and Addie have had a second son. Bessie's letter makes it clear that Addie and the two boys, DeLancey and Charlie, will be spending at least some of the summer at Meadowlands. Bessie hopes Jack will be able to join them for part of the time. She ends the letter with; "Kisses to the two boys from me. I am longing to see them again. I wonder if DeLancey will remember me." She adds what seems like a note of longing for a more sophisticated life. "I wish I could have gone with you to the *Taming of the Shrew*. Ever dearest Jack, your loving Sister."

Nearly ten months later, on January 1, 1888, and no doubt with many letters in between, Bessie writes to "Dearest Addie," chiefly about their recent Christmas celebrations and planned tea party. Bessie then relates a list of presents, a very common practice when writing to family members:

> Mother gave me a pair of moccasins for snow shoeing; Mod and Barc, *The Material Friend*; Mrs. Kingsbury, the Coits, Miss Sangster, Sarah Robinson, and Fay sent me books; Hattie gave me one too; Grace gave me a photo-frame and we had twenty one cards. Mother got three books, two tiles for teapot stands, and Hattie gave her a stand for holding yarn to wind. Willie sent her a case of knitting needles. Mrs. Symonds sent me the *Ill. London News,* Xmas eve, and a friend in Boston a subscription to the *Church Record*.

Anyone acquainted with Bessie would have no trouble choosing a present, knowing of her great love of books. In spite of having nine guests for a tea party "tomorrow evening" all is apparently under control and Bessie has time to continue her long letter. She lists those invited:

> Mr. and Mrs. Tom Peters, their governess Miss Ritchie, plain but charming, Miss Kati and Susi Peters, Miss Mary DeVeber, Hattie, Gabe (DeVeber) and Mr. Hatheway (clergyman at Jemseg), Everything is ready

for it is rather an undertaking to give a party without a servant to do as much as possible beforehand.

We see in this list the Victorian habit of formality even when writing to close relatives. The naming of adults without their titles only came into wide use after World War II. Why did Bessie go to all the trouble of having this tea party, having to prepare for it herself, with limited help from her mother? Partly, she was paying back hospitality received from the Peters and the DeVebers, but also it may have been to show Hattie what was expected of her after marriage to Mod in a little more than eight months.

Bessie was demonstrating that being between servants or having one suddenly leave should be no reason for a dull life. Hattie is clearly being considered as nearly one of the family and was probably already spending time across the river from her parental home in Gagetown becoming familiar with how the domestic pattern at Meadowlands is arranged. She would have also become well acquainted with Addie the previous summer and they may have established a sisterly affection for one another. Once Mod and Hattie were married, and Hattie would become the woman of the house, Bessie could return to nursing.

The next of Bessie's letters was written only seven days later, this time to Jack, with some repetition, but much which enlarges the picture of Bessie's life at Meadowlands:

> We are in the middle of a thaw again. Mod has just gone to Gagetown to bring Miss Ritchie and Hattie to tea and to go to Church with us this evening. We shut up the house this morning and went to Gagetown… Poor old Mr. Armstrong looks almost too feeble to hold himself up, much less conduct the Service but he got through very well. … If we have enough snow to make good travelling, Mod and Mr. Hatheway are going to put their horses together and drive to S. John. I am going too, to stay a fortnight as we have got a young girl to stay with Mother.

Miss Ritchie, "the plain but charming governess" is probably a similar age to Hattie and a good chaperon for her and Mod. Though engaged to be married, they could not properly spend much time alone, even in a cold sleigh.

A little back ground information is needed to understand the next part of the letter. Hattie's older sister, Mira, was married to Dr. Albert Casswell on September 14, 1887. There must have been some serious misunderstanding between the Casswells and the Scovils. Bessie writes:

> You know you cannot always carry the rules of etiquette to their logical conclusions. We asked the Casswells to dine on Christmas day although the Doctor has never been in the house since he was married and he quite often passes here. Mira never returned our visit nor did they even call after the tea party which was given expressly for them and to which they did not come.

Well, we now know one of the reasons for the tea party—to welcome the newly married Mira and her doctor husband into the social swirl. If the family records are correct, the couple had already been married for more than a year. The late timing of the welcoming tea party might have been the reason for the poor atmosphere. It was well known that Dr. Casswell had a gruff personality. Whatever the problem that caused this social alienation, it must have blown over by the time Hattie and Mod's children were born. Albert Casswell was the only doctor in the area and he attended Hattie and their births. My mother often mentioned her Casswell cousins in Gagetown, and the frequent visiting of the two households. One of the cousins, Frances, became her close friend.

During this break from nursing, Bessie was involved not just with domestic management: keeping an eye on her mother's health and happiness, writing letters to family members, engaging in the niceties of having the rector and others to tea or a meal. She was also writing books for publication.

Further in this letter to Jack, she writes: "I hear nothing of my book as yet. It is paid for so I am content to wait the publisher's time having now no pecuniary interest in the matter." Given the timing, she would have been referring to the first book she wrote, *In the Sick Room: What to Do, How to Do and When to Do for the Sick; the Art of Nursing.* This book was published sometime in 1888 by Clark W. Bryan of Springfield, Mass., but I have been unable to locate a copy. "Having now no pecuniary interest" means the publisher had purchased the book from her for a set amount, which precluded the payment of royalties on the number of books sold.

Bessie finishes the letter with a bit more farm news and her usual words of affection:

> We have made all our pork into bacon this year and hope it will sell well. Give my best love to Addie and many kisses to the darling boys. I am glad you have got into thick flannels. Ever dearest Jack, your loving sister, Bessie.

Eighteen eighty eight is a good year for preserved letters, which is fortunate as the fund of Meadowlands' news will become much less rich when Bessie leaves in the autumn of the year. Her next letter is to her youngest brother, Barclay, in New York and is dated February 26th:

> Dearest Barc,
> Your letter of the 20th did not come until last night. The roads are un-plowed between here and Welsford and Thursday's mail did not get in. It is raining today so it is doubtful if Mod and Mr. Hatheway will get off to Fredericton as they intend tomorrow. The travelling has been lovely on the ice and if it had remained good Mother would have gone with them. The change would have benefitted her and would have been a break in the monotony of the winter. We took Miss Ritchie and Hattie on a drive yesterday afternoon,

up the creek, through the canal and down this side of the island.

Most of the remainder of this letter is filled with the comings and goings and the marriages and illnesses of various relatives and family friends both in New Brunswick and New York, who would be known to Barc. A reference to the changing times appears in the following news. "Louise Allison's little boy has measles. She telegraphed for Pattie to go up and help her nurse him as she is without a servant. I hope the poor little man will not be very sick." In 1888 the quickest, most efficient way to communicate, where the service was available, was by telegram, which would normally arrive very soon after it was sent.

Bessie indicates she is pleased with her new chair that she purchased in Saint John, "The frame is cherry with a pretty carpet back and seat. It is a patent rocker, fixed on springs and is very comfortable." With this major purchase in February, Bessie may not yet have had plans to leave Meadowlands in September. Perhaps she had not yet been approached to take the position at the Newport Hospital. Or, if she had, the chair would be a fine addition for her mother to enjoy. She then includes farm news:

> Our nine little pigs are ten days old and all doing well. It will be a fine thing if we can raise them. It seems that Mod is already looking forward to being a married man with children to support so is enlarging the possibilities for income.

> Mod is going to have another wood shed and a new hen house built at the end of the new pig pen about where the old house stood. The hen house is to be divided by a lattice partition and large enough to accommodate about fifty hens. Abraham is to come the 1st of April to commence work on the building and will no doubt stay for some time when once he gets here. ... Many thanks for the papers, and the

Illustrated Magazine. Mother was much pleased with it. We were well supplied last week as Jack sent papers too. … Ever Dearest Barc, Your loving sister, Bessie.

I have only one more letter from Bessie headed "Meadowlands" written on March 4th, 1888 to "Dearest Addie," with effusive appreciation for the photographs of DeLancey and details of the Peters children's tea party.

> We are all perfectly charmed with DeLancey's photos. They are all excellent likenesses, but I like the one with his legs crossed best. The other is one of his expressions, I have often seen him look exactly like it, and it is hard to choose between. He is a noble looking child in either, no wonder people turn to look at him, dear wee man. The head is very handsome but I do not think it gives one as good an idea of him as the standing ones. When I saw the three cards I thought of course one was Charlie's. … Do have him taken as soon as you can. Fancy his being nearly sixteen months old and we have not even one of his sweet face! How lovely it would be if you were near enough for us to see you all often instead of such a long journey between us.

Bessie continues to be nourished by every crumb of information about her two nephews and is very clever in trying to extract a photo of Charlie, through praise rather than outright criticism. She continues with more compliments for Addie. "How beautifully you have made his plush coat and cap, the chinchilla must be very becoming to him." Even a description of the Peters children at tea hides a subtle compliment for DeLancey and another one for him at the expense of the visiting family.

> We had the six Peters children to tea on Thursday. They came about four and stayed until seven. We played

games and had high tea at 5:30. The twins are about four, Pearl and Ruby, their real names are Marguerite and Gladys, which seems to me much prettier. They are nice looking little fair haired things. DeLancey is as large as both put together and could easily spare good looks to furnish the entire family.

Bessie had been planning this party for some time:

I sent for *Sessions in Candy Making* and made chocolate candy and chocolate and coconut creams very successfully. Mod and Hattie helped me with the chocolate drops and you could scarcely have told them from the confectioner's only they were a little stout. The children were very good and seemed to enjoy themselves.

Again, discussion of servants comes up:

Why does Eugenie leave you? How much trouble you have had with servants since you went home [last summer]. Jane is very anxious to return to us. She says Mrs. Scovil was a mother to her.

More news about death and illness of family and friends in Saint John and elsewhere flows from Bessie's pen plus the good news that Louise's baby has recovered. Her last paragraph echoes concern for her mother's health and her ever present delight in her nephews:

Mother is still very well, but I dread the spring for her, it always upsets her… How proud your father must be of DeLancey's beauty. Kiss both the boys for me. With a great deal of love from us all to you and dear Jack. Ever your loving sister, Bessie.

A little more than six months later, on September 12, 1888, Hattie and Mod were married. The wedding took place at St. Paul's Church, Portland, New Brunswick, now part of Saint John. It was conducted by Rev. Canon DeVeber, assisted by Rev. C.H. Hathaway, rector of Jemseg. Though it seems quite a trek all the way to Saint John for the wedding, there were probably more residents, both family and friends, from that area who attended than from Gagetown. Hattie's mother, Susan Starr DuVernet grew up in the port city, so some of her relatives would have been invited. Mary Eliza writes on Sept. 16, 1888 to her youngest son, in New York:

> Dearest Barc,
> I wrote you a few hurried lines the day before Bessie, Jack & Addie left. I felt very lonely coming home alone after parting with them all, but soon went to work there was so much to be done. I sent Annie home while I was in St. John & the Wilsons attended to the dairy. Was it not too bad it was such a rainy day for the wedding—it poured—everything went off beautifully—a great many friends came to the church & all the connections. I never saw either Hattie or Mod look better.
>
> The bride had a lovely bouquet, the bride's maid ditto. We all were so sorry you could not have come on, it was impossible we know that. The cards all came safe and all your letters to me also and other papers.... Many thanks dear old Barc. I am very tired and must stop and go to bed ever dearest Barc. your affectionate.
> Mother

It is not clear in Mary Eliza's letter whether Bessie, Jack & Addie left for the U.S. directly from Saint John, a day or so after the wedding, but it seems so. Bessie would have been well packed and organized for her new life, before the wedding, plunging Hattie immediately into being the woman in charge after her honeymoon, which only may have been staying with relatives in Saint John for a few days, which was common in that period.

*   *   *   *

At thirty-nine, Bessie had commenced her second paid position and remained in it for six years. She appears to have given up her position as head of the infirmary at St. Paul's School in New Hampshire to emotionally support her mother after her father's death and help her run the domestic side of the farm, and, perhaps, because of her own "bad heads." There is no mention of "bad heads" in any of her letters from Meadowlands that I have, but they are only a small percentage of the letters she would have written over the course of her long life.

Bessie's next letter changes dramatically in place of origin and in tone. She writes from the Newport Hospital in Newport, Rhode Island on November 20th 1888, where she is now the Superintendent of Nursing and the head of Nurses' Training School. With her second brother, Mod, now married to Hattie and well in charge of the farm, her eldest brother, Jack, has had some thoughts about inheritance. Although he seems not to be thinking of his own benefit, he assumes he will outlive his older sister, which he did not.

In 1901, U.S. President Theodore Roosevelt shut down all trust companies as he thought they had too much influence and power in the economy. Jack was an accountant with one of them. He lost his job and never again had full time employment. His "friendship" with Bacchus intensified at this stage. Bessie propped up his finances, when required. Jack spent increasingly lengthy periods at Meadowlands and died there in 1917. Bessie outlived Jack by eighteen years, in spite of her being seven years his senior. But when Bessie wrote this letter to him in 1888, he still had thirteen years of employment and prosperity left. I will quote her letter in full as it gives insight into Bessie's thoughtful decisiveness and her concern for their mother.

Dearest Jack,
I will consent to lay the matter before the Supreme Court on these conditions:

That we all sign a bond agreeing to accept the decision of the Court as final;

That you and Addie bind yourselves not to enforce during Mother's lifetime or mine any legal rights you may gain, or be confirmed in by the decision and;

That you agree to bear the expense of the proceedings.

Both of the last two you have promised informally already but of course they must be put into due legal form.

As to Mother being told of the matter you know perfectly well that it would have been simply impossible to have kept it from her. Letters had to pass backward and forward on the subject and our home letters between ourselves have always been common property. You very much understate Mother's acuteness if you fancy that they could be withheld from her without her knowledge.

Oh Jack dear what a bother the whole thing is. You say to Mother that neither you or your family will be in any way benefited and that Meadowlands never will be divided. Why then did you not let it rest instead of making Mother so unhappy and stirring up so much hard feeling all for what? As far as I can understand a financial good to Barc somewhere in the distant future. When I think of it all it hardly seems possible that it is YOU who is doing it. I am, as always, Your affectionate sister, Bessie.

Jack must have backed down completely. Only a month later, on December 19, 1888 Bessie writes a short but normal letter to him:

> Dearest Jack,
> I did not know what you would like for Christmas so send you five dollars. Please buy yourself handkerchiefs, neck ties, or whatever you would like best. I have made Addie a sachet and ransacked Newport to find cotton to match the silk but could not. I was so hurried in Boston I had not time to look for it then.
>
> The Prayer book and Hymnal are for DeLancey. It seems impossible he is almost five and old enough to go to Church. … Do you remember the old book of Bible stories that was such a delight to you and Mod when you were little. They all go with my love and best wishes for a Merry Christmas.
>
> Do you have a tree this year? I am in the full tide of preparation for one for sixty people beside all the guests who are to be asked to partake of ice cream, cake, coffee and cocoa. It is no joke to get ready for such a party with a daily family of forty beside. I mean to be too busy to think on Christmas or I shall be home sick. Ever dearest Jack. Your loving sister, Bessie.

With Bessie launched into a position without school terms, she is no longer able to nip back to Meadowlands for nearly a month at Christmas. My next correspondence from her is nearly six months later, May 1, 1889 from Newport:

> Dearest Jack
> The holidays interfere so with everything. I am almost afraid this will not reach you on your birthday [May 2nd] but whenever you get it you will know that it

carries my love and good wishes for the day. I send $2.00, please buy some trifle with it as a memento. My birthday [April 30] went off very pleasantly. Mr. and Mrs. Coit sent me books. Hattie did me some work [probably embroidery] and Barc sent me a lovely little book. I had several cards and a good many letters.

I am just changing my cook. The present one has been here four or five years but she drinks and steals and after standing it until I could engage one who promised well I have dismissed her to her great astonishment and my great joy. The new one comes tomorrow morning. Bessie [Addie and Jack's third and last child, Elizabeth Adelie, is usually called Bess] must be a little darling with her blue eyes. When is she to be Christened?

Your garden will soon be lovely, this warm weather will bring forward the roses. Our grounds are beginning to look pretty. The lawn is very green, the tulips, daffodils and jonquils in bloom.

One of the nurses gave me the most exquisite pansies I ever saw yesterday. Most of them were immensely large and almost black.

Mother goes to S. John soon now. Mod was to go and take Percy on Monday. He says the water is rising very slowly and he hopes it will not be a high freshet.

Give my love to Addie and many kisses to the three children. Barc always tells me about them, particularly our Godson. [This was probably DeLancey, the eldest. Barc and Bessie must have been two of the usual three Godparents].

Wishing you many happy returns of the day, with love, believe me, Your affectionate sister, Bessie.

I have included the complete letter to illustrate how Bessie is adjusting to being away from Meadowlands and back at work, taking pleasure in her first spring in Newport, appreciating gifts, but still very concerned with the possibility of flooding back on the farm and the welfare of various family members. More than another six months pass before the next letter in my collection. The question of the ownership of Meadowlands had apparently not been settled.

Dearest Jack,
I am sorry you cannot come to Newport. I would very gladly bear the expense if that is the only obstacle.

I shall try to answer your letter in detail as I should if you were here. My "idea of the settlement of the whole question" is this. Meadowlands is taxed at $9,000.00 and if sold under the hammer with a clear title tomorrow probably would not bring that. Accepting this as a basis it leaves $3,000.00 in dispute. You have always said that you did not wish to disturb Mother or me in possession during my life time. It is a fair compromise that gives half to each of the disputants therefore I will give Barc $1500 at my death, securing it by a mortgage on the farm. He to give me a quit claim deed.

As to the other points in your letter. Barc has at present no assured title whatever to any part of Meadowlands.

Mr. Millidge tells me that the Canadian law does not permit an entail but turns it into a fee simple. If Father held the fee simple he had a perfect right to deed it to Uncle William and in that event my title holds good.

The Supreme Court is as likely to take this view of the wording of the will as the other. My chances are as good as his — Mr. Millidge thinks better — it is all a matter of uncertainty.

It was not fully understood at the time of the sale that I was to hold the farm in the interest of the boys. On the contrary it was given to me absolutely and that I so understood it is proved by the fact that from the time Mod went there in 1880 I have always spoken openly of my intention to leave it to him, which I should not have done had I been told that I was merely holding it for the boys. On the contrary Father said to me again and again, "The property is yours, never part with it as long as you live." The Canon said the same when I was in England. Neither of them appeared to doubt the validity of my claim, why should I then have suspected it? The Insurance came out of the property and had been returned to it. Barc did not contribute to the premiums which affected it and I cannot see that he is entitled to a share of it.

Barc was not "kicked out" of Meadowlands. He went at his own wish and request. I did the best I could to procure a situation for him and so did Mod. Many men have risen from much humbler beginnings. He was under no obligation to stay there. Mr. Kingsbury had given you a good start and I accepted his offer for Barc as the best we could do at the time. If Barc was "half educated," it was his own fault. We sent him to school and gave him all his time at home for study. He was not required to work on the farm.

Ned DuVernet [Hattie's brother] with less advantages than he had is preparing himself to be a doctor. Barc was simply wasting his time at home and showed no disposition to apply himself to get an education. I left school at sixteen and I have managed to make my way in the world. If I recollect aright you offered no objection to Barc going to the United States and he was some years older than either you or Mod when you began to earn your own living. Whatever money Mod has had has not been spent upon himself but has gone directly into the property. I wish Barc would write to me himself upon the matter.

I hope the children have born the summer well. Kiss them all for me and believe me. Your affect. Sister, Bessie

A lot of family history and half-history is contained in this one letter. I would like to know what "sale" she refers to. I cannot find any will of Samuel James Scovil, Bessie's father, in the N.B. Archives. As he was a trained attorney it seems unlikely he would not have made one. Bessie writes, "It [ownership of Meadowlands] has dragged on now through two generations and we do not want to carry it into a third." So it was never clean cut when the family moved there in 1880, six years after the previous owner's wife had died. I have questioned elsewhere why, when the Scovil family were urgently needing a home of their own, the farm was not made over to them earlier, especially as it was in the will of the original owner, Uncle Samuel Scovil, that it should go to Bessie's father. It is one of those family mysteries that will never be solved.

From the following letter written at Newport, R. I. on October 5th, the same year, 1889, we learn more.

Dearest Barc,
In answer to your letter of October 2nd which reached me today, I think that you start with a fundamental misconception of the point at issue.

I do not see why you "always understood that" I "held the farm in trust for the benefit of the whole family." When it was given to me, the Canon told Mother that the Master in Chancery gave me a full title to it. Both he and father assured me that the property was mine. Much was said of my holding it in trust for father and mother that they might always have a home upon it. This I thought was best secured by giving Mod such an interest in it that he would stay there and make a home for them which they could not have done for themselves for long. I immediately announced my intention to leave it to him and neither you nor Jack objected in any way. It is scarcely likely that I should have done this had I not believed the farm to be indisputably my own.

The bridge property [in Saint John, also willed to Bessie's father by his uncle Samuel Scovil] was to be your share. It will eventually be a valuable property so you were not to be cut off without something. In discussing the question of settlement you speak as if you had an unquestionable right to a third of the farm whereas the fact is that your title is at best a disputed one which you cannot establish without an expensive law suit that I am as likely to win as you are should we engage in it. This should be remembered in considering the terms of the compromise.

Of course I am anxious to have the question settled. It has dragged on now through two generations and we do not want to carry it into a third.

You do not derive any benefit from the farm at present, nor according to your proposition of leaving me undisturbed in possession of it during my lifetime will you do so as long as I live. At my death you would be in exactly the same position that you are now with no claim except the chance of enforcing one by a law suit. By accepting the settlement you would have $1500 in hand. I am eighteen years older than you are and likely in the course of nature to die a long time before you do. In proposing a compromise I take the ground that in a law court our chances of winning would be equal, where as Mr. Millidge thinks that mine are the best.

To bring the matter before the Supreme Court would cost a good deal of money which none of us have to spare. Why not let Fred Barker [a legally trained relative of Addie's father] on your side and Mr. Millidge on mine discuss the terms of settlement, if you do not agree to mine? Let me know what you think and believe me. Your affectionate sister, Bessie.

None of the family I have spoken with knows anything about a court case and I heard nothing about one from my mother so it looks as though either Fred Barker and Mr. Millidge settled the matter or Bessie's terms of settlement were accepted by Barc and Jack, probably the latter. Barc held no bitterness toward Bessie for her stand. He wrote of her shortly after she had written this letter that she was the dearest sister anyone could have. I have no doubt that before the Crash of 1929, as her stocks and shares in the Curtis Publishing Company climbed in value, that Barc felt her generous hand, as did other family members.

* * * *

Nearly a generation passes before Bessie's next preserved letter. The date is September 4, 1917, written from Meadowlands to Addie, which begins; "Jack has been writing you so regularly that I know you are fully informed about him."

Bessie's life and Jack's have changed entirely since 1889. Bessie gave up professional nursing in 1903 and returned to Meadowlands to look after Mod's five children when Hattie became ill and died.

Jack, now unwell, left Addie in the care of their daughter, Bess, and spent his last few years at Meadowlands, where he was cared for by Bessie. He was still on good terms with Addie and may have left New York to spare his daughter the responsibility of taking care of both her parents. Addie could rely on daughter Bess and Jack could count on the support and care of his sister. What his physical problem was is not clear, but there is some debilitating illness requiring nursing. It is generally accepted that he was fond of alcohol, but under his sister's eye that would not have been generously available, except for "medicinal" purposes, which might have included chronic painkilling.

Bessie's letter to Addie about Jack continues:

> The tenderness is very much better. His neck is not nearly as painful, so I hope the gland will not suppurate. We are using ichythol ointment and keep it bound up. He coughs very little and does not expectorate at all. His appetite is good and he sleeps a good deal though not always at night. He has nourishment six times a day. When it is damp or the wind is very high he stays in bed. He wears very thick flannels at night and has a down comforter, though he seldom uses it.

> He is able to read a good deal and has plenty of magazines and books. *The Times* would be a great pleasure to him, I am sure.

> Pattie Powys is coming from Winnipeg for three months; she leaves there on the 5th and will stay first with Aunt Grace [Robinson] in Montreal. She wants to come here but we cannot have her on account of the men.

The men include Jack and Mod and Roger, Mod and Hattie's youngest son, now twenty. Each would have occupied a bedroom. Mary, my mother and Bessie would have occupied the two remaining bedrooms. Mary giving up her room for one in the attic for a night or two might have been considered, but a month or more, even for a relative, was too long.

Elizabeth and Gertrude [Mod and Hattie's adult daughters] left yesterday and hoped to leave S. John for Boston tonight, if an extra Pullman were put on. They could not get reservations tho' they applied last week. Gertrude will have only a day in New York, possibly Sunday also, so she may see you. Elizabeth will stay in Boston for a week.

We have not heard from Morrie for a little time and are constantly anxious about him.

I hope Bess is feeling much better and able to begin work. My love to her and Charlie. Ever, Your loving sister, Bessie

Gertrude would have been nearly twenty-six so presumably had finished her course of study at Pratt Institute in Brooklyn, N.Y. and was now a fully qualified dietitian. She spent most of her working life at the Shaughnessay Hospital in Vancouver, B.C., eventually becoming the Head Dietitian, but in 1917 she probably held a position in the Eastern U.S. Elizabeth, twenty-seven, would have finished her studies in physical education training at Randolph Macon college in Virginia, and eventually acquired a teaching position in Winnipeg. It appears the sisters were spending their summer holidays at Meadowlands and were now returning to work via a short visit with American relatives.

Morrie, Mod and Hattie's oldest child was being held as a prisoner of war by the Germans and still had more than fourteen months before being released and returning to Meadowlands at the end of the war. Bess, Jack and Addie's third child and only daughter, eventually worked as a senior librarian at Columbia University. At this stage she was on her way to that employment. She married a New York born Episcopalian clergyman of Danish parentage, six years her junior and produced five children. Bess provided a home for Addie until her mother died, in 1928. At the time of this 1917 letter, Jack was slowly dying at Meadowlands. Both DeLancey and Charlie would have completed their theological studies by 1917, being 33 and 31 respectively. DeLancey was married with three of his eventual six children. Charlie may still have been living with his sister and mother, or at least within visiting range in New York, prior to marrying.

Thirty-seven days after Bessie wrote the above letter, Jack died. Her next surviving letter, addressed to Bess, was penned on Dec. 19th, a little more than two months after Jack's death.

> Dearest Bess,
> This will be a sad Christmas for us all. It is many years since we have had a break in our immediate family and even I, who had not had him at Christmas for a great while, miss your dear father now. We cannot but be thankful he did not linger and suffer through this cold winter. …
>
> We have been deep in politics and feel that we have little left to do now the election is over. General McLean, the Union [coalition] candidate for this riding asked me to organize the women voters of the parish of Gagetown, as this is the first time women have had the vote. It was given to the wives, sisters, mothers and daughters of soldiers. We had 45 in Gagetown and got 31 to the polls. The majority every where was overwhelming in favor of conscription. We have a majority of 40 seats in the Dominion Parliament. Quebec, being French Canadian, voted almost solidly against it.
>
> I hope the change to Philadelphia did both you and your mother good. She must have many lonely hours.

I am glad you are able to be with her instead of at the Library.

I am enclosing a very small gift, please get some little things for her, yourself and Charlie.

We dine at home, go to Morning Service at Jemseg and to tea at Mira's. Mr. Bennett leaves the parish next week so it is one last opportunity. Mr. Marshall also goes very soon.

We have had cheerful letters from Morrie from Furstenberg in Mickelenberg, Germany where he is now. He says it is a great help to be treated as an officer after their miserable summer. All food now goes through the Red Cross. We are not allowed to send any parcels.

Elizabeth is talking of going to Washington for a few days after Christmas for a change, before beginning work again. She decided not to go to her Uncle Robert [DuVernet] in South Carolina, as she intended at one time to do. Gertrude is very busy. We are urging her to resign in June, come home for three months' rest. She has not had a real holiday since she went to Pratt.

Mary got home on Saturday. She is not going back as the benefit is not commensurate with the expense. She does not look very well and her eyes are troublesome.

Roger is full of business, the men we have are not very efficient.

Uncle Mod joins me in love and many good Christmas wishes to you all. My love especially to your Mother. Your loving Aunt Bessie

I have included most of the letter as it brings us up to date on family members as well as the political reality for women — only partial suffrage. That Bessie is writing to niece Bess instead of to her mother, Addie, suggests the latter has lost some of her abilities though still able to travel, so not a complete invalid. Possibly Bess took an extended Christmas holiday from Columbia's library. Clearly the rift with Mira DuVernet Casswell is ancient history, having been patched up before Hattie and Mod's children were born in the late 1880s and 1890s. Morrie's imprisonment situation greatly improved when he was moved to a facility specifically for officers. Uncle Robert DuVernet was one of Hattie's brothers who owned a flourishing seed and nursery business in Greenville S.C. It appears that Gertrude is working as a dietitian in the eastern U.S. at this time. Mary might have been spending a term back at Edgehill School for Girls. I do know she spent a time at Edgehill when older so this is probably a reference. Bessie's comment about Roger and "the men we have" would be about the farm workers and farm management.

Bessie's next preserved letter was written a year and a half later, June 15, 1922 to Bess at 4 Chelsea Square, New York, surprisingly from El Dorado, Arkansas.

Dearest Bess,
Surprises on surprises! I do wish that I could be at your wedding but I see no hope of Mrs. Agnew being able to move by that time. I should so love to be there and see my new nephew, it is a great disappointment to be forced to forego it.

There is nothing in the way of wedding gifts to be had here so I'm sending you a cheque. Please buy some little thing as a remembrance of me and use the rest in any way you like.

Do write me the details if you can find time. What are you to wear and who is your bridesmaid? Constance will have sailed for England by then. Are you giving up the apartment in Chelsea Square and will your Mother live with you later?

Mrs. Agnew may not be well enough to travel for some time and I cannot leave her alone.

Has Charlie resigned his position in California? Are Beatrice and the baby with him and did the latter fully recover from the operation? I meant to have written your mother before this but my time for letter writing is very limited.

It will be nice for you to have DeLancey to give you away. How proud your father would have been to have been with you.

My love to your mother and very much to yourself Bess dear, I hope you may have many happy years. Always, Your loving Aunt Bessie

Bessie was seventy-three when she wrote this letter, well past the age of professional nursing, though once a nurse, always a nurse—a nurse for all seasons. She seemed to have a strong feeling of needing to care for Mrs. Agnew. This immensely fat, almost blind American woman came to live with Bessie, her brother Mod, and my mother, Mary, in the early 1920s, after they moved from Meadowlands to Fredericton. My mother disliked the woman intensely. I have a feeling this interloper was one of the reasons Mother eloped with my father as she was decidedly unhappy with Mrs. Agnew under the same roof. Mother said that anything Mrs. Agnew wanted was almost instantly provided for by Aunt Bessie, whereas my mother had to make a very good case for needing money for a new hat. Mrs. Agnew was not a relative so I assume she was someone Bessie met while she was working in the U.S. and with whom she had remained in touch.

Bess Scovil was thirty-three when she married the Rev. Charles Emil Karsten, whose parents had been immigrants from Denmark. Bess and Charles had five children in two year intervals, the last when Bess was forty-three. All survived except one, the second child, Elizabeth Adeline, who died four days after her birth. The eldest, the Rev. Charles Emil, Jr. is the provider of much material and inspiration for this biography. The other two sons, Jack and Beverly, were also both ordained. The surviving daughter, Anna Dorothea Barclay (Nancy) married an ordained man—not surprising, she told me, as they were everywhere.

The "Constance" Bessie refers to as potential bridesmaid would have been Constance Carr, granddaughter of Bessie's Uncle Jack Robinson, the youngest of her mother's ten siblings. I met Constance Carr in the mid 1940s in southern Nova Scotia, a charming, unmarried middle-aged woman, looking after an aged mother. Her name always appealed to me; my mother always referred to her by her full name as I think she was also intrigued by the alliteration. Constance Carr was a frequent summer visitor at Meadowlands.

Charlie (the Rev. Charles Barker Scovil) and his wife Beatrice had only one child, another Charles (Barker Scovil) who died in 1983, so it seems he fully recovered from "the operation" as a baby. DeLancey (Rev. John DeLancey Scovil) took over the job at his sister's wedding usually performed by the father of the bride. DeLancey and his wife, Dorothy Dudley Storer, were parents five times over having three sons and then twin girls. Two of the boys were eventually ordained as clergymen. Neither of the daughters, of course, were allowed into the family profession, although one, Georgiana, became a medical doctor, but too late for Bessie to revel in her great niece's accomplishment, of which she would have been immensely proud.

The last letter I have in Bessie's hand was written to Bess more than ten years later, October 13, 1932 from the home of her nephew, Morris (Morrie) Allaire Scovil, now, with his family, living and working in England. It is addressed to Elizabeth Adeline Scovil Karsten, at Zion Church Rectory, Dobbs Ferry, N.Y.—a suburb of New York City.

Dearest Bess,

Uncle Mod is getting on splendidly. There has not been a single set back. The stitches were taken out today and the tubes removed. I think the incision will be closed this week. He has been in hospital two months and has been so patient and cheerful through the whole ordeal. We hope to have him home in two or three weeks now.

I am very glad the setting of the old ring reached you safely. I think the box is the one given to my mother with the ring by her grandfather Anthony Allaire.

You say you have been playing lots of contract. I am too old a dog to learn new tricks. I was at an afternoon Bridge yesterday. Made a grand slam at auction and a good score though just short of the prize.

Cousin Sose [Robinson] is in London. Her son Bev. has just come back from Brazil and taken a furnished house for his wife and children so they can be together before he is sent off again.

Frances [Casswell] Jones has a daughter. She has been married for a year or two and is forty. She had a perfectly normal time and the baby is a fine child.

Roger [Scovil] was in Washington this month at a business convention and wrote very cheerfully from there. Roger Boy [Jr.] goes to S. School now and loves it.

Mary is having a very hard time and we can do so little to help her. Hayden is in America, he went via Montreal and will not be in New York.

I am very glad Charlie Junior is getting on so well at school.

Much love Bess dear to you and yours, especially Charlie. Your loving Aunt Bessie

Bess's "Uncle Mod," my grandfather, clearly had a serious operation. The postmark on the envelope for this letter is Paddington, a part of London where St. Mary's Hospital is located. The operation was probably carried out there. The nature of his ailment is not made clear, but my mother said her father was troubled with kidney problems, which were eventually the cause of his death, but this may be quite another matter. Mod lived for nearly another three years, so this surgical intervention, for whatever reason, was at least a temporary success.

The ring setting is still in Bess's family, with her daughter, Nancy Iredale, who lives in Philadelphia. Not only did Frances (Caswell) Jones (Mira DuVernet Caswell's daughter and Hattie's niece) produce her first child at forty but four years later she gave birth to another daughter, Attrude (Jones) Parker who, until recently has been living in her family home near Digby, Nova Scotia. "Roger Boy," Bessie's great nephew was only three and a half at this time, so the Greenville Sunday School must have delivered some pepped up Bible stories for him to "love" it. Mary, my mother, was indeed having a very hard time. Her first baby just took one breath and died after a four-day labour. Her second daughter, born in 1925, survived and because of Mother's determination not to raise an only child, I was born in 1929, though she realized long before that she had made a poor choice in suggesting that she and my father elope. Her plan to help bring happiness into her life and his was not sufficient to encourage him to give up binge drinking which he continued for the rest of his life, hoping it would ease the pain of an unhappy childhood and his terrifying experience in World War I.

Hayden Villiers, Bessie's nephew-in-law, her niece Elizabeth's husband, was in the habit of travelling to North and South America from time to time, looking for business for his manufacturing firm. My Aunt Elizabeth confided in me that these trips never once produced a scrap of business. She thought he enjoyed sea voyages and getting away from damp English winters. Hayden was the English manufacturing agent for Anthony Hoists, a Chicago based company. He headed, with Morris, his brother-in-law and a capable business man, a medium sized factory near Northolt, Middlesex where Tuffy Hoists were made. Tuffy Hoists was the brand name of the products manufactured by Anthony Hoists. It was commandeered during the World War II to manufacture airplane parts. When I visited the factory in 1949, it was back to making hydraulic hoists for placing heavy loads in the back of trucks.

Bessie at 83, with just two more years of life, could still hold her own at Bridge and was lavishing her love on the next generation of children. Charlie, already eight, was the eldest of Bess's four children.

This is the last of Bessie's letters in my possession, found in a trunk in the attic of Bess's house with many other family papers and kept by her son Charlie, after her death. After retiring from being a Canon of the Episcopal (Anglican) Church in Gardiner Maine, he and his English-born wife, Daphne, whom he met at Oxford University, moved to Readfield, Maine where he lived until he died in 2014. Charlie was always much interested in family history. I visited him in Readfield where I spent many hours discovering the contents of this treasure-filled trunk and was given thirty-one of Bessie's letters, in her hand. They are now in the possession of the New Brunswick Archives on the campus of the University of New Brunswick in Fredericton.

* * * *

The letters from which I have quoted are most certainly only a small fraction of the correspondence my Great Aunt Bessie composed and sent out over the course of her life. She was, along with being a prominent figure in the nursing profession, a professional writer, widely published. Her correspondence, while springing from the personal side of life, was engaged in with the drive and discipline of a person born to write.

In addition to the practice of maintaining and cultivating ongoing relationships with family members through letter writing, Elizabeth Robinson Scovil no doubt carried on a similar discipline of correspondence with a wide range of friends and associates. For Bessie, the practice of letter writing seems to have been a subsidiary profession. Thanks to her niece, Bess, who saved at least some of her Great Aunt's letters, and thanks to Bess's son, Charlie, who retained the collection, we have a direct window into this aspect of her life.

Chapter Seven

Household Manager at Meadowlands

"Bessie can make a succulent meal for six from a can of bully beef and a piece of string," said Uncle Jack to little Mary. Little Mary's interpretation of succulent was not the same as her Uncle Jack's. In fact, "little Mary" (my mother) told me many times that she did not think highly of her Aunt Bessie's cooking. The Lord might try to make her truly thankful, but it was a struggle. There was too much blanc mange and too little imagination. It is ironic that my mother's blanc mange — ah, that lumpless perfection — was among my favourite lunchtime deserts. I would salivate to think of it as I rushed home one block from the old George Street Fredericton High School. Another treat was steamed rice and raisins sprinkled with dark brown sugar and "washed with top-of-the-bottle."[15] The raisins were not those mean little ones now common, but generous, plump and moist — seeded raisins, or, as Aunt Bessie called them in her recipe for rice jelly, "stoned."

I am not certain that the heavenly rice pudding was in Aunt Bessie's repertoire, though I have always connected it with her, and as her recipe suggests she was in favour of marrying rice and raisins. With plentiful milk on the farm, it made good sense to use it in blanc mange, a quick way to make an easily digested and nutritious dessert, even though not popular with one of her charges. As for rice pudding, all the ingredients could come from the pantry with its huge, wooden bins for white sugar and flour that opened from the top and were pivoted forward on the diagonal when in use. Other dry ingredients were kept in large jars or tightly covered tins.

---

15 Layering a garnish of cream from the top of the milk bottle across the pudding.

Spices were in special canisters, marked "cinnamon," "cloves," "ginger," etc. all neatly fitting into a tin caddy. I remember, as a small child, the nostril jarring effect of the dark red spice tins, the gold letters blurred by brown and golden smudges, in my mother's pantry, which she had built as a copy of that in Meadowlands, though on a smaller scale.

The need to have a well filled pantry or larder was as necessary at Beaverbrook, the farm five miles from the stores and Amherst, Nova Scotia, where I lived until I was seven, as it was at Meadowlands. At Meadowlands a visit to a grocery store involved a trip across the Saint John River or a nearly four miles and back to Jemseg by horse and carriage or sleigh in the winter. Going to Gagetown by rowboat in pre-motorboat and pre-ferry days required planning. A trip there and back, with at least one visit to a relative or friend took the better part of a day. In the winter, when the river was frozen, a horse and sleigh lessened time for the journey, but the cold weather justified an even longer visit to catch up on gossip and to warm the chilled body. Buffalo robes for the legs and hot bricks warmed in the oven and covered with straw for the feet were helpful in keeping warm.

Twice a year—when the ice broke up in the Spring and when it was forming in the Fall, but not yet thick enough to hold a horse and sleigh—visiting Gagetown was impossible. These were times, at least two weeks in duration and usually more, when projects were undertaken that needed no outside help, or no more than could be found in Jemseg on the same side of the river. "When the ice goes out," was a favourite procrastinating expression my mother retained from her life at Meadowlands Even when the requirement could have been procured from Jemseg, a sleigh or wagon had to be made ready and a horse harnessed, taking a man away from more important work, or convincing a male member of the family the trip was necessary.

A regular journey to attend St. James Anglican church in Jemseg every Sunday morning, of course, would not have been an occasion for anything else except perhaps exchange of news at the church door. Such an outing sharpened the appetite as sermons were usually an hour long, and often snapped to a conclusion by the sound of my grandfather's pocket watch opened and closed with such deliberate vigour that the rector could not miss the message. By then, breakfast was a distant memory, so making haste to return home for dinner was welcomed by all.

Dinner, in rural communities, was the name given to the midday meal, where it was traditionally the heartiest meal of the day in order to sustain men and women throughout their afternoon labours. My mother continued the Meadowlands tradition of calling the evening meal "tea" although "supper" was becoming interchangeable with "tea" when I was very young.

In a letter dated March 4, 1888, Great Aunt Bessie wrote from Meadowlands to "Dearest Addie," her sister in law in New York, during one of her breaks from her nursing career, "We had the six Peters children to tea on Thursday. They came at four and stayed until seven. We played games and had high tea at 5:30."

In looking into this terminology, I find that in the English tradition "tea" generally refers to an afternoon cup and snack. "High tea" refers to the last meal of the day, one at which meat is served. It appears that afternoon tea started with the Duchess of Bedford in the early 1800's, who needed something to sustain her between lunch and dinner at 8 or 9 o'clock. It became the fashion among ladies of leisure. "High tea" was a more substantial meal, suitable for men in a working class environment, served around 6 o'clock. It developed into the last meal of the day for children and for families who wished to eat earlier.

Though English tradition was still strong in Victorian Canada, there were clearly changes that better accommodated the more vigorous lifestyle of the colonies, not least of which was looking forward to "dinner" on your way home from Sunday morning church over snow drifted or rutted roads and "supper" in the evening.

Self reliance and being prepared to cope with periodic isolation was a requirement of household management at Meadowlands. Having a good stock of grains, flours, and dried fruits along with the summer's crop of fruits and vegetables preserved in jars and stored in the root cellar made shopping for other staples scheduled as needed. The farm itself provided a continual supply of milk, cream, and butter, and pork, chicken, and beef.

* * * *

In visiting Meadowlands for the first time when I was ten, Mother described the cellar as filled with "preserves." When I stood on the cellar's dark earth floor with her, I did not imagine the rows of colourful jars, which, in the past, weighed down the shelves lining the stone walls. Instead, my eyes flew to the low ceiling, and that is where they stayed. A layer of sawdust was stuck to the ceiling! How could that be? I was used to seeing sawdust on the ground. How could it have risen to the ceiling of the basement of the Meadowlands house? Mother provided the answer.

Every Fall, the house was "banked" with a trough of sawdust heaped up all along the foundation of the house as insulation. Boards were anchored into position to hold the sawdust in place. The Meadowlands house was on flat intervale land near the shoreline of the St. John River. When the winter ice broke up and spring floods came, the river often over flowed it's banks and spread over the land around the house. If it rose high enough it would wash the saw dust into the cellar and fill it with water. Sometimes the Spring freshet would even flood the first floor of the house. When it receded the sawdust that had washed into the cellar and floated on the water was left sticking to the ceiling.

My mother explained how this unwelcome visitor caused a great deal of work. Threatened with high water, everything made of iron that could not be moved to the second floor had to be greased to prevent it from rusting. This included the kitchen stove. All preserves and root vegetables in the cellar had to be rescued, too, though by April there would not be many left. One particularly bad year, my mother told me, they set up a small stove elevated above the water that had flooded the first floor so they could build a fire and prepare hot meals. One year the water was so high a canoe was tied to the railing of the verandah.

The level of flooding each Spring depended the depth of snow cover in the forested watershed of the river in northern Maine and New Brunswick and the speed of its melting. A quick, warm thaw would mean high flood waters downstream. A long cold spring with slow melting would mean minimal flooding. It is hard to imagine the mess left behind at Meadowlands when the water receded from high level flooding. And it is hard to imagine Bessie, with her nurse's training, her sense of good order and sanitation, dealing with the clean up and recovery. Some measure of this troublesome and exhausting ordeal would have to be repeated with each Spring freshet.

However, the deep soil of the interval terrain along the lower St. John River was among the best farm land in the province and seasonal flooding was part of what made the luxuriant hay fields of Meadowlands so sustainably productive. Spring cleanup after the freshet was a small price to pay for the natural abundance of the farm and a relatively affluent and secure way of life. When the river returned to flowing between its banks, Bessie's household management, with the assistance of a live-in cook and house maid, went back to providing not only her usual succulent meals for the family, but for planned and unplanned visitors.

My mother said it was Aunt Bessie's management that organized Meadowlands to accommodate visitors. Brother Jack probably meant his remark about bully beef and a piece of string as a compliment for quick planning. Unexpected visitors would mean an impromptu upgrading of meal preparation. And Bessie, my mother often said, "controlled the purse strings." She was the one family member who could make money at will by writing another article or composing a new book for selling to an eager publisher and her North American audience. Her personal financial security enabled her generosity. Family members could depend her for assistance for special or even on-going expenses. Jack, especially, had reason to be grateful to Bessie for her generosity over the years. He was not likely to criticize her cooking, except perhaps in an oblique way to tickle his own funny bone.

Miss Scovil's hospitality was well known. My mother said a Curate could smell Aunt Bessie's finnan haddy ten miles away on a Friday. Next to family members, men of the cloth were favourite guests. There were a number of ordained men in her family. She nourished deep religious feelings and wrote books on religious subjects. Entertaining parish pastors and other Anglican Church officials as they visited the area would have been a welcome event that helped relieve Meadowland's somewhat isolated situation and provided stimulating, intellectual conversation.

They were, on the whole, also welcomed by my mother, though some she found boring and some, in her late teens, too forward.

She described a certain tall Englishman, a Curate who later rose to a very prominent position in the Anglican church, as being unusually unattractive. He used every excuse to sit next to her, and consumed a large second helping of finnan haddy. Her indifference must have acted as a tonic for his efforts. Much to her embarrassment, this persistent admirer returned the next day with a button in his hand, which he said he had found in his pocket and thought it might be hers. Mary's indignant, negative reply cooled his ardour.

On other occasions, after young clergymen had been well fed, Mary was required to ferry them across the river to Gagetown. By her late teens she was an accomplished operator of all kinds of boats on the river. When Bessie saw an advertisement for the newly developed outboard motor for use on rowboats, she took the initiative and ordered one from the manufacturer. When it came, Mary insisted on learning to operate it, which she mastered.

At one point, when she was motoring two well fed curates from Meadowlands to the wharf at Gagetown, the motor quit midstream. Motors were erratic in those days and this was not unheard of. Mary did everything she knew about how to get it restarted, including "stripping the engine," which meant cleaning the fuel intake line, but without success. As they floated downstream, the two Curates became thoroughly alarmed, especially when their Captain said, "You will have to pretend there's curtain between us." (Dear God, is she going to strip herself?). Mary shouted out a loud "Damn" as she gave the starting cord another mighty pull. The motor sputtered to life, she opened the throttle, and off they went. This must have been a relief for the curates, even though the strengthening effect of Miss Scovil's lunch may have lost much of its benefit. Clearly, the Devil, who obviously inspired their slight but energetically determined Captain, had to be acknowledged as also "moving in mysterious ways."

*   *   *   *

Aunt Bessie's recipe for finnan haddy, baked with half milk and half water also nourished me on many Fridays when I was growing up, as it did my own two children. A variation on this became "Aunt Bessie's Fish Pie," the recipe for which appears in the Lord Amherst Chapter of the I.O.D.E.[16] cook book in the mid 1960s placed there by my cousin, Courtenay Scovil Purdy.

> 2 C. milk
> 2 C. cooked flaked fish
> ½ C dried bread crumbs
> 2 Tbsp. flour
> salt
> 1 egg
> dash cayenne pepper
> ¼ C. parsley
>
> Heat milk and add flour, a dash of cayenne pepper and salt to taste. Pour over well-beaten egg. Fill baking dish with a layer of sauce, then one of fish, then the rest of the sauce. Top with bread crumbs and parsley. Bake 20 minutes at 375 F.

Writing this brings back memories of that satisfying casserole with its crispy, golden topping, and the need for an exploring tongue checking for an escaped bone. "Aunt Bessie's Fish Pie" was likely sometimes made with shad at Meadowlands. They were part of the St. John River's abundance. The off-putting feature of shad was the preponderance of bones. What a great labour of kindness

---

16   Imperial Order Daughters of the Empire. A charitable organization dedicated to enhancing the quality of life through education.

to all, especially to children, to turn de-boned shad into fish pie. Aunt Bessie's Fish Pie lives on elsewhere. Over the years, when visiting my first cousin Barbara Villiers Wootten in England, the delectable and historic Aunt Bessie's Fish Pie has been cooked by one great niece and enjoyed by two.

A few years ago this same cousin gave me her mother's hard cover copy of the *Fredericton Cathedral Memorial Hall Cookery Book, Third Edition, Containing Many Additional Recipes, 1920.* On the inside cover is written in my aunt's hand, "Elizabeth R. Scovil, 169 Langside St., Winnipeg, Feb. 13th, 1921." This was great Aunt Bessie's niece, my mother's sister, who was working in Winnipeg as a physical training instructor, prior to marrying Haydn Villiers and moving to England where she lived for the remainder of her life.

Miss Elizabeth Robinson Scovil is given credit for four recipes in the first edition of this famous book: Cheese Potatoes, Royal Sandwich, Manchester Pudding, and Lemon Marmalade. My mother used to laugh at what she saw as the absurdity of "Royal Sandwich" as a name, considering the ingredients. She may have been in on discussions regarding the title. I seem to recall her saying that. If so, she obviously lost in her efforts to douse Aunt Bessie's tendency to accentuate the positive. I cannot go into raptures over either of the first two contributions and fortunately my mother did not perpetuate them. However they should have an airing as an example of "tested" and acceptable recipes of the time.

CHEESE POTATOES

Cut enough cold potatoes into small pieces to fill a pint measure, cover with a pint of white sauce, spread a layer of grated cheese over the top and cover with bread crumbs moistened with water; bake half an hour.

ROYAL SANDWICH

Mix 1 cup of flour, a pinch of salt and two teaspoons of baking powder to a batter with 1 cup of milk; pour into two buttered Washington pie plates and bake. Have ready a mince made of any cold meat, seasoned with pepper, salt, celery salt, or poultry dressing as preferred; heat it with a little gravy or melted butter and boiling water, and spread between the cakes. Gravy can be served with it if desired.

The following contribution from Bessie is a good example of the book's more extravagant recipes:

MANCHESTER PUDDING
Half a pound bread crumbs, pour over them 1 pint scalding hot milk, add ¾ cup sugar, 2 tablespoons butter, 3 eggs well beaten, pouring a little of the hot mixture on them before adding a teaspoonful vanilla. Pour into the bottom of the mould 2 teacups jam; add the batter and steam two hours in a covered mould.

Another of my Great Aunt's recipes suggests rows of golden jars on shelves in the cellar at Meadowlands, destined to cover toast on snowy school mornings:

LEMON MARMALADE
Six lemons sliced very thin, and each pile of slices cut in quarters, cover with 10 cups of cold water and let it stand twenty-four hours. Boil until the rind is perfectly tender, add 2 cups of sugar and simmer for twenty minutes, or until the syrup jellies.

I am disappointed, however, that Aunt Bessie's Queen of Puddings was not included. Mrs. H. V. B. Bridges' version seems to have been accepted first. Hers, a custardy mixture with bread crumbs and jam is not at all like Aunt Bessie's humble but delicious concoction that my mother continued to create. It had layers of white bread with a handful of those fat "stoned" raisins hiding among the folds, vanilla flavoured milk mixed with an egg poured over and baked until set — a frugal way of using stale bread and catching the milk before it went off in pre-refrigerator days. This was a tongue burner, if it were served directly from the oven as the bread seemed to hold the heat. I learned to be patient, and sometimes added the cooling influence of the "top-of-the-bottle."

The cultural period and historic significance of the *Fredericton Cathedral Memorial Hall Cookery Book* is nicely illustrated in the Foreword to the third edition.

> This is the Third Edition of what has been known as the *Fredericton Cathedral Cook Book*. The proceeds of the sale of the First Edition were applied as a contribution to the Organ Fund of Christ Church Cathedral, Fredericton. The proceeds of the sale of the Second Edition were contributed to the Restoration Fund of Christ Church Cathedral, which was struck by lightning and partially destroyed by fire on the night of July 3, 1911.
>
> It is proposed and intended by the Editors of this Third Edition, to apply the proceeds to the building Fund of the Memorial Hall, to be erected upon the Cathedral property.
>
> The recipes contained in the First and Second Editions of this book have been again carefully revised, and only the most useful of them are reproduced herein. Some of the old recipes containing wine as an ingredient have been retained, but care has been taken to select of such recipes only those that permit of the satisfactory substitution of fruit syrups or fruit juices for the wine. Many additional recipes appear in this edition, especially recipes for canning of fruit, vegetables, fish and meats. These canning recipes are most excellent; the directions very clear and simple and good results

are unfailingly obtained if the directions are carefully followed.

The fact that each recipe has a name or signature appended to it is not intended to imply that the recipe is original, but rather that it has been used and is approved by the person over whose name it appears.

The fourth paragraph suggests that the Temperance League was active in its objections to the inclusion of wine in recipes appearing in the first two editions. The last paragraph is normally not added to community cookery books assembled in this way, but it does relieve the contributor of potentially being regarded as a thief.

Reading the names attached to the recipes is like reliving my introduction to Fredericton in 1940 at the age of ten. Of course, I did not meet them all; many were dead, like Lady Ashburnham of pickle fame. Lady Ashburnham's Pickles are still a staple in the Fredericton community and throughout New Brunswick. These departed worthies—her ancient friends and relations—were often mentioned in conversations with my mother.

Though Bessie and her household did not move from Meadowlands to Fredericton until the early 1920s, she made regular trips to the city with the incentive of visiting relatives and attending the Anglican Cathedral. And, of course, she had lived in nearby Douglas for the better part of nine years before she began nurses training in 1878. In many ways she would have considered herself and been considered by others as part of the Fredericton social mélange. A known supporter of church causes, and as the author of several books on religious subjects, she was a well known and appropriate person from whom to solicit recipes for inclusion in the Cathedral Cookery Book.

As the introduction stated, three editions were published. I have quoted from the third one which was published in 1921. A copy of the second, published in 1911, is safe in the New Brunswick Provincial Archives. Three of Bessie's four recipes that appeared in the first and last edition are also in the second edition: Cheese

Potatoes, Royal sandwich, and Lemon Marmalade. Manchester Pudding was omitted from the second edition. The Archives also has a copy of the first edition. It is undated and the pages have come loose from the binding. It uses an expression no longer current—"a quick oven," meaning a hot one.

Many of Bessie's relatives and friends contributed recipes to 1911 edition of the *Fredericton Cathedral Cookery Book* including Mrs. John Robinson (Moose Meat Pie and Jugged Hare), Mrs. Arthur Carr (was a Robinson), Mrs. R. F. Randolph, Mrs. Dibblee (was a Robinson), Mrs. H.V. Bridges, Miss Edith Gregory, Mrs. Balloch, Mrs. Mira Amelia DuVernet Casswell sister of Harriet (Potted Partridges), Mrs. DeVeber, Mrs. J. de Lancey Robinson (American Rarebit), Mrs. Wm Robinson (Shortcake), Mrs. Wm. Scovil (Pepper Relish)—all names well known to me.

The advertisements included in this vintage cookery book are almost as entertaining as the recipes. The Fred B. Edgecombe Co. Ltd., which was a clothing store across from the Normal School (now the Justice Building) on Queen Street, Fredericton, amusingly links their business and the business of the book:

Edgecombe's Garment Department
Dame Fashion's most approved styles
LADIES' AND GENTS'
Coats, Suits, Dresses, Kimonos, Waists, Evening
Costumes, Corsets, Dress Trimmings, etc.
Cooking appeals to the Inner Wants—Our
Garments are for External Use Only Inspection
Invited. See Our Specialties in Fur Garments.
FRED B. EDGECOMBE CO. LTD.
Agency Perrin's celebrated kid gloves
City Railway and Ocean Steamship Ticket Office
Telephone 106   Fredericton, N.B.

Another business made the most of advertising in a "recipe" book:

A RECIPE FOR THE BLUES:
Eat Well, Drink Well, Sleep Well, and
ATTEND REGULARLY
THE GAIETY THEATRE
550 Queen St. Fredericton, N.B.
The Capital's Big Photoplay Theatre
4 Shows Daily: at 2.30, 3.15, 7.15 and 8.40

The advertisement, on page seventeen, from the Enterprise Foundry Co. Ltd., Sackville, N.B. with an illustration of an Enterprise Monarch Steel Range, comes with this bit of appropriate doggerel:

> We may live without love, we may live without books,
> But where is the man who can live without cooks?
> And e'en if the cook and her book are all right,
> If the stove is no good, then there's trouble in sight.

> Such trouble can be avoided if you have in your kitchen an
> Enterprise Monarch Steel Range

Bessie obviously prevailed upon her cousins and other family connections to place some of the forty-seven advertisements, covering twenty-six pages in the 1911 edition of the *Fredericton Cathedral Cookery Book*. Page nine shows the Saint John Robinsons responded enthusiastically:

T. B. & H. B. Robinson
Insurance St. John N.B.
& J. M. Robinson & Sons
Bankers & Brokers
Members Montreal Stock Exchange
Market Square
Saint John N.B.
Montreal Moncton

The Starrs took all of page five:

R. P. & W. F. Starr
Coal
Scotch and American
Anthracite
Old Mines Sydney, Springhill
Reserve and Cannel Coals
Shipped Promptly to All Points in the Maritime
Provinces
R. P. & W. F. Starr
49 Smythe St. 226 Union St.
St. John. N.B.

W. F. Starr (Frank) was the first cousin of Harriet (Hattie) Lavinia DuVernet Scovil, Bessie's sister-in-law, Morris's wife.

* * * *

Organizing food preparation for the family and farm workers at Meadowlands was not as daunting a burden as it would have been if Bessie had not already experienced heavy responsibilities in the nursing profession. Spending the summer of 1903 there to help Hattie through her last months gave Bessie a gradual view of what was required. By September she was in full control of the domestic scene. After Harriet' death, she conducted an extended search for an adequate housekeeper, thinking that if one was secured she could return to nursing. No housekeeper that met her requirements could be found. As time passed, and it became clear that Mod (Morris), her brother, was not likely to remarry, Bessie retired from professional nursing and over the next two decades remained at Meadowlands to nourish and nurture the five Scovil children—Morris, Elizabeth, Gertrude, Mary and Roger—into young adults.

While Bessie became fully devoted to the domestic world of family and farm life, she remained professionally engaged in the world of nursing through her reading and writing. She kept up with advances in health information. She was writing and publishing regularly in professional journals and in a best selling popular magazine. She was a continual advocate for upgrading the quality of nurses' training and for the welfare of nurses. A decade after coming to Meadowlands she published, "Food for Nurses" in the *American Journal of Nursing*, vol. XII, no 12, September 1913. This was not just a theoretical presentation but a challenge to training programs and hospitals to heed her advice and put her recommendations into practice. Elizabeth Robinson Scovil naturally applied the same knowledge of food, proper nourishment, and good health practices to her management of the family at Meadowlands as she did to the welfare of nurses.

When we look at the trajectory of her experience, we see a person who integrated everything she learned into the conduct of her life. From operating the infirmary for a prestigious school for boys, to private nursing, to being the Superintendent of Nursing at a major hospital and the Head of its Nurses' Training School, to celebrated author of child care books and professional nursing journalism, to household management at Meadowlands, the life of Elizabeth Robinson Scovil was a combination of being of service to others and a strong commitment to personal excellence.

Chapter Eight
Epilogue: Final Years & A Familial Quest

In 1924 my Great Aunt Bessie and her brother, Morris, sold Meadowlands for $20,000 and purchased a house on King Street in Fredericton. Meadowlands, according to the news story of its sale in the *Daily Gleaner*, was "one of the largest and finest farms on the St. John River." Mary and Roger were still part of the household, but were soon to strike out on their own: Roger to employment in a seed and nursery business owned by a relative in South Carolina and Mary into elopement and marriage that led to her settling near Amherst, Nova Scotia.

In 1926 Bessie and Morris sold their King Street house in Fredericton and thereafter spent fall and winter in South Carolina living with Roger and his family and spring and summer in England living with Morris and Hattie's oldest son, Morrie and his family. This arrangement seemed to suit everyone concerned; the two families had the intermittent household assistance of a grandfather and an aunt with substantial financial resources; Morris and Bessie had the pleasure of being in close association with the two families and of enjoying moderate climates year round.

Morrie was no doubt grateful for Bessie's organizing and financing his move from the life of a farmer at Meadowlands to that of a sophisticated business man, not far from London, able to send his children to superior schools rather than to the Gagetown Grammar. Bessie referred to Morrie as "my darling boy" in letters when he was a prisoner of war in World War I and gave him a significant keep sake in her will. Madeline, Morrie's wife was clearly fond of Bessie, appreciating her intellect and her knowledge of nursing, her own choice of professional training as well. Morrie and Madeline had three children, Courtney, Anne, and Richard. Their house, in Bishop's Stortford was large enough to comfortably accommodate the six month visits of Bessie and Morris.

Morris's oldest daughter Elizabeth and her husband, Hayden, also lived England. Their three hundred year old residence, Ridgewell House, was located in the small, historic village of Little Missenden, near Amersham in the county of Buckinghamshire. They had two young boys, George and John and in late 1934, a daughter, Barbara, born a few days after Bessie died. Although Ridgewell House looks imposing, it had only three bedrooms plus quarters in the attic for the maid. Bessie and Morris visited, but likely did not stay there for long periods.

Bessie and her niece, Elizabeth, seemed to have shared an interest in Spiritualism, which was very popular in England in the 1930s. On at least one occasion they visited a clairvoyant, in London, a half hour's train ride from Little Missenden. I have a notebook that includes the partially legible results of the consultation. It was found among Bessie's belongings after her death by Madeline and brought to Canada along with other of her papers when she and the children left England at the beginning of World War II in 1939. The notes are on the subject of George and John's health, especially the conditions of their chests. I find it difficult to believe that Bessie would have placed any credibility in the findings and advice of a supposedly clairvoyant Spiritualist, but perhaps Elizabeth was keen and Bessie wanted to support her.

In the early to mid 1930s the boys appear to have spent their winter holidays learning to ski in Switzerland. Improving their health may have been the chief reason. Health promoting retreats to mountain locations of fresh, dry air were popular for those who could afford them, and for good reason. The damp winters of England with its pervasive coal-fired air pollution from residential and industrial uses was intuitively regarded as bad for one's health, especially for those with "weak chests," as the concern was expressed in those days.

So with six month "summer" stays in England with Morrie and Madeline, and six month "winter" stays in Greenville, South Carolina with Roger and his wife, Rose, and eventually their three children, Roger, Rosemary, and Barclay, Bessie and Morris moved into their final years. "Roger Boy," as Bessie referred to him in letters to distinguish him from his father was born a few months before I was in 1929. We became close friends through our teen age letters when we were attending university and through visits when I lived in England and he travelled to Europe on business trips.

At one point when we were remembering our Great Aunt Bessie and Grandfather, cousin Roger said he thought their long visits must have been a strain on his parents, having to create a three generation household in a house designed for just two. Bessie recorded that she always made sure their extended visits were not a financial burden to either of her nephews. Roger's wife Rose, was also a trained nurse so the two women would have had a mutual interest. Rose also had strong religious leanings which would have appealed to Bessie. Rose was a member of the Oxford Group which eventually became the Moral Rearmament movement.

In my previous book, *Meadowlands: A Chronicle of the Scovil Family*, published in 2020, I devoted a chapter to Bessie's last months at Morrie's and Madeline's home in Bishop's Stortford. The story I tell in *Meadowlands* is creative non-fiction. It is based on fact but when exact facts are not known, as in conversations, creative non-fiction supplies the narrative in order to provide a probable and more fully developed story. Much of that chapter is founded on my visits to the town of Bishop's Stortford, my own experiences of living in England with two small children, and my knowledge of Morrie and Madeline's children, Courtenay, Anne, and Richard after they moved to Amherst, Nova Scotia in 1939, where I was also living. We shared the same grandfather, their mother's father and my father's father.

The actual last days of my Great Aunt Bessie are not exactly known to me or to anyone else now alive. However, I now have access to her death certificate and that of her brother, Morris, thanks to my daughter, Holly Sutherland who resides in England. Bessie's certificate is as follows:

> Twentieth November 1934; Name: Elizabeth Robinson Scovil; Age: 85 years; Spinster of no occupation, daughter of Samuel James Scovil, Solicitor, deceased; Cause of Death: Angina Pectoris; certified by T. M. Morris; Mr. A. Scovil, Nephew, in attendance, 11 Windhill, Bishop's Stortford; Twenty-first November; H.D. Field, Registrar.

The death certificate is hand written and not at all clear, but at least it provides several facts: Bessie died of heart problems, as I thought; her "Darling Boy," Morrie, was with her when she died (the initial of his middle name, Allarie, is used on the certificate); she died at his home and not in an institution. I did ironically smile a little to see that Bessie was registered as having "no occupation." To list all her "occupations" would have required several lines of writing. Morrie would have known but obviously did not intervene which seems regrettable but understandable in the circumstances. Bessie would have been happy with "Registered Nurse."

Morris, Bessie's brother, died only a few months after his sister, which may indicate how attached they were. Bessie was eleven years older than Morris, several siblings having died in infancy between her birth and his. Morris would have been the lovingly cherished little brother who survived and, along with his family, benefited greatly over the years from her sisterly concern and steadfast support.

Not only did Morris depend on his only sister in many ways while growing up, he continued to rely on her when he took over the nine hundred acre farm of meadows and woodland after their father died in the early 1880s. Bessie's nursing and writing careers made her financially independent and eventually wealthy. She considered that through inheritance, she owned the farm, which she named Meadowlands. She was more than willing to help Morris make the farm a viable operation.

Income from selling thoroughbred horses and hay made the farm financially viable. With Hattie's death in 1903, Bessie returned to Meadowlands to take on household management and the care of the five Scovil children. She frequently covered extra expenses such as sending Mary, her youngest niece, to Edgehill boarding school for girls in Nova Scotia. In addition, she financed Morrie's two years of advanced education at the newly established Agricultural College in Nova Scotia.

When I eventually tracked down Bessie and Morris's shared gravestone in 1997, I thought it completely appropriate that my grandfather should continue to share his dependence on his sister, even in death. According to Morris's death certificate, dated April 4, 1935, he died at Haymeads, Bishop's Stortford. His address is given as 11 Windhill, Bishop's Stortford, his son's home; Occupation: Retired Farmer; Cause of Death: a. Uraemia [kidney problems]; b. stone in bladder; c. postectomy 1 year ago; Details of informant: M.A. Scovil, son, in attendance, 11 Windhill Bishop's Stortford. Haymeads appears to have been the forerunner of a small hospital, perhaps what we would call a nursing home. It was located just around the corner from 11 Windhill, making frequent visits by Morrie and Madeline easily accomplished.

* * * *

On Sunday, September 1, 1997 I decided to visit Bishop's Stortford, a few stops on a train toward London, to see whether I could find Bessie's grave. I was staying with my daughter, Holly and her family in Cambridge. They were away for the weekend and I did not bother to put on the radio or TV before I left the house. When I arrived at the railroad station I asked a woman at an information kiosk how many Anglican churches there were at Bishop's Stortford as I was looking for a relative's grave. I was told St. Michael's was the most prominent. It was located at the top of the hill, easily visible from the station. However, she said, it might not be open today. I asked why. With tears coming to her eyes she told me, "Princess Diana was killed last night."

By the time I reached St. Michael's, it was 12 noon and the congregation was just leaving. In the empty church I sat a few pews from the front, trying to digest the shocking and unlikely news of Princess Diana's death. Unable to do so my mind strayed to thinking of years ago when my Great Aunt Bessie, my Grandfather, Uncle Morris, Aunt Madeline, Courtenay, Anne and Richard all sat, possibly in the same polished pew, looking up at the same ornate pulpit, the same stained glass windows, the same altar, the same choir stalls.

The church was completely empty. There was no one around, not even a verger to ask where I might find graves from 1934, so I started looking at those surrounding the church. They were far too old. I asked a person nearby who pointed me in the direction of a more recent graveyard a ten minute walk away. It was an impressively cared for cemetery. I looked up and down the many paths where every imaginable name and sentiment was etched on small, medium and large stones, under occasional shady trees, but no success. Then I noticed, across a road, what looked like another cemetery. I found no Great Aunt or Grandfather, but there was one stone, off by itself, a cross with the name of my cousin, Richard Scovil, and his dates on it. The dates on his cross were 1928-1947. In 1945, when World War II ended, Richard felt he should return to England from his protected life in Amherst, Nova Scotia, and do his two years of National Service, which was compulsory for English young men of over eighteen. Although Richard was under no obligation to do this, now living in Canada, he felt more English than Canadian and presumably wanted to establish his residence there. He returned to England, joined the army, served for a short time, broke his leg in a training accident, and was invalided out. He then found employment with the Shell Oil company, developed polio, and died of it six hours before his parents, Morris and Madeline, arrived from Nova Scotia by aeroplane, a still an unusual, but by far the quickest, way to travel. In this case, not quick enough.

Richard's early death was a double blow for his parents and elder sister, Courtenay. When Madeline brought their children to her original home in Amherst, Nova Scotia, in September 1939 there were three of them. In a few short years, only Courtenay remained. Anne, the middle in age, was a vivacious young teenager, fond of horseback riding and at age 14 was already jumping. Late one October afternoon in 1941, Anne and her friend, Molly Simmonds, were bicycling back from Sackville to Amherst, after spending the day riding on horses at a friend's home. A car without lights on in the early dusk did not allow enough room for the bicycle on the outside. It collided with Anne, sending her flying. She hit her bare head and was killed instantly. Unfortunately, she had taken off her protective riding hat and in the early 1940s bicycle helmets were not worn. Another aspect of this tragic accident is that Anne was riding on the outside, nearest to traffic. In England, where Anne learned to ride a bicycle, it was common to ride two abreast and the drivers of passing vehicles allowed for it. I remember always cycling single file, one behind the other, in Canada.

Although no Scovils had lived in Bishop's Stortford since Morrie sold their house after the war, it was the last place Richard called "home" before he left for Canada in 1939. His parents would have wanted him buried near his Great Aunt Bessie and his Grandfather, but that was apparently not possible. Though saddened and pleased with my findings, I decided to contact the Urban District Council offices for more information, which I did by phone from Cambridge.

On a subsequent trip to the cemetery, and equipped with a map showing identifying grave numbers, I found what I was looking for. The location was at the far end of the grave yard, beyond all those epitaphs and memorials I had read and passed on my previous search. There it was, a simple cross about waist high, of York stone, white on one side and pale grey on the other. It stood at one end of a six by two foot raised bed, gravel covered with stone edging. I was told the reason one side of the stone cross was so white and the engraved lettering on it was so clear was because it was found face down and righted after I made my inquiry.

How long had it been lying face down? I knew the area had been bombed during the war. A bomb exploded on part of Morris's former house. Bombs could well have fallen near the cemetery, dislodging the recently placed stones. Bessie and Morris's stone would not have been put in place until 1935 or perhaps 36. Bombings occurred just six years later, not enough time for noticeable weathering or for lichen growth on the face of the stone. I made a sketch of the grave, the cross and the wording on it. The little red book in which I made the sketches and wrote the inscription was tucked away in a safe place, but over the years just where that is has escaped me. I hope it will one day miraculously reappear. However, I remember the inscription reasonably well. Along with her name and dates, Bessie's birth place was given as Meadowlands, New Brunswick, Canada.

It is highly unlikely this is literally true. Although this farm was owned by a member of the Scovil family at the time of her birth, her parents lived in the city of Saint John. It would have been strange for them to be visiting a distant farm, far from the amenities of the city at the time of their daughter's birth. The Farm at Scovil Point was known as just that until Bessie named it Meadowlands when she first saw it in 1880 after she had graduated from the Nursing School at Massachusetts General Hospital in Boston and was visiting her parents who had recently moved to the farm after inheriting it. Perhaps she was so attached to Meadowlands that she asked Morrie to put on her gravestone "born at Meadowlands." It had long been written on her heart.

Under Bessie's details on her stone were those of her brother, Morris — name, dates of birth and death, no place of birth. I took photos of the long sought grave and returned later with Holly when we photographed one another standing beside it. During the summer of 2021, Holly returned to the cemetery, planning to take more photos, but much to her surprise and disappointment all had fallen into ruins and she found it impossible even to locate the area she was seeking. The more modern cemetery across the road, where Richard is buried, appears to have taken over as the functioning one, with many more graves than when I was originally there.

The ambiguity of exactly where Bessie was born prodded me into further research at the Provincial Archives of New Brunswick.

I found that places of birth in the Province of New Brunswick are easily found if they occurred in the last one hundred and fifty years or so, but this information for those born in 1849, as Bessie was, is only available in baptismal records held by churches. Scovil Point and Jemseg, the nearest village, were in the district of Cambridge related to Cambridge Narrows a few miles away. There is no baptismal record of Elizabeth Robinson Scovil being born in the district of Cambridge or in Gagetown, across the river from The Farm at Scovil Point. But neither does her name appear in the baptismal records for 1849 in the most likely Anglican churches in the city of Saint John. Babies were normally baptized within a few days of birth or certainly within a few months. So now, finding no evidence either way, I am left to wonder—perhaps Bessie was not stretching the truth. Perhaps The Farm at Scovil Point was the place of her birth and the record of her baptism, wherever it took place, has gone missing.

When travel becomes comfortable again, I intend to make another pilgrimage to Bishop's Stortford. In the mean time, I prefer to think of my Great Aunt Bessie's and my Grandfather's graves headed by that pristine cross of white York Stone with their busy productive lives recorded in a few words and numbers, plus that bit of perhaps fiction, perhaps not, "born at Meadowlands." I am now glad to remember that when I was there, I sprinkled some earth and forget-me-not seeds among the gravel on the grave. I like to think there may be some of these persistent and well named flowers still flourishing amidst the ruins.

Acknowledgements

Many thanks to my first cousin, the late Roger M. Scovil of Atlanta, Georgia (eldest child of Roger P. Scovil, my mother's younger brother), whose book, *A Scovil Genealogy*, published in 1992, was a great help in keeping track of birthdays and other details. The late Canon Charles Karsten of Gardiner, Maine (grandson of my great uncle, Jack Scovil, Bessie's brother,) made the contents of his mother's trunk (cousin Bess) available to me, which included letters between Addie (Jack's wife) and Aunt Bessie. I am especially grateful for access to this primary resource material and for his general encouragement. The granddaughter of my uncle Morrie, Anne Purdy of Amherst, NS, was generous in giving me family photographs and articles, some of which I used in *Meadowlands: A Chronicle of the Scovil Family* and some of which have been used in *A Nurse for All Seasons*. As well, I thank members of my two writing groups, "Wolftree" and "Woolastook," whose years of supportive encouragement allowed me to think of myself as a writer. The many expressions of reading pleasure prompted by *Meadowlands* encouraged me to complete *A Nurse for All Seasons*, which had been started decades earlier. Special gratitude goes to Alison Calvern who nursed my writing ambitions with weekly sessions of herbal tea, expertise, and special care. Finally, and in many ways most importantly, I thank Keith, Ellen, and Brendan Helmuth at Chapel Street Editions for their enthusiasm, attention to detail, and good humour.

About the Author

Virginia Bliss Bjerkelund is a Maritimer, born in Amherst, Nova Scotia, educated in Fredericton, New Brunswick, followed by nearly 30 years of living in England where she married and brought up a daughter and son, now both retired. She returned to Fredericton, re-married, travelled widely, practiced Social Work, and is active in the cultural life of the city. Virginia is the author of the non-fiction novel, *Meadowlands: A Chronicle of the Scovil Family*, published in 2020 when she was 90.

www.ingramcontent.com/pod-product-compliance
Lightning Source LLC
Chambersburg PA
CBHW051132120626
46547CB00012B/772